COSMIC CRYSTALS!
Working With New Crystal Skulls

Paulinne Delcour-Min

© 2025 by Paulinne Delcour-Min

All rights reserved. No part of this book, in part or in whole, may be reproduced, transmitted or utilized in any form or by any means, electronic, photographic or mechanical, including photocopying, recording, or by any information storage and retrieval system without permission in writing from Ozark Mountain Publishing, Inc., except for brief quotations embodied in literary articles and reviews.

For permission, or serialization, condensation, adaptions, or for our catalog of other publications, write to: Ozark Mountain Publishing, Inc., P.O. Box 754, Huntsville, AR 72740, ATTN: Permissions Department

Library of Congress Cataloging-in-Publication Data
Cosmic Crystals: Working With New Crystal Skulls by Paulinne Delcour-Min -1948-

An extraordinary book that shines a spotlight on crystal skulls.

1. Spiritual 2. Crystal Skulls 3. Healing 4. Metaphysical
I. Delcour-Min, Paulinne, 1948 II. Crystal Skulls III. Metaphysical IV. Title

Library of Congress Catalog Card Number: 2025931799
ISBN: 978-1-962858-40-3

Cover Art and Layout: Victoria Cooper Art
Book set in: Times New Roman and Castellar
Book Design: Summer Garr

Published by:

PO Box 754, Huntsville, AR 72740
800-935-0045 or 479-738-2348; fax 479-738-2448
WWW.OZARKMT.COM
Printed in the United States of America

For Altai

and for everyone who has ever been intrigued by crystal skulls.

Other Books by Paulinne Delcour-Min

Spiritual Gold
Holy Ice
Divine Fire

Table of Contents

Acknowledgments

Talking With Crystals   i

Chapter 1   1
Moon, the Amethyst Deva, and the Shaman Stone

Chapter 2   19
Arapo, Zeb'n, and Waking the Sleepers

Chapter 3   26
*Solange, Hapi-atzi, Radiance, Moon, Stardust, Mars,Cloud,
Charles Lapis, Fred, Hunter, the Skull of Dreams,
Shallimar, and the Sleepers Tell Me More*

Chapter 4   45
Can Skull Beads Function as Crystal Skulls?

Chapter 5   55
*The Cosmic Crystalline Matrix, the Twins, Quartz Speaks
and I Become Light*

Chapter 6   66
Merlin's Skulls and Skull Cleansing

Chapter 7   78
Ancient Stones and Telluric Energies

Chapter 8   87
Egyptian Mysteries

Chapter 9   97
*Choosing and Naming Your Skulls, Traveling Bags and
Instant Repairs, How Skulls Communicate, How To
Meditate With Your Skull*

Chapter 10   107
Florence and the Standing Stone

Chapter 11   117
Mariam

Chapter 12   122
*More From Hapi-atzi: Merlin's Advice On Working With
Your Skulls*

Chapter 13   130
Evangeline Mo

Chapter 14 *Stardust and Exploring the Shadow With the Shaman Stone*	139
Chapter 15 *Solange and Moon Reveal More*	152
Chapter 16 *Hapi-atzi, Hope, and the Cintamani Pearls of Fire*	165
Chapter 17 *The Face, Golden Feathers of the Sun and the Dragon Raffim*	175
Chapter 18 *The Dragon Raffeem and Arwen the Bird Skull*	187
Chapter 19 *The Ancestor Skull*	200
Chapter 20 *"Hitchhikers" and Crazy Buying*	207
Chapter 21 *Kai*	231
Chapter 22 *Postscript: Visiting Castlerigg Stone Circle*	235
Skull Sizes	255
Skull Suppliers	257
Bibliography	260
List of Illustrations	263
About the Author	265

Acknowledgments

The Mystery of the Crystal Skulls started my journey with the skulls—I very much wanted to know more! So thank you, Chris and Ceri, for writing that famous book. I met the late Nick Nocerino, with his ancient crystal skull Sha Na Ra, and a sitting with Sha changed my life when, in answer to a question, I saw a vision in the skull's crystal depths (Michele Nocerino, his daughter, continues his work today). Next, I met Bill Homann, guardian to the most famous crystal skull in the world, the Mitchell-Hedges, and from that skull I received a message for *Holy Ice*, my second book. So Nick and Bill, thank you for helping me along the way, and thank you Michele, because like Bill, you generously gave me photos for *Holy Ice*.

Very big thanks indeed are due to my husband, Ye Min, who whole-heartedly came on the journey with me. His good advice and support proved vital. I owe a debt of gratitude to Ozark Mountain Publishing for helping me realize my dream, and thanks go to my editor, Jill Worley, who was an absolute joy to work with.

I thank all those who supplied the skulls, and especially Tracy Queen and Bruce Mitchell, because of their kindness. Tracy is at www.the-crystal-tree.co.uk and Bruce trades on eBay as silverli740. I also thank Mike Sharman, who trades on eBay as nigri_671, and I must single out the team at www.crystalskulls.com and www.ancientcrystalskulls.com who supply fabulous skulls, and where you can sign up for their informative, free newsletters, and VIP alerts (without which I would not have Amersandi). A big thank you goes to Katie Beardsley for her kind gift that brought Hope and the Shaman Stone. I thank the mineral kingdom for all the help I was so freely given, and dare I say it, Merlin.

I value the sharing platforms offered by skull groups on Facebook, noteably Explorers of Crystal Skull Mystique, administered by Adriana Stella Olday, and Wisdom of the Skulls, administered by Kathryn Jones. Also The Mitchell-Hedges Crystal Skull Meditation Group (Europe), whose regular meditations while I was writing the book were inspirational. And my thanks go to Vikki (Elmera) Cunningham, for her contribution, and to Maggie Hall, for acting as first reader. I shall always be grateful to Isabelle Crummie, Guy Needler, and Veronica Fyland for all their help and encouragement at the start of my writing career. Last, but not least, is my dearest friend Hana, who believed in me, whose old laptop I still use for my writing to this day, and who dragged me into the digital age. Hana, you and your twin sister, Lamya, are very special souls.

Bless you all.

TALKING WITH CRYSTALS

I have loved crystals ever since I can remember. They are pure, beautiful, and mysterious. They whisper to our subconscious of magic, of ancient times, of powers unseen. They hold a promise of protection and healing. Crystals have always been something very special, and this book is about communicating with them.

I am a past life therapist who loves crystals, and at mind, body, spirit exhibitions I would load my table with pieces of rose quartz because it attracted people to come up and speak with me. The lively heap of beautiful pink stones was a magnet and an ice breaker. Past life therapy is an abstract concept to sell, but I noticed the crystals were easy...and that nearly everyone loves a little bit of crystal treasure! Even children.

Yes, humans and crystals go deep.

We are naturally drawn to them.

Looking back, my deeper connection with crystals began the evening the organizer of a past life conference came over for dinner. I had been a speaker at his conference and he brought his wife to meet me. During the meal she declared she was a witch. I thought, as a witch, she might be interested in crystals, so I brought out my favorite large piece of quartz to show her. She asked if I had ever met its guardian. I had to say no, because the possibility of communicating with a crystal had never crossed

COSMIC CRYSTALS! *Working With New Crystal Skulls*

my mind. The dinner party was many years ago now, but the idea took root. From what she'd said I was expecting a fairy to be associated with my lovely crystal. I had meditated for years, although never with a crystal, but I thought it worth a try to see what I could find.

I got a bit of a shock. I met no fairy, but a distinct and quavery voice piped up in my mind's ear. High pitched and oscillating, it clearly said I was its guardian for this eye blink in time. It said human lives were short compared to a crystal's lifespan and that to a crystal, a human lifetime seemed no more than the shadow of a cloud passing over the landscape of Earth.

The simple quartz crystal I was holding in my hands was talking down to me as it patiently explained the situation from its own point of view. It opened my eyes to the fact that crystals do have a consciousness, and that they are willing to communicate with us—if they feel like it! If they feel it is worth their effort. Otherwise, they just ignore us. But our crystal skulls are different. They are made for that very purpose and that is what makes them so rewarding to work with.

Crystal skulls are deliberately shaped in our image.

The crystal is carved down until it takes on the shape of the bony protection that shields the seat of our own personal consciousness, the human brain. When the crystal has been transformed into the shape of a skull, we can switch it on as if it were a crystal radio, a two-way radio running on telepathy.

Crystal skulls are potent symbols of wisdom and consciousness.

To any who find them sinister or creepy, I would say that if crystal skulls were meant to be symbols of death, then they would be carved with suture lines scattered over their smooth crystal craniums. Suture lines are the shallow lines that show where the edges of a baby's bones fused together to make up their skull, and as humans, we all have suture lines on our skulls which will be revealed after death, when flesh falls from bone. But a typical crystal skull does not have these lines. Instead, it is polished smooth because it is designed to work in the same way as a crystal ball. That's right, like a crystal ball, crystal skulls are

TALKING WITH CRYSTALS

scrying tools, and as such, they are in line with fortune-telling traditions. Every old or ancient crystal skull I have ever seen has had a polished rounded cranium, with no sign of any suture lines that would snag the eye and distract from looking within. We use a scrying tool when we seek information that is beyond the reach of our senses and conscious awareness; with a skull we need to be able to look into the crystal depths like a window into our subconscious. Then the mind projects symbols and images onto the crystal of the scrying tool in order to convey the information we are seeking into our conscious awareness.

However, crystal skulls are much more than scrying tools. Reflective bowls of water are scrying tools too—but they don't talk back to you!

There are many Native American legends concerning crystal skulls, and ancient crystal skulls have surfaced in various parts of the world, including Central America, Tibet, and Mongolia, but few people will ever get the chance to have an ancient crystal skull of their own to work with. But that does not matter a jot, because today anyone—even me—can enjoy having a crystal skull in their life because thousands and thousands of lovely new crystal skulls pour from the world's crystal workshops. Their production is inspired by the myths and legends of the crystal skulls of old, and just like their ancient counterparts, these new skulls are powerful tools to be worked with. Their carving may be recent, but the crystal they are carved from is as old as the hills. In fact, it is the very same crystal that the ancient skulls were made from, and the same crystal entities work through it.

I know, because this is what happened to me...

CHAPTER 1
Moon, the Amethyst Deva, and the Shaman Stone

It was the autumn of 2020 and I was hatching a plan. I wanted to take crystal skulls to the ancient stone circles of Britain. My book, *Holy Ice: Past Lives and Crystal Skulls,* was just out and I was curious to see how the circles' energies would interact with a crystal skull.

There are over a thousand of these mysterious places dotted around the British Isles, where around five thousand years ago huge stones had been shaped, transported, and set into place, enhancing the natural energies in the landscape. My husband and I live on England's north east coast, and we were looking forward to an exciting road trip with a couple of skulls when my book's success led to an astonishing request.

In an Amazon review, posted in the US on the 29th of November 2020, Altai wanted more—more than just past life memories—and wished I'd write about working with new crystal skulls. Well! I had thought my writing days were over, because the last book in my trilogy, *Spiritual Gold, Holy Ice, Divine Fire,* was already with the publishers—but here was an inspiring and exciting new project. So thank you, Altai. It was a logical next step, but one I would never have thought of. I was going to need a whole heap of new skulls, in different sizes and types of crystal, to make the book interesting, and to see what different kinds of skulls had to offer. But by now Britain was in winter lockdown because of the COVID 19 virus. Our road trip had to wait because all non-essential travel was forbidden, and crystal shops, like all other non-essential shops, had been forced to close.

But there was still the Internet...

Within hours I began to hear the silent calling of a life-size quartz skull, eager to come to help with the new book. Tracy and Louise, at The Crystal Tree in Essex, stocked my books alongside their beautiful crystals, and during lockdown they posted videos of their stock on Facebook to sell it. I was tempted to buy their Tibetan quartz skull. When Tracy held it up to the camera and asked, "What is this skull saying to you?" it shouted out, "Buy me!" But it was too small to be the one I sensed calling and I hesitated.

I told Tracy exactly what I was looking for. By an amazing coincidence she had just got a skull from the wholesalers. It had not gone in the shop yet. Could this be what I was looking for? She sent me a video of it. I found the synchronicity compelling. I trusted my intuition and had faith that this *was* the skull that was calling.

It arrived at my home on the 5th of December 2020, and the nagging sensation of calling ceased. Miraculously, a few short winter days after the idea for the book had been sparked, a life-size quartz crystal skull was in my hands!

It had been in a hurry to get to me, but it was in no hurry to tell me its name. I meditated with the skull and all it said was, "The Goddess wears many veils, and so do Her skulls..." Its quartz did indeed have many veils in it, as cloudy areas are called, and there were a few small, feathery inclusions of red iron oxide too. This blood red pigment is properly known as hematite, and in the form of red ochre it had been held sacred at the end of the last Ice Age, when a Goddess culture held sway around the world. Archaeologists find it in ancient graves from this time, and from a past life experience I write about in *Divine Fire,* I know this was seen as "Mother Earth's blood", and used to symbolize the Great

CHAPTER 1

Goddess's blessing on the departed.

I took it as both a blessing and a good sign.

The name, when it finally came, was beautiful: **Moon-Over-the-Waters-of-Life**, conjuring up images of reflection, of light and silence, of night, and of a cosmic womb seeded and thriving with life. At eight inches long and weighing twelve pounds, Moon remains by far my largest skull.

Every crystal skull has its own individual character.

The type of crystal will contribute something to this, as different sorts of crystal have different properties that we can't help but sense and respond to. The character of the carve will mean that some faces naturally attract us, while others may even repel us, but much more important than a skull's superficial appearance, is the character and quirky nature of the indwelling crystal entity it has attracted to it. Crystal is the natural habitat of a subtle life form—a crystal entity, otherwise known as the crystal's deva. "Deva" is another name for nature spirit, and crystal devas are part of the hierarchy of nature spirits and maintenance entities that assist in the universe's evolution. Like angels do. The Bible describes hierarchies of angels, and you could view the crystal deva that has chosen your skull for its home to be a little like its guardian angel. I usually refer to the deva as **the skull's essence.** Because that is what it is, and when we communicate with crystal skulls, it's the essence we are communicating with. The essence doesn't care if your skull was carved by someone famous or by a machine—because it is the piece of crystal itself it is interested in. It all depends on how big the crystal's footprint is in higher dimensions.

We humans see the 3D body. But we live in a multi-dimensional universe. We personally have an energy field, called an aura, we have soul and spirit, etheric and astral bodies, too, that exist in higher dimensions but are anchored to us through our physical body here—so, do not imagine all you see is all there is to a crystal, and when a crystal has been carved into the complex curves of a skull, an energy that would not be interested in ordinary crystals has access to it. This is the **Collective Crystal Skull Consciousness,** often referred to as the CCSC.

3

The Collective Crystal Skull Consciousness exists in higher dimensions where the laws of physics are different, but that does not stop it from accessing 3D, where it is bound by neither linear time, nor by any of the other constraints of 3D as you and I are. This Consciousness is like an ocean of intelligent awareness, where knowledge and information has been stored and shared down the ages, and is still being added to today. It is accessible to all skulls everywhere. It is supremely intelligent, telepathic, and psychic, and it resonates with human consciousness; even to the extent of affecting our reality by tweaking energy threads at the 3D level of our world in order to engineer coincidences, synchronicities, meetings, exchanges, and even mistakes, all to bring about a desired outcome. This intelligence pulls skulls to their guardians and is protective, benevolent, and healing. It helped Moon come to me. It is here to help us, and that is why crystal skulls can be such a joy to work with, and how they have a mysterious and uncanny ability to know things which should be absolutely impossible. As will be demonstrated many times in these pages.

Left to right above: Moon-Over-the-Waters-of-Life and Solange

CHAPTER 1

Left to right below: Hapi-atzi and Radiance

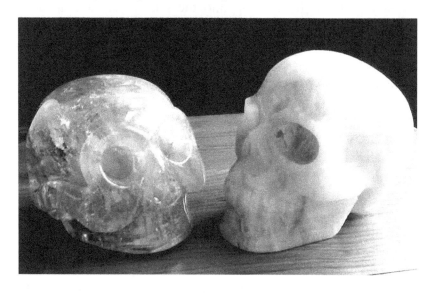

Nor does size matter when it comes to one-to-one relating with a crystal skull. Two inches, or even less, is plenty big enough for a skull to give you astonishing experiences.

Which means crystal skulls are within the reach of everyone, and there is no need to chase after huge expensive skulls by "master" carvers, or fall prey to skull snobbery about how old your skull is. Inexpensive, magnificent little crystal skulls are out there, all ready for the picking! Choose one that takes your eye and I suspect it won't be long before you have more. I've found skulls enjoy company, and we human caretakers and guardians benefit from them in so many subtle ways that few people stop at one.

I asked Tracy about Moon's provenance, but she could give me no details. I asked Moon, and she told me she had been carved in China by a man who loved his work and took pride in it. She said his family had been stone carvers for generations, and showed me his ancestors standing behind her—the picture of that

COSMIC CRYSTALS! *Working With New Crystal Skulls*

in my meditation was clear and sharp. However, China is a big country...China stretches up into the Himalayas and includes Tibet, an autonomous region within China. That whole area has long been associated with crystal skulls...was Moon from there? But wherever she was from, love and care had been poured into her and had woken her up.

To take this further, I meditated again and asked my inner guides to help. Guide Hera held Moon towards me, eyes facing mine, and told me to visualize breathing in some of her energy. I visualized Moon's energy swirling around inside my head and then aligning with mine. It made interfacing easier. Moon is only a thought away now and I just have to picture her face and ask my question to get an answer—though for important matters I would meditate and do things properly. But there isn't always time for that when you're internet shopping for new skulls!

Having a crystal skull is such a positive experience that I soon started looking for more. One night at the beginning of February 2021, I was on the Internet looking at skulls when I revisited the Tibetan quartz. I asked Moon what she thought. She wistfully said she would like him for a brother, and she would like sisters of amethyst and aquamarine, too. So "buy me" no longer fell on deaf ears. When he arrived, he declared his name was **Solange**. I looked it up—it meant "sun (Sol) angel (ange)." Solange has a tiny feathering of golden healer on his underside, which is what yellow, sun-coloured iron oxide is called when it stains crystal. And, as my husband, Ye, said, I now had "Brother Sun and Sister Moon."

Moon's sisters were to be found on the other side of the Atlantic.

Deep purple amethyst **Hapi-atzi** was on eBay after a storage locker sale in California. The only clue to her past being a brass tray in the same sale, depicting the Mayan calendar and engraved with "Souvenir from Teotihuacan."

Brazilian aquamarine blue beryl **Radiance** was found on Etsy. She arrived in a box from Canada along with **Fred**, a winged skull in Mexican crazy lace agate, and **Stardust**, a star being skull in Madagascan flower agate. The seller had tucked in

CHAPTER 1

a gift of Dalmatian jasper, a darling little skull called **Hunter**. He may have been very small, and not chosen by me, but Claire, at New Earth Magic, had sent me a treasure in Hunter. I had no idea how helpful he would be.

Vibrant blue **Charles Lapis** was soon followed by **Cloud**, a grey labradorite skull shot through with flashes of blue and gold, which arrived on my birthday in March. Then I sent for a Preseli bluestone skull, the same Welsh bluestone as the inner ring of Stonehenge. This stone was considered so important 5,000 years ago that they transported it 150 miles from Wales to Stonehenge. We couldn't resist calling him Elvis Preseli until he said it should be "**Mars**." Charles, Cloud, and Mars are only two inches long, but that's plenty big enough to give them power.

Left to right: Stardust, Hunter, Cloud, Fred, Manos the Black, Mars, Charles Lapis

My collection was growing. But unless I worked with them, there was no point to getting them, and so I meditated with every last one I'd ever owned—even individual skull beads—and recorded the experiences. This is what makes the book. It is the skulls' voices that hold wisdom, not mine. I have been astonished where a skull can take me. I hope sharing my journeys in the inner world will inspire you on adventures of your own, and help you benefit from the comfort crystal skulls offer when you hold their smooth, cool, soothing crystal bodies in your hands and welcome them into your life.

In April 2021, a friend offered to help me with my research by buying a companion for Moon.

I had wanted a *nice* skull to honor Katie's kind gift, because I would be sending her a photograph of it and wanted her to be proud of it, but the one that was attracting me the most was damaged. I hesitated. There were other, more perfect skulls in the same stone, but the damaged one was by far the most appealing—I loved the crystal markings of the dream chevron amethyst and couldn't forget it. I kept going back on the Internet to have another look. That skull haunted me, and so, despite it not being perfect, I followed my intuition and bought it. I am glad I did, and you will see why when you read what happened next.

We waited for the skull to arrive and my friend wondered if its name was Hope. The word kept coming to her, and then I came across this quote,

> *"Hope sees the invisible, feels the intangible, and achieves the impossible."*
> *– Helen Keller*

Well Hope was certainly to do that!

The skull came in the post and I gave it a gentle cleanse to wash away the energies of travel, but there was no chance to work with it until first thing the next morning. My husband, Ye, had brought me a cup of tea in bed before going out.

The house is blissfully quiet.

I pick up the skull at my bedside and settle into a meditation. I ask its name. The dream chevron amethyst answers.

"I am **Ramasa Metri**, but I have many names and hope is

CHAPTER 1

my purpose. I am here to engender hope. No matter how battered your human hearts and your bodies may be by the ravages of time and life, hope springs eternal."

"Hope is life and keeps you in body."

"Hope of success, happiness, achievement, loving relationships with others—be they plants, animals, crystals, people, stars, inner guides, or the intangible levels of life experience. Hope is my purpose and not my name, but there's no harm in calling me after my purpose, **Hope Ramasa Metri**."

"My physical crystal body is not whole, but my etheric and higher bodies are. The small pieces that broke off during carving serve a purpose and go their own ways; they serve in other capacities. Do not worry about them."

Why did I pick you out? I ask. *Why did you call so strongly to me though there were others like you that were whole?*

"Because I can serve you well and we are in harmony together, you and I. Perfection has its limits and can render spiritual tools sterile and dead. We are to be used, not kept as 'perfect' ornaments. I embody the conflicting forces of nature in a way that contains and tames them to some degree, though they create an inner tension within me, hence the fault lines in my crystal. This gives me power. It does not diminish my power. I am more effective because of this."

May I enter your crystal? I ask.

The skull gives permission and I find myself on a narrow sandy beach facing a crumbling amethyst cliff. The cliff represents the side of the skull. A blue-gray sea edges the beach, and a small trickle of fresh water is flowing into the sea from the base of the cliff. It flows from a wide fissure in the rock. I enter the fissure. It opens out into a cave. Light sparkles from crystals scattered over the cave's walls. The light is coming from me! I can see it catching here and there, reflecting off polished facets on the walls. The roof of the cave tapers up into darkness high above me. A voice booms out, "I'm glad you have come to seek communication with me, because it's time to converse with the Amethyst Deva of Earth."

I am so startled and overawed that I have to finish here.

I need a strong cup of coffee before I can go any further…

and it's just as well I'm coming out of the experience, because the house erupts with noise as Ye unexpectedly returns early from his errand. After coffee I resume the meditation, feeling much more awake and grounded this time. I am not a morning person at the best of times, and I usually meditate at night when the house is quiet and Ye is asleep. But I was eager to get to know my new skull. I'd wanted to make sure I'd chosen the right one. I slip straight back into the experience.

In the sand of the cave floor an amethyst cube is serving as an altar. It is an upwelling of the bedrock of the cave, its polished top as smooth and cold as the skull's crystal. "Lie down on this," booms the voice. I feel the cold stone beneath me, and it sharpens my connection.

"I am the Amethyst Deva of Earth. Listen well. For as long as life holds tenure on this planet/space rock, I will be valued for my qualities of protection and purification. I am a master stone, created by Gaia (Earth's spirit) to help her fulfill her purpose. She seeks to experience, to integrate and process, to transmute and transcend, eventually to exist solely in higher dimensions. My purpose is to help her in this. I am a processor stone. I integrate experiences and turn them into profound wisdom. I collect and transmute the experiences of life forms, including those of other crystal life forms."

What emotion does amethyst hold for Gaia? I ask.

"Ultimately it will be joy in achievement, though along the way I will be called on to integrate, process, and transmute pain, suffering, degradation, and destruction—for the journey is long, even by the standards of crystal life. We record the life of our planet and hold and process her emotions for her. We are her 'organs of feeling' if you will; water collects her memories and we store what water knows. Those of us who work with human guardians also store their memories, too, so Gaia has access to, and retrieval of, the human experience. At the moment, she is preferring sea creatures' experiences—dolphins, whales, octopuses for example—because they do not waste their lives on fear and greed as many humans do. Enjoy Earth's bounty: her beauty, her sunsets and weather, her rocks, and the myriads of

CHAPTER 1

companion life forms she hosts, and try to step lighter on her as you live your life."

Was this the right skull to buy? I ask.

"You know it is. Stop doubting yourself. Just enjoy the hope and beauty of Ramasa's crystal. The niggle of 'missing bits' is a low human concern. Once in skull shape, the energies are sealed in, no matter what damage may befall the skull's crystal. Nothing can take away its power. Not even if it's in pieces, if the pieces are kept together."

Should a skull ever be repaired with glue? I ask.

"Water based glues are best, as they can be soaked away and do not create an energy barrier between the crystal pieces."[1]

"Come back and work with me again. There is much you need to know and much that I want you to put in your book." (!)

That was Tuesday, the 27th of April 2021. That it knew about the book left me speechless. I was intrigued by the promise of more to come, but meeting the Amethyst Deva had been beyond my wildest dreams. You never know what a skull will show you or tell you, and size is nothing when it comes to the magnitude of the experience you can have. The tiniest skulls have taken me on jaw-dropping journeys. A case in point was a black obsidian skull, hardly bigger than my fingernail. It had been slipped in as a free gift with a larger purchase, and this is what happened the first time I worked with it.

I tuned in and asked its name: **Manos the Black**. He is male. Despite his tiny physical size, now that I'm in the inner world, he is huge. I have to visualize climbing up three steps to enter a door in his smooth black side. I grip its black doorknob and step through. I see starlight—and step off a narrow ledge into space. Now I am just consciousness, I have no body. I watch stars die and stars being born, I watch them dance through Time as music surrounds me like a film soundtrack. Suns and black holes ebb and flow…

"Everything is going to be okay," Manos says. "It is all part

---

1   I looked into this and found "Crafter's Pick, The Ultimate! Non Toxic Water Based Super Glue bonds metal, plastics, glass and more. Dries clear." I haven't used it on a crystal skull but it sounds good.

of the Dance of Life, and when 'bad' things occur they are only triggers and catalysts for change. Change is life, and life is eternal; be happy as you adventure through Creation! Come to me when you want to swim in the sea of stars and want to feel the flow of Creation, when you want to dance through Time. I am physically small, but I offer you the bigger picture. Size is nothing. What's small at the 3D level can equal higher dimensional gigantic! Laugh, because it is true and it is the cosmic joke."

I returned mind blown.

Katie's gift also brought me a strange little skull, with crystals on its crown, that arrived in May. I was curious to see what I would find when I worked with it. As usual, first I study it closely under a lamp. This helps me tune into the crystal. I link in with Source and visualize bringing the light down around me, and as always, I ask in the archangels: Michael to keep me safe, Uriel to help me perceive the truth, Gabriel so everything is imbued with love, and Raphael so healing will flow forth from the experience. Then I focus on the skull.

I ask its name.

It will not tell me.

I move on to the next question and ask if it is willing to work with me.

"Yes, that's why I've come to you, why I caught your eye and persisted."

May I enter your crystal? I ask.

"Yes."

I visualize standing outside it. Its side is polished, smooth and shiny like a crystal wall. No obvious door, so I run my hands along it and when it yields to the pressure of my fingers I find a revolving glass door. This takes me in. The door was concealed by a slight flash of chatoyance in the crystal bedrock. It is there, but only when you look the right way.

I pass through.

It is twilight. I'm in a jungle. I hear animal noises and water— that means a river near by. The animals are coming to drink. There are birds. I see their large shadows passing overhead. This is the magical, liminal time between night and day. The time magic can

CHAPTER 1

happen and shapeshifters go hunting their prey…

I'm wondering where that thought came from, and I ask who the shapeshifters are.

"Shamans journeying to find evil spirits of disease and slay them. The birds are shamans in disguise. They are in the trees."

"I am a shaman stone. Neither a skull nor just a crystal, I walk between worlds and can shapeshift my consciousness between crystal and skull consciousness. We can go hunting, you and I. Hunt for your enemies and disable their intentions, render them harmless, show them a better way to be with the help of the angels."

"I am heavy because I can draw on much power: most of me resides in higher dimensions, in the realm of angels' crystal cities—like those that will cover the earth when she has ascended much higher up the frequencies, and is no longer in 3D; when the sun has reached out fiery fingers and taken her to its bosom."[2]

Moon said you have the brains of a child, but could be entertaining—what do you say to that?

"Moon joked. She knows my power is greater than hers at times of my choosing. You feel my power; it's not a child's energy. Entertaining? There is a novelty value to my appearance, but entertaining I am not. That is not my function, you chose me for deep, dark work. I offer to work with your shadow and to assist in its integration. Moon looks the part, but I have the power. She is kissed and blessed by the Goddess and carries Her mark upon her crystal,[3] but Moon holds too much light to help you with shadow work. She has other skills and abilities for you to discover. Come to me when events, things, or people niggle and rankle you."

"We will chase down the shadow aspect at play in the situation."

"Yes, Moon made a joke, but she did get you to buy me, so she has her ways to achieve the team she wants. You have assembled a powerful and surprising team that offers a wide spectrum of

---

2   When the sun becomes old and is what NASA calls a red giant.

3   Inclusions and feathering of red iron oxide, which is an ancient symbol of the Goddess's blessing.

COSMIC CRYSTALS! *Working With New Crystal Skulls*

help. Use us. Frequently. And watch your world evolve and the success you deserve will flow to you."

"Audience terminated. That's enough for now."

I exit by the revolving door.

I am back, aware of being in my bed and aware of my bedroom around me once more.

I thank the angels, the skull, God and the Goddess—the Divine Source of All That Is.

It is one o'clock in the morning. I need to ground after that, so—cocoa and supper. Looking back I can understand why it withheld its name, a name gives you power over the person or being. This skull is very different and I shall simply call it the **Shaman Stone**.

Next day I photograph it with Hope Ramasa Metri.

I was eager to show Katie what her gift had brought, but when I print out the photo I am astonished to see a white emanation coming out of Hope to touch the Shaman Stone. Now crystal entities are beings of light, they look like a white ether, and have been caught on photo by other people in the past. Years ago, the UK Kindred Spirit magazine published an article on Harry Oldfield. It featured a photograph of his discovery of a crystal-dwelling photonic entity which had emerged from a crystal, and when startled it had shot back inside. Harry pioneered electrocrystal therapy.[4] In the US there is video footage of just such an entity emerging from a crystal skull called Max. You can see it at: howtoraiseyourvibration.blogspot.com/2011/11/max-crystal-skull-also-called.html

To check the photo is what I think it is, I decide to give Hope Ramasa Metri another visit. I settle down to meditate.

I visualize standing outside the skull.

There are noisy seabirds nesting on the amethyst cliff as I slip in through the fissure to enter the dark cave. Again, it seems I'm giving off light, a steady pale glow, but then I realize it's not me at all—the light is from my guardian angel.

I ask the skull if I may speak with it.

An echoey "yes" filters down. The voice sounds far away at

---

4 http://www.electrocrystal.com >harry

CHAPTER 1

first, then gets stronger.

I ask about the photo—is the white, curvy emanation the crystal deva?

"Yes, giving you proof of my existence and you are to put it in the book. I was imbuing the Shaman Stone with greater connection to interface with you."

I ask about Hapi-atzi, my first amethyst skull.

"I love that skull because she is of my own amethyst crystal body and we resonate in harmony. She has suffered neglect, even though she was always safely stored. She is delighted to be called on to work with you. You and Hapi have interesting ground to cover.

I ask the deva's opinion about two other amethyst skulls I'm considering adding to the team. One is very like the Shaman Stone, and the other has extravagant deep purple chevrons at the back of the cranium.

"The first will be a joy to work with and the second will increase the energy field for our work together."

But I was warned off a kambaba jasper skull that had caught my eye. (It would be a long time before I got permission to buy that one…for a good reason, it turned out. I wasn't ready for it yet). The amethyst skulls did join my team, and you will be hearing from them in chapter 3.

I ask if there is anything else it wants to tell me.

"You are too tired now, but another time we will discuss Earth's magnetic resonance as it relates to human consciousness."

I want to clarify if this is the amethyst deva or the skull itself I am talking to. (By which I mean if it's the overarching Amethyst Deva of Earth, or if it's the individual devic crystal entity that has made this skull its home and can tap into the Collective Crystal Skull Consciousness). I'm informed it is the Amethyst Deva of Earth who is using the skull as a two way radio.

"I am with this skull because it is carved of my amethyst stone body, but I can be in many places where my stone body occurs, and all at the same time. I will be here when you come to me. Make your intention clear, tell the skull (meaning the skull's devic entity), beforehand, and set up the expectation. Then it will always work."

15

COSMIC CRYSTALS! *Working With New Crystal Skulls*

In all four photos the Shaman Stone is on the left and Hope is on the right. The photos were taken in quick succession because I was planning to pick the best and delete the rest. At the time I did not notice the curvy, white light shapes passing between the skulls. The first photo in the sequence is above, the second is below.

CHAPTER 1

The third photo in the sequence is above, the fourth is below.

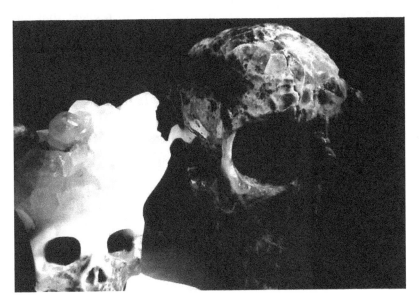

COSMIC CRYSTALS! Working With New Crystal Skulls

Will you speak to me through other amethyst skulls? Or do they have their own voice and personality? I ask.

"They do, but I can cut through and override them. They are learning to individuate, that's why working with people like you is good for them. We are like a group soul, but as everything in the universe is to evolve, amethyst crystal is no different. Same as for animals where there is a group soul that individuates into multitudes of tiny evolving pieces. The pieces all come together in the group soul, and each time a piece incarnates, it gathers more experiences and understandings and by this means the group soul evolves."

"This goes on throughout Creation."

"It is an unfolding pattern remarkably constant wherever there is consciousness and life forms. What you understand as a 'life form' is but the tip of the iceberg, so to speak. Remember, the whole universe is sentient. Humankind are so limited in their spectrum of sense input from their sense organs that they have no idea that rocks and mountains dream, that clouds feel, and rain drops chatter to each other; trees talk and insects sing. The Creator is alive, meaning that within the Creator resides all consciousness. The universe is the Creator's energy expelled to coalesce into matter which forms the material world—that energy is the Creator's—and so it is alive. All of it. So therefore everything, every gas molecule, every atom, is alive. It's just that you are too limited to notice, or to be able to register that fact for yourselves. Some of your mystics have seen it and know, but mystics have never been accorded the full respect that their blessed experiences deserved."

"Humankind will evolve and will learn that this is true, in the end. Already your scientists (quantum physicists), have found human consciousness can change the behaviour of matter, so that's a start."

"You are tired. Audience terminated."

I thank the deva and leave the cave.

Outside, the seabirds shout, "Told you, it's true, everything is alive!" Apparently I hadn't been able to understand them when I went in. As far as I knew, they were just shrieking raucous bird noises then. I wave farewell to the birds and return.

I'm aware of being back in my bed, back in my cozy bedroom.

I thank the angels, the skull, and the Creator who is our Source.

18

CHAPTER 2
Arapo, Zeb'n, and Waking the Sleepers

When I'd been planning to visit stone circles, I had bought a skull called **Arapo**. From the moment I saw his face on the Internet I felt a strong connection with him. He was sandstone, and evoked childhood memories— when the world was a magical place and I had adventures played out against our local hill's sandstone rocks. Then, just before Altai posted the review, I'd got a second skull to take with me. This one was quartz; **Zeb'n** was fierce, her energy a cross between Zena warrior princess and Grace Jones. I wanted her to protect Arapo and amplify his efforts at tapping into the standing stones at the circles. Quartz is a good amplifier and a powerful crystal. It is a really good stone for a skull, though sandstone is not an obvious choice. I just liked it.

However, visiting stone circles was not going to be happening anytime soon with lockdown, but something else definitely was. Every new moon, and every full moon, Bill Homann gave an evening meditation live on Facebook with the most famous crystal skull in the world—the Mitchell-Hedges. Ye and I enjoyed these events, and we brought our skulls into the living room with us to participate on Zoom. Once the meditation had started there was ample silence to check in with your own skulls during this time of heightened activation.

Left to right: Zeb'n and Arapo

One week, at the end of February, fierce Zeb'n startled me by bursting out with, "I'm going to wake up the children!"

She meant the few small skulls I'd gathered over the years. They had fallen deep asleep as the years passed by because I had never worked with any of them. So, after the meditation, when the skulls were returned to their places in our therapy room, I grouped "the children" in a circle around Zeb'n, joking to Ye they were attending Zeb'n's school.

The school ran throughout March 2021.

I checked in on them days later and it looked like four had been socked on the jaw. They looked bruised and the fluorite skull now had missing pieces, with no fragments to be seen. The four damaged skulls had been bought way back in 2007 to represent the elemental summoning skulls of Atlantis when I was writing chapter three in *Holy Ice*, but over the years I had lost sight of their purpose as a visual aid for book talks, and they had recently insinuated themselves into the growing skull community. It had seemed a shame to waste them, shut away in their gold cardboard

CHAPTER 2

box, mimicking their place of containment in Atlantis. In *Holy Ice* I explain how the elemental summoning skulls were used to interfere with the weather, causing storms at sea and famine in enemies' lands. They had needed to be locked away to keep them from mischief, and the thirteen quartz skulls in Atlantis's main temple had sat directly above them, pressing down on them to keep their energy contained. Of course there were more than thirteen quartz skulls in Atlantis, but the thirteen were the famous ones that made it into legend.

So, to prevent the four skulls in question being further damaged, they were removed and stowed away back in their gold cardboard box, and placed beneath the skulls' table in our therapy room, directly below Moon's trusty bulk. Moon would keep them in order. Meanwhile, on the table top, Zeb'n continued the school with the rest of the sleepers. I wondered if Zeb'n had shown them who was boss!

They had only been stand-ins for the mischief-making skulls, the ancient trouble makers, but there is such a thing as sympathetic magic. I had bought them for that purpose—they had never been dedicated to it, but nor had they been released from it. I decided they were best left to sleep, tucked up safely in their box, until further guidance.

The school finished and I worked successfully with all the graduates.

How did Zeb'n do it?

All is revealed when I enter her crystal.

On April 6th I settled down to meditate with her. She is forceful and surprisingly heavy for her size. We had communicated several times already, and she had explained that when crystals feel heavier than you might expect, it is because they have a lot of material in higher dimensions funnelling energy into them.

I had never entered her crystal body before. This would be a first.

Tuning in to her I hear her say, "I am your rainbow bridge to the Divine."

She grants me permission to enter.

There is no door in her side—but she opens, revealing a wide,

COSMIC CRYSTALS! *Working With New Crystal Skulls*

gorgeous staircase of rainbow crystal that sweeps up and around from a lower ballroom of light, where a golden Celtic harp plays to itself. Sparkling cadences of music vibrate gently throughout the chamber.

I ascend the staircase. At the top there is an upper level of clouds and rainbows and light. Then I notice that a big rainbow connecting with the top step arcs up, forming a rainbow bridge leading into the Kabbalah's Tree of Life. Zeb'n's essence comes with me as we cross over the bridge and enter Tipereth, the sphere at the heart of the Tree. We make our way higher, up the pathways of the Tree to the sphere of Binah, the Great Mother, to meet with Moon-Over-the-Waters-of-Life.

The skulls "talk" to each other, and me, but it is all too far above my head to hear or understand, and the experience has a dream like quality now. I am given to understand that Zeb'n has recently entered the service of the Goddess, she has received a blessing and now carries a sprinkling of the sacred red marks in her crystal that were not there before... this is part of the dream sequence, I will not find them in her 3D physical form, though her crystal body does look different after this—more lustrous and intricate.

I thank her for waking up "the children."

And I'm given to understand it was her harp that did it— the vibrations of her harp. (So play music to your skulls, and especially make it a harp CD!)

We leave Moon's essence in the sphere of Binah, and return, sliding down the rainbow bridge, back into Zeb'n's crystal crown. Her essence remains within her crystal, and I go down the staircase and out. A roller shutter comes down behind me.

Ooooh! What a fabulous experience that had been.

I had tremendous respect for Zeb'n after that. I had never suspected a tie-in between crystal skulls and the Tree of Life. If you would like to read more about the Tree, I recommend Dolores Ashcroft-Nowicki's book, *The Shinning Paths, an Experiential Journey through the Tree of Life*. I've read it and reread it, over and over, because I love the imagery. But for me it has to be Archangel Michael who is the angel of Tipereth, sphere of the

CHAPTER 2

sun, rather than Dolores' placing of Raphael there, wonderful though the archangel of healing is. He is out of his element in the sun. (You will understand why I say this when you get to chapter nine).

As soon as your lovely new skull arrives, work with it. Your yearning for it, your focus on wanting it, will have activated your desire body and already you have a preliminary energy connection with this particular skull, even before it reaches you.

We live in a sea of energy. Our body is a collection of cells vibrating with the energy of life. We have a physical cellular body, and in higher dimensions, we have soul, spirit, etheric, and astral bodies. A sub function of our astral body is our **desire body**, and this goes from active to passive according to our response to things. If we see something we want—a certain skull say—our desire body shoots out tendrils of energy that wrap around the object of our desire. The tendrils of energy form cords, and our energy flows along the cords. If we lose interest, the cords shrivel and drop away, but if we remain interested, the cords strengthen and more of our energy flows around what we desire. In extreme circumstances we become consumed by our wanting, it can literally be draining for us. But for crystal skull purchase, this is good, and we can use our desire body to our advantage. The tendrils of energy we have wrapped around the crystal skull we long for mean we can make a connection even while awaiting its arrival—and our energy link with the skull is always strong when it has newly arrived.

Take Arapo for example, back in the autumn of 2020.

I really wanted that skull and had panicked in case some one else bought him first. He just seemed to leap out of the laptop's screen to make a connection with me. Sedona sandstone, traveling via Canada to the UK, at a time when there were postal delays… the days passed slowly. I was drifting off to sleep one night, idly wondering when my lovely new skull might arrive, when I saw him in my mind's eye very clearly. He announced his name. He said he would be another week in the post, and that as soon as he arrived he wanted to visit the beach, meet up with the local

COSMIC CRYSTALS! *Working With New Crystal Skulls*

sandstone and its rock pools—and that he had something to tell the sea!

I live by the coast and the sea is only a few minutes away.

He said he'd seen the sea in my aura when we connected on screen.[5]

He arrived the afternoon of Halloween. I took him down to the beach to catch the ebbing tide, but after a couple of gentle waves, the sea smacked him over and aggressively swept in. For a heart-stopping moment, as the monster wave drained away, I feared I'd lost him. There were plenty of other lemon-sized sandstone rocks on that beach, and knocked over, I couldn't see his sweet face.

I did wonder what on earth he had said to the sea.

I asked him.

He had fond memories of his old friend the sea from eons past, when he was sand and later stone, and he had wanted to say "hello." But when he was touched by the waves he was shocked to realize the extent of the sea's pollution and degradation in the millennia since then. I suspect his surprised and unflattering comments were not diplomatic, nor well received. La mer had been insulted. I suspect the Lady of the Sea had slapped him!

First time I meditate with Arapo he declares, "I am a bridge for you between the seen and unseen worlds."

After gaining permission to enter, I visualize slipping inside a fissure in his sandstone side and passing through, coming out in a valley surrounded by high red sandstone cliffs—red like Sedona, red like Arapo's stone—red, with bands of blonde sandstone and fossilized mud threaded through.

The valley has a lake in the center and greenery surrounds it, it looks fertile. There are fish. I climb rough steps in the sandstone cliff to my left, and stand on a high, natural look-out platform. From here I can see the sea in the distance—far away, out through the valley and beyond. And I remember Arapo's fascination with the sea.

5   Including the vision of the sea that the ancient skull Sha Na Ra had shown me in 1998 when I asked if I should go to live there. I had an irrational fear of tidal waves, but on the strength of the vision I knew it was the place I should be. Arapo said the vision was still printed in my aura.

CHAPTER 2

A UFO lands in the valley. It has come for water from the lake. I observe, but there is no communication. Then I return, feeling there will be more to this story. It felt a long time ago, before there were people.

To sum up, as soon as your skulls arrive, work with them. Keep them near you for your energies to acclimate. Keep them by your bedside for a while, because some communication will be subconscious, some in dream state. Let them attune to the vibration of your voice and your touch. Talk to them. Use sound to cleanse and awaken them: Tibetan tingshas, bells, or crystal bowls, and of course, harp CDs. Gregorian chant, classical music, and in fact any harmonious music is suitable. Feel it in your body and feel if the skulls reach out or withdraw from it. People do not all enjoy the same music and why should crystals be different? Crystal is always vibrating, and quartz oscillates at a constant frequency, which is why it is used in time pieces and electronics. In all things crystal skull related, follow your intuition; feel it in your body, does it feel right? Or does it feel wrong?

Never give your power away to a skull. No one is a perfect channel. Distortion is always a possibility in any communication, so use your common sense and discernment. "The skull says…" is never an excuse for what common sense would contradict. That said, when we share our world with crystal skulls we do ourselves a favor and open to the wonder and enchantment of life. We open to a treasure house of skills and abilities we may never have dreamed we had. To be drawn to the skulls in the first place, I would be amazed if you have not got a strong past life connection with them, and a skill set already at your finger tips. (And for those who wish to learn more about tendrils of energy and the cords we create in our lives, I recommend Denise Linn's book, *Energy Strands, the Ultimate Guide To Clearing the Cords That Are Constricting Your Life*).

CHAPTER 3
Solange, Hapi-atzi, Radiance, Moon, Stardust, Mars, Cloud, Charles Lapis, Fred, Hunter, the Skull of Dreams, Shallimar, and the Sleepers Tell Me More

Looking back, it was the arrival of Solange in February 2021 that really began the series of one-to-one meditations I planned to do with all my skulls. I needed to be systematic to make sure I discovered each one's character and what they could offer me. No point splashing the cash just to have them sit on a shelf like ornaments! They were meant to be tools to enhance my life. So I entered each skull and let an experience unfold.

When I first began I felt most comfortable entering through their left side, though you should always go with your own feelings here. Perhaps you'd prefer to enter through the eyes, for example. Every meditation I do starts with a simple protection, as with the Shaman Stone in the first chapter, and I always ask the skull for permission to enter. On visiting a sacred site, you would ask the spirit guardians for permission to enter and it's the same with a skull. You're trying to build a relationship with the energies that work through it and respect is important.

Tibetan quartz **Solange** gave me a disturbing experience the

CHAPTER 3

first time I entered the inner world to work with him. I found him filled with water, his eyes capped over and covered up. I wondered what this symbolized. I visualized removing the eye coverings and was given to understand they symbolized the Chinese government's interference in the affairs of Tibet, and that the water symbolized grief. I was concerned for poor Solange, so I tried again.

Next time, the water has gone and a spiral staircase leads me up into the crown area. Here, panoramic windows are set in curved walls and show me the mountains of Tibet. It is a brief experience, but things have shifted, and afterward I re-examine Solange's crystal body under my lamp. At the point I'd visualized entering, I see a staircase and a human figure suggested in the cloudy veils; it is uncanny. It hadn't been there before and I felt welcomed by the skull.

As the meditations piled up, they often followed a pattern.

On entering, I'd come into a ground floor area where steps would lead me up to a second, higher level in the crown. It was a very different experience with each skull, and not all skulls presented this two-tier arrangement, but both Solange and Hapi-atzi did.

Amethyst **Hapi-atzi** is next. When I entered, I found myself standing on a dark purple stone-slabbed floor, but what's strange is that I recognize the staircase. It is the same staircase that had taken me into a past life in *Holy Ice*, a past life where I had met Merlin. This time it takes me up to a large room in the crown of the skull...and in the center of the room I see a big oak table.

Behind the table stands Merlin—it has taken me to meet Merlin again!

We speak.

A sudden rush of emotion overwhelms me as memories from the past life swamp me. I can't handle the rush of feelings and have to leave—but I will be back—I know I will be back, and I will be better prepared next time. This was only a brief experience, but it was fantastic and uplifting, and all will be revealed later in the book. The Celtic past life had been full of tragedy, but I was overjoyed to meet Merlin again. It had taken me completely by

27

COSMIC CRYSTALS! *Working With New Crystal Skulls*

surprise, though I did know you could meet up with guides and departed loved ones through the dimensional bridge offered by a crystal skull.

When it comes to aquamarine **Radiance**, I wanted to ask her if she was happy with her name, because it had been chosen for her by the seller. She replies, "Radiance is apt, for I radiate peace and joy, gentleness and love." She gives me permission to enter and I find a sliding glass door in her side.

It has a sickle moon-shaped door handle and opens easily. I pass through into a chamber where aquamarine velvets are strewn around and there are luxurious velvet hangings and soft carpets. The colors are all the soothing, pearly, blue-green shades of aquamarine crystal.

There's a big soft bed. I want to sink into it.

Radiance says, "I offer rest when you are sore oppressed, and peace when you work, so you may enjoy your work and achieve more and feel better. I am in essence a healing skull, with a high harmony vibration which can restore yours. My job is to harmonize the skull team and help Moon. You need peace and rest, and joy in your work. That's why I've come—to assist you."

I sink into the bed, a four-poster bed draped in beautiful hangings.

Radiance says, "I offer deep peace."

I hear the sea murmuring and silver bells tinkling outside this lovely chamber. I go to a window and open it to hear the sea better; a light breeze wafts sheer voile curtains and now I hear mermaids sing.

"You may return at any time," says Radiance.

Two days later it is **Moon-Over-the-Waters-of-Life**, and this will be the first time I have explored inside my mysterious Moon. The essence of her name is reflection: moon reflecting sunlight, water reflecting moon.

I enter the inner world and see Moon before me.

On her left-hand side I find a door with a circular silver doorknob, beautifully embossed with a picture of the moon's phases above an ocean. I open it and pass through into a cathedral of light. A soft voice is humming in this luminous space. This is

CHAPTER 3

Moon's voice and a bright spotlight now shines down on me.

"Listen," says Moon in a resonant feminine voice. "We have made a good start, you and I, and you hear me. I am linked to the Galactic Federation." The spotlight beam now begins to feel like a tractor beam, and I float upward. Am I being lifted on board a UFO? A Galactic Federation UFO? Is this the beginning of an astral abduction? I decline the experience. I say I don't want that, and I am gently returned to the floor. But it does leave me wondering if perhaps a contact had taken place...one not remembered, because such memories tend to be buried deep in our subconscious. Skulls and off-world entities have always been linked, even in legend, where the skulls were seen as gifts from other worlds. But I wasn't expecting this and I'd had enough.

Moon was huge inside and I suspect she has many other rooms inside her crystal, not just the lofty cathedral-like space I'd entered.

I face up to my ET contact experiences in *Divine Fire*. Like many experiencers, I had missing time in childhood and I have an unexplained scar on my body. You have no control over when these encounters will take place, and you are powerless to stop the experience, or control what happens.

I retrieved the memories through regression and found I had had physical abductions and astral abductions during sleep. I have had many a nightmare of being hunted by aliens and being betrayed by tracking devices implanted in my body. So, you will understand that while alien crystal skulls are very popular these days, many repel me.

Until I found **Stardust** I thought I would never, ever, buy one.

But her enchanting crystal and her kind face won me over.

Looking at my past life connection with aliens helped me, because when you've seen yourself as an ET, it takes away the fear and you understand them better. But it took me months before I went back inside Moon, but on the plus side, being in Moon made me feel my vibration had been raised.

Now Stardust's delicious flower agate is from Madagascar and when I ask her, "What do you offer me?" she answers, "A

COSMIC CRYSTALS! *Working With New Crystal Skulls*

window into the past. You may research Lemuria and Atlantis with me."

Around a fine fault line on her left-hand side, Stardust has a little golden healer coloration in her crystal. This draws me to it and in the meditation I walk in through the fault line. I emerge and see a landscape laid out before me; this land is fertile, with forests of tree ferns, ancient trees, and lush growth. A pterodactyl flies overhead. It is Antarctica a very long time ago. There is a river.

I'm looking down on the river from a vantage point high on a mountainside and I see a huge vista sweeping before me.

I see a UFO.

Stardust says, "You have never been alone," by which she means humankind has never been alone, that star people have been visiting Earth since before we began.

I leave, returning through the fissure provided by the fault line.

Little **Mars Preseli** provides a very powerful experience for me.

He says the creamy-white spots scattered over his stone body represent stars, and when I find a door in his side, it has a creamy-white ceramic doorknob just like the spots of his stone. He announces he is my gateway to the universe and the stars.

I pass through and enter his stone body.

Inside it is as black as night.

Then I realize I'm standing on a black world, looking out at the universe. I see multitudes of stars in the sky, and feel a very raw and very elemental powerful feeling in my body. A fireball flies down from the sky and I think it's a bomb—is this war? Am I in a war zone?

Hastily I climb up some black jagged rocks to my left and from this new height I look down to see a chasm filled with volcanic fire, a natural force of nature. The projectile rock—it's not a bomb—falls safely into the chasm and disappears. It is all natural, it is not a war. Mars' message is **when you shift your viewpoint you understand things differently**. I'm in no danger here, though the raw forces of nature carry destruction, they are

CHAPTER 3

part of the universe, part of life. They are not evil.

A black dragon lands. It is not evil. But it is raw power, primordial energy, and I come to understand that it's all a part of me. I have to be comfortable with this energy and not afraid of it. It's "Kali" energy, destruction before creation. Very powerful, raw, and dark, the hidden side of life. Very old and basic and universal—and it leads on to transformation. This energy is "the boiler room of the universe." This energy is personified as Kali, the ancient Hindu goddess, whose depiction always shows her dancing, wearing a necklace made from the skulls of demons she has killed. Sometimes in life we need to embrace our Kali energy—which is not going to be comfortable for those around us, but it will bring change and transformation.

Now because I've felt resistance to the name he chose, before I finish the meditation I check his name with the angel of truth, Archangel Uriel. I can't help but think Mars is a big name for such a little skull. Uriel holds out a cauldron. I pluck out a folded paper, open it, only to find "Mars" written there. I burn the paper and throw its smoking remains into the chasm.

Mars it is then.

After all, Mars is a star, a whole world. But when we look at the sky from Earth, Mars is no more than a tiny pin point of light. It's all in the viewpoint, as he says.

The Hindu pantheon has Kali as Mother of the entire universe. She is a goddess, ready to fight evil, a demon slayer and a divine protector. Her skin is shown as black or dark blue and her mood is terrifying and unruly. In one of her four hands she holds a man's severed head, representing the sacrifice of human ego needed to access her cosmic knowledge and protection.

Kali represents justifiable female resentment and rage. She is part of the human psyche I had not understood before.

Cloud is a gray labradorite crystal skull the color of rain clouds. His body has blue and gold flashes. When I found Cloud's particular skill, I was certainly glad I'd been drawn to get him. At this time I was having bad dreams about spiders each time I met a certain person, and it felt like psychic attack.

I go in through Cloud's side and up a spiral staircase into the blue flash area of his face. Here there is a heavenly fragrance. I continue up into the gold flash area around the eyes and brow, and here there is music—music of the spheres and of angelic choirs—it's gorgeous! I see light raying down into the skull from heavenly realms, and looking up I see the light stretching all the way up to the Divine. Wow, I think. Truly wow.

Then I see how this skull can draw on that light for shielding and protection. Cloud can flood the house with this higher dimensional light and put a mirror wall around it to make the house invisible to the eyes of evil, or invisible to those who wish me harm. The mirror has a speckled, flickering quality. It is not flat and static, but has depth and constant movement, it scatters and deflects.

I was well impressed with this little skull.

Cloud is now our "Head of Psychic Security."

He prefers to perch by the beeswax candle on the tall angel candlestick on the skulls' table, rather than join in with the other skulls below. He fits like a glove in the elevated position and says it makes it easier for him to cast the protection energies around.

I have certainly noticed a difference since he came. No more spider dreams now.

Cloud, Mars, and a skull called **Charles Lapis** are only two inches long, but they have taught me that two inches is an excellent size—small enough to be extremely portable, yet strangely powerful. Charles is exquisitely carved from a very vibrant blue lapis lazuli stone. Little Charles has almost the same carve as Moon, though his nose is not drilled right through. When I sit down to meditate with him I find a door with a pyrite knob, just like the little speckles scattered through his stone. I enter and find a spacious area, its floor covered in rich blue tiles. I see a staircase to my left, spiraling upward. I climb up the blue treads into the crown area. Here there is a rich blue sea. I swim in it. It is warm and relaxing, and I head for a tropical beach of warm sand and palm trees. The sand is nice, comforting. A blue turtle-being comes up beside me and we talk, or rather communicate telepathically. It says we've been together, that I was once its mate and we were happy and successfully raised lots of baby hatchling

CHAPTER 3

turtles—it says it loves me and misses me. I cry because I realize I love it and miss it, too, I miss the warmth and easy connection we had between us in that past life. Tears sting and flow, take me by surprise.

It tells me Charles Lapis is the Keeper of Records, that Charles has the key to the records. I'm told that lapis lazuli equals wisdom and knowledge, and that beautifully carved Charles has precision in his functioning. We have a long "talk," the turtle and I, and it says we will meet again—perhaps even in real life, in ordinary reality, in connection with crystal skulls—because he is a man now, a man with sandy colored, short, curly hair. (!)

Well.

I take my leave and swim back to the steps. I descend the spiral staircase with the blue treads. I thank Charles and he tells me I can always return and meet the blue turtle again, or other beings I've loved. And if you'd told me before this experience that a piece of lapis lazuli could bring me to tears, I wouldn't have believed you.

Shallimar, Erin Nuummi, the Skull of Dreams, and Tiger

COSMIC CRYSTALS! *Working With New Crystal Skulls*

Years ago I sent for a gold flash Nuummite skull, but I let it slumber away until Zeb'n woke it up. Nuummite is a very ancient black rock only found in Greenland and is believed to be over three billion years old. It can contain glints of blue, copper, and gold. It is said the inclusions in the crystal look like shooting stars in space. This is true, and may explain why I had the following experience. Or at least why the beings first contact me through this skull.

I learn her name is **Erin.**

Erin Nuummi I call her.

I have permission to enter and see that her door has a diamanté doorknob with a gold collar around it, redolent of the gold flashes in the stone. I step through and I'm standing on polished black tiles and can see nothing in the darkness within Erin—until a meteor shower lands like a fall of golden stars. But they are not stars. They are space craft. And out of the craft come gold-skinned aliens who advance on me. I wonder if I should be afraid.

One comes right up to me, he's just a bit taller than me and he says, "You are one of us." I look down at my arms and to my surprise I see I am like them now. He says he is my brother. He says to come and see Mother, as she is dying...and somehow I know he's right. I get in his craft. We return to his world, and on the way I feel the dimensions shifting, causing a physical sensation in my body, like a 90 degree backward twist.

Walking on his world I see bluish rocks, purple trees, orange sand, and a pink sky. To look at, the world is not unlike Earth, except that the colors have changed with the dimensions. We go into Mother's simple dwelling and she is lying down. I hold her hands and feel her love for me. She asks how my Earth mission is going—have I achieved it? I say yes, my three books are out in the world now. She says she misses me and hopes it was worth it, and that I should look after myself and nourish myself with the beauty Earth can provide: the beauty of the waves where I live; the beauty of plants and flowers; the beauty of crystal skulls, and of my friends. She says that I should enjoy the beauty of life on Earth while I'm there. I feel overwhelmed and soon take my leave.

CHAPTER 3

My brother and his friends return me to Earth and the dimensional shift seems more acute on the way back.

Then we fall like meteors.

I get out of the craft and stand in the darkness inside Erin and wave goodbye to them. I exit Erin and thank her, the angels, and God for the experience.

That was something to think about.

"I hope it was worth it," stuck in my mind. It had put me on the spot and felt very judgemental. Fancy having to justify your Earth life to an ET parent.

An ET parent you didn't know you had.

Earth's gravity is punishing on a body. Our spindly, lanky ET bodies were made for life in much lighter gravity than Earth's, and our lives lasted much longer on our home planet. So my Earth life is short to an ET parent who knew me before I volunteered to incarnate as Paulinne. From Earth's perspective, these aliens would be classed as energy beings and not be seen as solid at all. The dimensional overlap provided by the crystal skull allowed me to interact with the ETs and see them as solid, because they were as solid as I was while in my astral body. But "Home" was part of the dark matter of the universe, 95 percent of the universe is dark matter and dark energy that cannot be seen from our 3D level of existence. Our scientists only glimpse its shadow, but they know it is there.

Though these aliens looked much like the ETs usually known as the Grays, our skin was different. We were golden skinned— proper shiny metallic-looking golden skinned. I have always liked gold as a color, and perhaps that's why it draws me, because it reminds me of home…

But the aliens hadn't finished with me yet.

The next night I meditate with **Fred**, another of the new skulls that had arrived in chapter one.

Fred is Mexican crazy lace agate and you will remember he came with Radiance, Stardust, and Hunter in early April 2021. Fred told me his name before he arrived. He has wings on his head, like Hermes, and like the wings on the Caduceus. He was listed as a winged traveler skull, and that turned out to be very

COSMIC CRYSTALS! *Working With New Crystal Skulls*

apt.

When I sit down to meditate with Fred I visualize opening a door in his side and pass through into a desert. It's night here. It feels like New Mexico. There's sand all around me and I can smell desert sage. I see a circular UFO has landed to my right and I go over to it. The aliens look like last night's aliens—same gold spindly bodies and black almond eyes. They say I am like them... but I'm extra tired tonight and keep falling asleep. I have to cut the meditation short and end here.

The next night I try to get more of the story.

I enter through the door in Fred's side and I'm back in the desert again. There's a new moon and I can see by its light that the UFO is still here. I go over and ask the ETs why I'm in this form—because again, I have a gold body and black eyes like theirs. They answer it is to help me relate to the alien side of my nature.

Then they say, "We've come to take you somewhere."

They say, "We travel the universe, but we always come home, and that's where we are going now."

I get in their craft and this time we land by a sea on our home world. I stand on lavender-blue sea cliffs. It is sunset on the world, and in the dying light the sea winks with phosphorescence as oil-bright colors pop and swirl on restless waves. The pink sky is flushing magenta.

It is very peaceful here and the air has a lavender scent.

I have always longed for this place, and never known where to find it. In a past life in Spiritual Gold I mistook it for Venus, because Venus has the same color of sky, but this world is much larger.

It feels good to be home and I'm given my own craft.

I will be able to return here whenever I choose.

My brother sets up an auto pilot so it will do the return journey unaided, though he does accompany me back this time.

When we land, we open the dome on the top of my circular UFO and get out. The other ETs came with us in their craft and they take my brother home with them. "My voice is my passport," is all I have to say next time I want to open the dome, and the

CHAPTER 3

auto pilot is primed for repeated return journeys. But before my brother goes he says, "We travel the cosmos. Come into Fred and call us if you need us. Fred has a portal to the cosmos within him."

I wave goodbye.

And when I thank Fred, Fred winks!

This Hermes skull can take me home—Fred is my portal—I just need to settle down with him and meditate. The thought that I have an astral UFO tucked away inside the portal within a small skull makes me chuckle. It is an outrageous idea! But skulls act like mirrors and can show us hidden aspects of ourselves. And they can do a whole lot more than that, too.

Tiny Dalmation jasper skull **Hunter** arrived as a gift with Fred. His body is a pale cream stone with black spots, like those of a Dalmation dog. He's only an inch long, but he tells me he is for "Hunting new skulls," and "If you need something come and tell me."

The door in his stone body has a black doorknob, as black as one of his spots.

I enter and find myself in a spacious area with a cream colored carpet, as creamy as the stone. I look around and see a fixed, robust, wooden ladder to my left. The ladder takes me up, and I enter an upper area where spacious windows line the crown and a big telescope is set in the third eye. The telescope is trained on looking out. Hunter says, "This is how I find what I'm hunting for!" He tells me I need to focus the telescope on what I need, visualize it strongly, and then ask him to bring it to me without stipulating how. Leave it to him to find a way.

So I did.

Of course it is a more subtle function than just asking for a heap of cash, but the money you need may come to you in different ways. Skulls work by tweaking energy threads in the world, by engineering synchronicities, mistakes, events, kindnesses received, meetings, etc. This means they can pull things to you, and this is how crystal skulls have earned their reputation for manifestation. In a very short space of time I asked Hunter for help with a steep dental bill I'd been presented with,

COSMIC CRYSTALS! *Working With New Crystal Skulls*

and it got mysteriously halved when I came to pay, without a word of explanation. With Hunter's advice the purchase of two more skulls became possible; remember the amethyst skulls I'd wanted at the end of chapter one? Well, so far, I'd not had the funds to send for them, but that was about to change—because often there is another way to go about things. Also, the book wholesaler sent me free copies of my books to thank me for helping them rectify a mysterious postal mistake. We were able to redeliver a parcel that had been sent to us in error, so that it got to the right person who lived nearby, and my books were a gift to thank me. And to top it all, a very unexpected royalties check arrived for *Holy Ice*, my skull book. Though it had only been out a few months, it had already earned back the publisher's advance and more.

I was most impressed by Hunter.

Now **Marco Quartz** is a small, transparent quartz skull. He is male and he was my first ever proper skull, bought at a mind, body, spirit event way back in 1998. Before Marco I'd only had a necklace of tiny quartz skull beads. I had always meant to meditate with Marco, but in twenty three years I had not got around to it. He was a sleeper, but after Zeb'n's school I settle down to meditate with him and he tells me his name. He says, "Good evening," in a deep male voice; such a big voice for such a little skull.

He grants permission to enter, and I go straight in, but get nowhere, so I come out and try again. On the second attempt I open a transparent door in his side. It has a black shiny doorknob... and once inside, his clear quartz body is all dazzling light and crystal—but then I see grass—and I'm in an Alpine meadow, near the edge of a cliff. Then I fly—I float off the cliff edge and soar, because I'm a bird now, a stork with big white feathers and long legs. As I fly, Marco tells me what he offers me, "I can help you astral travel, help you fly like a bird. I give you freedom to travel. Your traveling days are not over yet." I like this. I fly over a forest and decide to visit a troubled family member. I fly to their home and look in through a window. I don't pick up much, but even though I'm only astral traveling, I feel very conspicuous as a great big stork! I don't know why Marco made me a stork—

CHAPTER 3

perhaps next time I'll be something smaller...or perhaps the stork hints at issues to do with babies? Hmmm...

Left to right: Jago Jasper, Malcolm Isua, Shanash Rose, Marco Quartz, Melandra Ruby Ro Quartz

I ask the angels to send love, light, and healing to all my family, and return through the door.

Meanwhile, the skulls that Hunter helped me with had arrived.

I had been so impressed with the Shaman Stone, that when I saw an amethyst version from the same seller, I really wanted that one, too, plus another of the dream chevron amethyst skulls which had particularly beautiful markings. They'd arrived gorgeously boxed in black velvet on May 20th, and by then the seller had become a friend, arranged a generous discount, had a copy of *Holy Ice*, and was happy to wait until June for payment!

I had rather cheekily nicknamed the skull with the amethyst crystals on its head "Skully Bonce," which is comic slang for "Skully Head," but when it arrived it said I was to call it the **Skull of Dreams**. It also said it was androgynous.

COSMIC CRYSTALS! *Working With New Crystal Skulls*

The crystals on Skully's head sparkle and catch the light. They draw me to them, and I enter through the roots of the crystals. It's like being in a hall of mirrors. The mirrors are showing me happy times from the past; show me being Mum. Show me younger and happy, when my children were small and everybody got on. Then they show me that the troubled family member incarnated with a problem. The mirrors are showing me that over the years the problem has grown, and that is what is at the root of things. *What do I do?* I ask.

Skully says, "Heal the etheric ice splinter in their energy field from a distance—we can work together on that. It is good you found me and that you persevered to bring me to you. We will do this together, you and I, and then move on to bigger Earth healing projects. You can call me Skully, but know I am the Skull of Dreams. Farewell…Truly, truth is in the roots of crystals."

The words the skull uses echo down the years to me from a long lost dream. I vividly remember scribbling them down one night while half asleep, way back in the days when I kept a dedicated dream journal at my bedside, long before I had any children. **Truth is in the roots of crystals**. I didn't know what it meant and couldn't remember the dream, but it sounded too important to ever forget.

The skull's words had given me food for thought.

Scully had sounded confident that we could right the situation and move on to other things, but it was going to take time. It is ethically wrong to interfere with karma and freewill without the permission of the other person. You can't just go around forcing healing on people, however well intentioned you may be. But you can send love, light, and healing to that person's higher self and guardian angel, and ask that it be used for the highest good. So…I wrote out my request on a small piece of paper, then folded it up and tucked it away beneath Scully on the skull table. The Skull of Dreams was on the case, but I knew there would be more to do on this.

CHAPTER 3

The new dream chevron amethyst skull that had come with Skully gives her name as **Shallimar the Beautiful**—then she says she is, "Just kidding about 'the beautiful'." But I'm not so sure about that when she makes me go up an elegant curved staircase with hand rails before I'm allowed to reach a door in her side. It is thirteen steps up to a very stylish dark purple door that bears a golden doorknob. When I enter, I find graceful palms and impressive large plants inside, and everything is very lush and luxurious.

What does this skull offer me? I ask.

"A chance to relax and gardening tips!" is the surprising answer.

I can't resist asking how to help the palm plant we have in the therapy room, because it hasn't grown in a year.

"Mist it," Shallimar says.

I ask about a sickly garden plant.

The answer comes that it doesn't like the sea air where I live—it must go! And time was to prove Shallimar right on both counts.

In the center of Shallimar, hidden in a clearing set within a verdant tropical jungle, I find a secret garden. There is a table set round with comfortable garden chairs. I sit down and bask in the warmth and the sunlight. The light feels soothing and healing as sunbeams stream down around me, filtering through soft green foliage. In the distance I hear bees hum, happy in their work.

Shallimar says, "I am here to make you feel happy, expansive, and at peace. That's my job. Visit often."

Is there anything else I should know about you? I ask her.

"Gradual flow will build our understanding. You were drawn to my garden of peace, that's why you bought me." Shallimar is a beautiful, kind, and gentle skull. Before we finish she tells me, "If you use me first at bedtime before Shanash, I will make Shanash more effective."

Now **Shanash Rose**, the skull she means, met the Mitchell-Hedges skull at a conference in Edinburgh in 2008, which is when we bought her. Shanash had slept soundly ever since, until Zeb'n woke her up. When I enter her rose quartz crystal body I find soft, fluffy clouds linked by ladders, and it reminds me of an old fashioned Snakes and Ladders board game I had as a child. You threw dice to progress on the board, hoping to climb up the ladders and avoid sliding down the snakes. There are no snakes in Shanash, only ladders and clouds. I have fun climbing from cloud to cloud and when I reach her crown I see the setting sun. Beautiful colors fill the sky, flooding her crown and infusing the clouds there with the colors of sunset. Shanash signals it is the end of the day, a time for rest, a time for relaxation and sleep, a time to unwind and sleep in the softness of a cloud.

The world was a simpler place when I was a child.

Shanash can help me recapture that.

It is strange how some skulls are very definitely male or female, but others are more androgynous. The next skull, **Melandra Ruby Ro Quartz**, is another androgynous one. Melandra came from the same event as Shanash, and was also a gift from Ye. She is clear quartz, and despite the name she has given me, there's nothing of ruby I can discern about her.

In the meditation I'm standing in front of a high, transparent quartz cliff, which is Melandra's crystal body. I enter the cliff through a fissure in the rock, and emerge on the far side of the fissure, where a wide vista of a plain spreads before me. Black thunderhead clouds fill the sky and roll across the plain. There's lightening, snow, then rain—and a lake fills up to my right. The storm passes and there's a rainbow in the sky. The sun is out and the rain has created a lake—frogs appear, croaking loudly, then an alligator...

Melandra says she is to help me with learning "Patience with the weather of life." She tells me not to let storms in life get me down, that sunshine will always follow; lightening comes first, then rainbows. The message means not to stress/push/grumble at myself for not getting the things on my list of jobs done. Instead, I should just observe and float. At this point I'd been struggling with brain fog and exhaustion following my second COVID 19 vaccination, and I was feeling bad about not getting much done, so this message helps me.

Now, red jasper has long been considered a stone of protection,

CHAPTER 3

which is why I sent for **Jago Jasper** years ago. But until Zeb'n woke him up, I didn't know how he could help me. He says he offers me "Shelter when cruel winds blow."

With Jago I had to overcome a sense of darkness before I could link into the angels at the very start of the meditation. I enter him by knocking on his door to ask permission. "I thought you'd never ask!" he says, and that's when we establish his name.

Once inside, I am standing on a creamy white fleece of a carpet, a luxurious sheep's wool carpet, but the rest of the space inside Jago is empty and most of the floor is tiled with polished red jasper stone, like his body. Looking through a window I can see it is dark outside, and in the dark and desolate landscape cruel winds are blowing. But a cozy carpeted slope takes me upward from the entrance to a large welcoming room in Jago's crown. This, too, is carpeted, but with a much deeper, thicker, curlier fleece—it's very comfortable—it's like a huge bed which you sink into. Through the windows I see it's still dark...and the winds blow like they do on Mars; like the dust storms on Mars, but it's warm and cozy here within Jago.

Jago Jasper is a guardian and protector for when life seems harsh. His red stone has a cream band around the teeth and I think that gave rise to the image of the fleece.

Malcolm Isua was another sleeper. At 3.85 billion years old, Greenland's Isua is almost as old as the planet and is gray in color. Malcolm offers me "A window into elemental realms."

I open a door with a sparkly doorknob and go in. I am standing on a gray world just before dawn, looking up at a sky filled with stars and dominated by the wheel of the Milky Way. Dawn comes and I swim in a shallow sea where there is underwater vegetation and lots of green fronds and fish. I swim to an island fringed with black volcanic sand. I walk on the sand and see smoking volcanoes in the distance. Now I become an elemental being— and that's when I realize I was one all along in this experience. I see other elemental beings swarming out of the nearest volcano; it's like the volcano is breathing them out, and I join with them and ride on the clouds scudding past. I have fun shaking the clouds to drop out their rain. ...And that's when I know I've been through many, many lives experiencing the elemental realms. I remember being quartz, growing, filling up fissures in host rocks with my crystals…then I'm swimming in the sea again, and I go back to the gray place where I started. I pass through Malcolm's door and return.

That was a very long time ago when life was just beginning on land, when plants and soil were first forming.

The next meditation is with a tiny tiger's eye skull which came as a gift with a larger purchase a long time ago. It tells me its name is **Tiger** and adds "For though I am small I am mighty!" The door in its side has the golden chatoyance of its body, and there is a gold lever handle to open it by.

I step through into a landscape of gentle hills.

Here it is sunset at harvest time, and the fields are full of golden barley corn swaying in the evening breeze. It's a lovely warm evening and the air is filled with bird song. The sky is on fire with the setting sun, and I'm standing in the mouth of a cave, looking out on this fertile land. I feel peaceful and happy and rich with the abundance of nature and the gifts of Mother Earth, Goddess Gaia, to her children. Here I am well satisfied with life.

Tiger tells me he is my "abundance" skull.

This is the skull to meditate with when I want to feel abundant.

I'm drinking grape juice from the vines and I'm told I will always be well fed by Mother Earth, and she is pleased I'm here. Her cave offers me shelter and comfort and I'm told I am always welcome here.

Tiger says, "Just know I'm here for you." Tiger is a very comforting skull, one to help forget worries. I wish I'd found out about Tiger years earlier! I wish I'd not waited so long to work with my skulls. Don't make my mistake.

CHAPTER 4
Can Skull Beads Function as Crystal Skulls?

Tiger and Manos the Black are the tiniest skulls I have—only the size of a fingernail, but this does not stop them from functioning as skulls; size doesn't seem to matter. Skull beads are often larger, at about an inch long, but their stringing holes are drilled right through them. This must scramble their energies, surely, but does it put them beyond use? Can they still function as skulls? I wondered.

I had seven skull beads carved from different types of crystal. I'd bought them in 2012 all strung together on a thong. I had hoped to wear them and had always intended to split them up and rework them into other necklaces. I cut the thong but couldn't decide which bead to put with which. So I decided to ask the skull beads themselves, to meditate with them and seek their opinions—all the while wondering if indeed they were capable of having opinions!

The first I sit down with is of green aventurine. It tells me to call it **Mahrasi** and says it is female. I visualize opening a door in her side and pass through, deep into her crystal. I find myself under the sea; it is dark and green and there is a lot of plankton—but the hole affects my experience. I feel it weighing down on me when I am inside the skull. At the start, the hole had made it

COSMIC CRYSTALS! *Working With New Crystal Skulls*

difficult for me to get into the skull. It tried to suck me into itself, tried to funnel me through and out the other side of the skull. In fact, the hole almost cheats me of my experience.

How does the hole affect you? I ask Mahrasi.

"It bothers me, but does not stop me. We are not meant for our voices to be heard separately, we were created to be with others. We are happiest as a team where we can compensate for our wounding (by which she means the drilled holes). We have exchanged our individual journeys for a collective journey, at least for a while."

I ask if she wants to stay with the other crystal beads.

"Yes, in one necklace. It matters not which order we are in."

I ask what she can help me with.

"Remembering the past. Wear us for regressions."

Mahrasi was the only bead where the hole was a problem—perhaps because it was slap bang through her center, while the other beads had been drilled higher than that. But apart from Mahrasi, I was surprised by how well the beads could function as skulls.

The second skull bead calls itself **Petri of the Seven**. Petri is a very pale amethyst—and "of the Seven" tells me this bead is very committed to being with the others. I open a glass door in his side and step into a circular room where pale lilac, magenta, and purple windows span from floor to ceiling. The colors shimmer and are fading softly into each other. Translucent voile hangings are casually draped over the windows and more divide up the interior space. I hear a harp. A breeze as warm as a Mediterranean summer evening carries floral scents to me...this is nice. It is peaceful here and good for transmuting stress. The feeling is "**all will be well.**" Nothing negative holds here or can enter. This is a quality of amethyst and Petri offers me a calm, peaceful space where harmony reigns and any discord I may have been carrying is transmuted.

Petri says, "I offer peace, release from worry, and upliftment. I am here for you. Visit me when you need my gifts. I also do this work for the place I find myself in—your home for example—and join in the planet-wide amethyst activities, for this is our

CHAPTER 4

function. This is why Earth gave birth to us. I am a processor stone, as all amethyst is. We all function thus, from the smallest of particles to the largest formations."

I return.

I thank the angels, the bead, and God for the experience, as always.

Peter the Red is the third bead I meditate with. He is rhodocrosite, and like Mahrasi and Petri, he tells me he wants to be strung together with the others.

I ask how he feels about the drilled hole.

"It's not ideal, but it is done. We survive. We still function. We do not need to be in any particular order because a necklace forms a circle."

I prepare to enter his crystal and find a brick porch built at his side, sheltering a door with a red doorknob. I open the door and pass through. At first it is dark inside, then lights come on and it's like a surprise party. There's a band playing loud jazzy, South American carnival music—with trombones! It's a festival! It's a party! Peter says, "Enjoy life, that is what I encourage you to do. No worries, be happy!" The space is full of people celebrating and dancing, who shout, "We are celebrating your book's success!" The people do a conga. Peter says, "I just want to show you that this new "skulls endeavour" you are working on will be a success. Come back to me for advice in the future. And when the Desert Glass comes, wear it often. This will hasten success."

The Desert Glass was Libyan Desert Glass. I had used the first royalties from *Holy Ice* to send for a pendant of this tawny-colored glass set in silver. I wanted to celebrate the fourteen years I'd toiled on my books with something beautiful and it certainly was. This substance is only found in one place on Earth, scattered across a remote area of desert between Libya and Egypt. It could only have been created in a high-energy event a long time ago—it is a very mysterious substance indeed and you will be hearing more about it later.

The fourth bead calls itself **Tiger of the Seven**; it is tiger's eye stone and it glints with a lovely golden-brown chatoyance as light moves across the surface. As I prepare to enter his left side,

COSMIC CRYSTALS! *Working With New Crystal Skulls*

I find flower pots on either side of a wooden door. I knock, and when the door opens I go in.

All is darkness inside...then dawn breaks, and I'm in a jungle. There are birds and monkeys, I hear jungle cries and see flowers beginning to open to the sun...next I'm in a desert. Cacti flower around me, there have been rains and the plants have come alive to set seed...next I am over the sea, and I go to an island. Here there are tropical trees, coconuts, flowers, sand...and there is a volcano on the island. I go on up to the volcano and look inside. It's hot, smoky...next I see ice and snowy wastes. This is Antarctica, and I'm whisked off to the pole...

I am given to understand this is a skull to show me the beauty and variety of Earth. Tiger of the Seven says, "Enjoy Earth's beauty. Keep me with the group, we work best together. I am small, but can take you far—anywhere on Earth you want to go—mountains, forests, sunsets and sunrises, riding on clouds, watching rain and thunderstorms..."

Then I'm taken back to a garden, I recognize the pots and plants—it is my own garden! I have been returned home because it is time to leave. I open the door in Tiger's side, and as I pass through, I realize the pots sitting outside the door remind me of those in my own garden, which is where I enjoy Earth's beauty on a daily basis.

However, when it comes to the fifth bead, a black obsidian bead calling itself **Janus the Black**, it is a very different story. Janus the Black has had enough of being with the others and now wants to be with Manos the Black, tiny little black obsidian Manos first mentioned in chapter one.

Janus was the name of the ancient Roman god with two faces who lends his name to January, even today. One of his faces looked backward to the old year, while the other looked forward to the new, and I suspect my Janus had found his second face in Manos. (They sit together on my skull table like shiny black twins after this, but the others will get their wish to be strung together.)

I ask if the hole bothers him.

The answer is "No."

I'm given permission to enter and find three black stone steps

CHAPTER 4

on his left side leading up to a shiny black door. I open it with a golden lever handle and pass through into a dark cave.

I see cave people sitting around a fire. Their shaman is wearing animal skins, headdress, and mask, and is all decked out in his full regalia. It is a naming ceremony. Each year they are given a new name, their names reflecting their achievements and hopes. So it is a summary of what their year achieved and what dreams they hope to fulfill in the coming year…for example: Wise Mother of daughters Flower and Star, with New Child Coming.

(At this point I am made aware it is also the case with our crystal skulls—each skull's caretaker gives their skull a name, even if just a nickname, and that is how the skulls like it. It helps them to work with you; as you pick a name, it is automatically tuned to your vibration and to theirs, by your intention. A name is a sound signature. So with each human it will be a different name that is appropriate, because each human has a slightly different vibration. Famous skulls have a stage name, but when they change hands, their new guardian will have their own nickname for the skull. The most famous of them all is the Mitchell-Hedges, once called the Skull of Doom by Mr. Mitchell-Hedges, but now known as the Skull of Love by its present guardian, Bill Homann.)

The people speak in Click language. They make clicking sounds with their tongues rather than using words like we do. They are happy. They have a big dry cave and there is plenty of fire wood in the locality, plenty of fallen trees, plenty of food and game. These are fertile lands, with a kind, warm climate and abundant water in streams and rivers nearby.

The cave people have shining eyes and new fur garments. They are prosperous and happy. They have tools and herb lore and medicines, and they have a huge network of communications with other tribes. They trade successfully with travelers from afar, who come in boats and overland. They are at the cutting edge of achievement for their time. It is autumn. Next they will prepare for winter and lay in stores. Their big cave means they can store an enormous hoard of dry fire wood—splendid riches for them.

Janus says, "Come to me to feel happiness, success, and achievement. For you deserve to prosper. You honor us and for that, we thank you."

Iron Cloud, the sixth skull bead, is a gray, heavy, metallic-looking hematite bead who wants to stay with the others. I meditate and enter the inner world again where he towers above me like a great gray cliff. He tells me I need a password. I have to say his name three times, and then a hatch opens in the cliff. It looks dark inside, but I enter.

Inside it is huge, a great echoing space like a hanger. There's activity, men are making something. This is the future. They are making a machine for visiting the sea bed to study marine life and assess the damage that has been done.

How does this relate to me? I ask.

"You will be there. That's why it concerns you now," Iron Cloud says. I realize in this future I'm part of a team planning to assess the breeding habitat for species of fish, and hoping to repair it where possible. We will be planting a kelp forest. Where there is a will to repair, there is hope for the future.

The seventh bead is **Zatis**. Zatis is a clear quartz trans skull (by which I mean female, but wanting to be male), and this is the only skull so far that it did not feel right to find a door in the left-hand side. Instead, I go in through the left eye.

I am flying through the air now, a cloak streaming out behind me…there are birds. I go to a sea bird nesting site on the cliffs of an island. I can understand the birds as they gossip and call out to each other—because I am a nature spirit now. I realize the "cloak" is just energy streaming out behind me. I am elfin to look at now. The birds can't see me, nor can humans…I'm checking up on the birds: are they breeding successfully? Seems they are. I report my findings to a hierarchy of nature spirit caretakers. Here I am pure energy, not solid at all in a physical sense. I can spin and glide and power through the air. I ride the wind.

I return through the eye of the skull.

Zatis put me in touch with an aspect of my elemental self.

One Christmas, when I was writing *Holy Ice*, Ye gave me a bracelet of seventeen half-inch, clear quartz skull beads. Their turn comes to be meditated with.

CHAPTER 4

I ask their names.

They reply, "We are a council of skulls, the **Council of Seventeen**. Yes, we have individual names, but we prefer to work as a collective. We have been together long enough for us to attune our individual energies to one symphony. We can sing with one voice and communicate with one voice, though our decisions are the result of conference."

"We collectively have the power to create a portal. We can suck undesirable energies into the portal we create, and transfer them out of your way, to a place where others are well equipped to deal with them in higher dimensions. We offer you protection and can travel with you. You should wear us more and work with us. Wear us on your left wrist where energy enters. This will also help with your feelings of tiredness, as we charge the incoming energy and amplify it for you. Relax! Glad you found us! You can work with us individually, but there is no need for that. Wear us, use us. The more you do, the greater our power to help you. Wear us and see your fatigue disappear."

But I do enter one bead through its side by means of a glass door with a crystal doorknob. I find I am standing on a floor like a mirror. I stand on the mirror and bask in light. Light is everywhere, the shadows and darkness of backache and tiredness wash out of me as I fill with waves of light, and the light is displacing the darkness. It is a lovely experience and when it is over, I return.

Buzz Aldrin, the former US astronaut, has a bracelet like mine and he has been seen on TV wearing it. You can see him with it on the website www.crystalskulls.com, where Buzz speaks of his crystal skull bracelet as being good luck to ward off evil spirits. Like me, he is convinced the skulls offer protection. They have kept their word and I only wish I'd worked with them years earlier and understood how much they could help me.

COSMIC CRYSTALS! *Working With New Crystal Skulls*

The Council of Seventeen

Now the beads I have had the longest are on a necklace I made after my friends Chris and Ceri gave me a copy of their book, *The Mystery of the Crystal Skulls*. I was well impressed by the book and by its talk of the ancient Native American legends of thirteen ancient crystal skulls, the size of human skulls that held information on our origins, purpose, and destiny. The legends say the skulls held answers to the greatest mysteries of life and the universe, and they foretold a time when this information would be vital to the very survival of the human race—and although the skulls have been scattered and hidden, one day they will be reunited so their collective wisdom can save us from disaster.

CHAPTER 4

The Council of Thirteen – an Earth crystal deva bead to the right

Inspired by the legends, I had strung thirteen inch-long clear quartz skull beads into a necklace. The beads were interspersed with pearls to symbolize the pearls of wisdom the ancient skulls held. I wore the necklace the day I went to the Wolf Song 1X World Peace Elders tour when it came to Northumberland in the UK at the September equinox of 1998. That is when I had a life-changing sitting with the ancient crystal skull Sha Na Ra, when I saw a vision in the crystal, and received the answer to a question. But despite that, I'd never worked with the beads.

COSMIC CRYSTALS! *Working With New Crystal Skulls*

When I sit down to meditate with them in 2021, the beads tell me to call them the **Council of Thirteen**. They say, "We are crystal beings choosing to work with humans because we answered a call. We heard there was a need and we came. Some of us are not Earth crystal devas, and you can tell who we are because the crystal bodies that host us have a different carving style; there are three Earth devas amongst us and ten from other star systems you are in harmony with. Wear us more. We are attuned now to work together. We can protect you, and we do. We are joyful to be together. That is all you need to know for now. We are the Elrands. We all have names. Enter at another time."

I was dismissed!

But when I look at them again now, I do understand why ten have a different style to their faces.

CHAPTER 5
The Cosmic Crystalline Matrix, the Twins, Quartz Speaks and I Become Light

Worlds and crystals form when interstellar gases combine. The crystals become part of the crystalline matrix that permeates the universe. All the crystals in the universe are linked through this matrix; crystals connect up and can tune into each other through the matrix. Crystals are like bugging devices sprinkled throughout Creation, implanted into the material worlds. Higher beings can work through them and use a planet's crystals to tune that planet, and thus they can affect the vibration of the worlds.[6]

Though crystals hold a lot of information, they can tune into even more elsewhere by simply accessing the crystalline matrix and downloading what is required. And because humankind has worked with crystals for thousands of years in a healing and shamanic context, over time the Collective Crystal Consciousness has amassed a huge amount of information about the human body, mind, heart, and spirit and its maladies and cures.

Crystals heal us by interfacing with our psychic, magnetic, and bioelectric energy, as well as by connecting and conferring with our body consciousness and soul. Crystals heal by strengthening and stimulating our own inner healing systems, and by bolstering

6   *Divine Fire* page 146.

failing energies, or by rerouting energy that has become blocked, trapped, or its pathway broken. Crystals can transmute blockages and raise our frequency in order to lift us out of harm's way, and crystals can draw upon a seemingly limitless supply of other-dimensional force; it flows to them from higher dimensions.[7]

And although all crystals are part of the massive crystalline matrix that permeates the entire cosmos, crystal skulls are particularly adept at tuning in to the matrix, and that is why your skulls know everything about you. Your skulls are rewarding to work with because they offer a mirror that reveals hidden parts of your psyche, and they offer you healing and personal growth. Your crystal skulls know you better than you know yourself! You will see this illustrated time and again in these pages. My skulls have accessed my records and told me many things about myself I did not know.

I was enjoying working with my skulls much more than I could ever have imagined. So in June, hungry for more skulls, I bought the twins Bethsherida and Alsherida. They were two little matched skulls cut from the same geode, both with tiny, delicate, twinkling quartz crystals growing out of one side of their faces. I just couldn't resist them when I saw the little darlings on eBay.

Alsherida is male. His crystal tips protrude from the right-hand side of his face, and so I plan to meditate and enter on the left-hand side as usual. I settle down and start the journey into the inner world. I find microscopic crystals twinkling in his gray rock side as I climb up winding steps to a ledge. From here I see a cave opening higher up in his side. I go up.

I enter.

It is dark inside the cave...but there is light here and there, where the rocky chambers that honeycomb this skull in the inner world are open to the sky, as though the crystal tips are light wells bringing in light.

I come to a huge central cavern with a pool at its heart and see springs feeding it. There is an elaborate water system and drainage so it doesn't overflow and the water is always fresh.

---

7   *Crystals To Go* by Edwin Courtenay, page 64.

CHAPTER 5

Musical sounds come from the water as it plays a water harp. Light beams down through a clear crystal roof like a crystal dome. It is very tranquil in here, very calming.

Alsherida is to the left and Bethsherida to the right

What does this skull offer me? I ask.

But I'm too tired, and keep fading in and out of the meditation. Alsherida says, "Come back tomorrow."

So I do.

The journey starts and I retrace my steps up to the ledge and enter the dark cave above. I pass through other chambers until I'm in the huge central cavern again, the one with a crystal dome roof. The large pool is here, and the water music.

I ask if I should enter the pool.

I am given to understand that I should. There are steps down into the warm water. I swim to where water is bubbling up. I float over the bubbles and the bubbles massage me. It is very relaxing.

COSMIC CRYSTALS! *Working With New Crystal Skulls*

A voice booms out, "Can I have your attention? Listen well, for I am Quartz and these are my children, (*by which Quartz means the twin skulls*), treat them kindly and they will reward you greatly with visions of the future, **your** future. Use them to settle matters regarding your future. They are indeed kin, and work in harmony together, you will find out how in the months to come."

I ask if I will get to visit the standing stones I'd planned this year.

"Some, not all; more next year," comes the reply.

Quartz why are you speaking to me? I ask.

"Because you are a part of me—or were once a part of me—and you and I are linked still."

How can I best serve you? I ask.

"By listening and interacting with my crystal body. I can nourish you. Put these two skulls out on the table in your garden to soak up the sun and the moonlight there, and watch them come alive and become charged. They will work the more strongly for you then."

How do the crystals on their faces help? I ask.

"They are antennae and collect and beam out energy. You yourself have had bodies like these crystals, you relate to the crystal side of the face, although you currently reside in a human body, as represented by the other side of the face. These skulls marry together two worlds: human and crystalline in a different way to a normal crystal skull—more raw and earthy, more elemental and powerful when taken to the circles of standing stones. Take them with you when you visit, and also take Arapo, Zeb'n, and Moon. That's your core team. Take Charles Lapis, keeper of records, for he can read the records in the stones, and take Jago Jasper for protection from old energies that may reawaken at the sites. Wear a visualized cloak about you with a hood up to cover your head and hide your eyes. Your cloak is purple, Ye's is blue. Your lining is golden. Visualize it well and the site will welcome you. For so it is. Farewell."

Needing to get out of the pool now, I swim to the steps. I stand at the top of the steps and bow, with my hands together. I say, "Thank you" and then a strange cry rises in my throat:

58

CHAPTER 5

Aieeeee…echoes through the cavern. Quartz has stirred some ancient feelings in me that are seeking release.

I leave and make my way back to the ledge, then back down the steps.

I thank the skull, Quartz, the angels, and the Creator, and I feel very grateful for the profound experience.

Bethsherida has a feminine energy and the crystals along her left side sweep out like a pair of angel's wings. It was Bethsherida's wings that first caught my eye on eBay. She is slightly larger than her twin. It doesn't feel right to enter her left side through her crystal tips, so I fly in through her left eye.

A thick, creamy-gray substance surrounds me.

It feels kind of blank because there is no sound in it, then I realize it is cloud—I'm flying in cloud, thick clouds, not ragged, thin cirrus clouds. I'm flying into the sunset. Everything goes orange/pink. I dissolve into the light and beam out over the world, gilding the trees and shimmering on water. As light, I explore and run everywhere, glance at everything. I explore and greet Earth. She talks to me. She gives me an account of her state—a status report, and I transmit this back to the sun. This is how the intelligence behind the sun knows the health of the planets and can retune them. With the status report considered, the solar emanations will adjust the balance required, and coded information for Earth will be sent out with the new light of a new day.

Quartz says, "This is a process that is always in flow; a system of checks and balances; part of the universe's ongoing expansion, unfoldment, and growth in an evolutionary context. Earth welcomes the light. It is a language and shows her she is not alone. The contact with light reassures and comforts her. It is like a child hearing its mother's voice. The sun is the mother for the worlds that circle her. She gives them succour and feeds them. She teaches them and educates them into a galactic awareness of their part in the body of Creation. Like cells in a human body, suns grow old and die, and planets are created from their dust, and then they get old and die in their turn. It is cycles of birth and

COSMIC CRYSTALS! *Working With New Crystal Skulls*

death until the Great Recall, when the Creator breathes back in the energy that was exhaled (in the Big Bang). The cosmic dance will have an end before another rebirth, and the dance will be born again, each time refining and achieving more splendor for the Creator of All. For so it is. Fare you well."

I am dismissed. Time to go home.

As light, I touch a cloud, then transform, and I fly back through the clouds and out of Bethsherida's eye.

I'm back in bed. Mind blown.

I thank the skull, Quartz, the sun, the angels, and the Creator of All.

Then I'm off downstairs—in search of cocoa and toast to ground myself after that amazing experience!

✳ ✳ ✳

I think about what Quartz had said. Crystals and light—though they are born in a dark womb deep in the earth, crystals do have an affinity with light. Let me share a past life experience from *Spiritual Gold* with you to illustrate this. The memories come from one of my crystalline life form existences retrieved when I was searching for information. In the meditation, I told my inner guides what I was looking for and we all went up into the stars and we came to a doorway made of lines of light.

I opened the door slowly and stepped through.

I found I was looking at a very bright scene. Very bright white light infused the sky above me, and white sand shimmered below me in the glare. I was looking down from the entrance of a cave, but the rock at my side was so smooth that at first I thought I was in a temple doorway. The entrance was pyramid-shaped, but naturally formed.

When I look at my body I am mineral—my body is a pyramid-shaped crystal. It is translucent in places, transparent in others, smooth-sided and absorbs light. I am absorbing light until I have enough energy to move. I know an area beneath my base has the ability to ripple forward and will carry me slowly across the terrain spread out before me.

CHAPTER 5

That is how I will emerge from the gestation cave.

A friend joins me, comes from behind me...more are following...we are leaving the cave. We flow down from the entrance and cross the white sand, seeking a patch of the dark rock that makes up our mountains and is the bedrock of our world. We are seeking a high place, drawn by the light—the sunlight will be even stronger there. When we find such a place, we will settle.

We pass others of our kind, already rooted in the places they have found.

When we find a place of our own, we will no longer move. Instead, the base area of our bodies will dissolve the rock we are on, allowing us to form roots. We mix the atoms of rock with our own, and filaments grow from us that penetrate the tissue of the rock. We absorb ever more sunlight, and as we do, we grow upward toward the light, and downward into the bedrock of our planet.

That is our job, to grow. We do it well.

We will do it until all the planet is covered in crystal, until crystal penetrates its heart to the core, grounding the light. We "sing," we vibrate in our happiness at being here, at absorbing the light. For in the light is the love of the Creator and it nurtures us.

For we rightly see who we are. We are the consciousness, the brain of our world. We are its sentience, and we hum with the rhythm of the universe in a hymn of thanksgiving to the Divine Creator of All. We are happy beyond measure. No darkness clouds our world. We have never known the darkness free will brings, for we simply complete our purpose the best way we can. What else is there to do? Nothing. We are at total peace, fulfilling our world's dream of evolution. For we grow and grow and hold ever more light. Our world is filling with light. Light is in its very tissues because of us. It will be a world of light, forming a necessary balance to dealings elsewhere in the cosmos. This we dimly understand because it is whispered to us in the light. The photons of light bring us messages and wisdom and joy, and we rejoice in the love of being. Being part of the Plan, being able to assist our Creator and fulfill our destiny.

In that past life of mine we sang, vibrated, rooted, and grew to the light until we covered our world, until it all sang and every molecule was sentient and sang. The planet evolved, we were more obviously a part of it than humans are on Earth, where you and I appear to be so separate. But we are not as separate as we look, I was told by the guides.

✳ ✳ ✳

I had been so impressed with the twins that in July 2021 I bought them a sibling from the same seller. This little skull was of the same stone, but wore its crystals on its crown. When it arrived it told me it was androgynous and said to call it **Beamoth**: "Bea" from beauty and "moth" from a life form with wings for nocturnal journeying...

After being transformed into light last time, I'm wondering what is going to happen this time! Whatever comes next?!!

I ask permission to enter.

I find myself standing before a huge gray cliff, sparsely scattered with tiny glinting crystals. No door to be seen. I knock on the cliff and a hidden door swings inward. It is dark inside, but a flaming torch in a sconce on the wall offers me light. I lift it from the sconce and take it with me as I pad forward into the echoing darkness of a huge cavern. Somewhere water is dripping. I keep on, and cross the rocky floor to the far side where a lighted passageway beckons to me. Wall torches line the passage as it leads me down, and down, until I'm in a huge cave with soft golden sand on its floor. Big crystals of quartz now gleam on the walls and dance in the flickering light of flaming torches.

I must be in higher dimensions, in the etheric levels, because I'm given to understand this cave is a womb of Mother Earth. This is a gestation cave for energies that shimmer and twinkle in the air around me.

I'm told these are "seed energies" that will leave the cave and drift away to lodge in valleys, to lodge in nooks and crevices, or perhaps catch onto rocks, or sink into sand—and once they have lodged, they will attract actual 3D seeds. The seeds of Earth blow

CHAPTER 5

in on winds or fall with the droppings of birds, and it's where the "seed energies" await them that they will root and put down a 3D body. There they will manifest and bloom. These "seed energies" are a preparation, they make things possible. They offer potential, and they will drift out of the cave of their own volition, but they can also be steered by nature spirits and guided to likely locations. This is an ongoing process as life ebbs and flows across our planet.

I ask if there is anything else I should know.

"Only that it concerns you in a small way, for you render this service while you sleep. You leave your physical form asleep, and in your astral body drift off to caves like this and catch onto the drifting energy as it readies to leave. And you guide it out, and lodge it for the nature spirits to take over the next day. Many of Earth's people have nighttime tasks and these change on a regular basis. This is yours right now. This is the mechanism behind nature reclaiming spoilt or denuded land. This is part of the ebb and flow of life across the world. Be of good cheer, for the healing of devastation is always in flow!"

I thank the skull for explaining.

It feels like something I've always known but had forgotten…

I turn to go, feet sinking into the soft sand before I am in the passageway and on my way up, toward the darkness above. I still have my torch to guide me across the dark cavern. Gratefully I replace it in its sconce on the wall and open the door—there is a handle on this side of the door, though there wasn't one on the outside.

I leave, closing the door carefully behind me.

I'm back in my bedroom.

Later, I find there is another of these little skulls with the same seller on eBay. I'm trying to be sensible and stop buying skulls, but I may yet send for it. Skulls are addictive—and after seeing elemental potentials with this one, whatever would the next one show me? I had to find out.

It arrived on a Friday and spent the day soaking up sunlight on a table in my garden. It wore its quartz crystals on top of its head, and underneath, near the base, there was an area of yellow ochre, which set it apart from its three siblings.

COSMIC CRYSTALS! Working With New Crystal Skulls

I meditate with it the next day.

The name it gives is **Yello-mani-urua**. As the name is revealed, I feel the sweep of it spanning from modern European through to the ancient languages of India and Australia.

Again, I stand outside a gray cliff. There is yellow ochre in the rocks and glints of tiny crystals. I see a gray door and grip the matte black doorknob. It opens inward. It is dark inside.

Then a searchlight shines down. I hear, "Welcome, come right in." Though it is dark, it is warm and flowers scent the air. I smell jasmine, and feel a warm breeze around me. The searchlight moves and picks out trees...palm trees, at the edge of a beach. I move out of the darkness toward them and find myself gazing across a moonlit ocean. A full moon and myriads of stars shine down on me, and I hear the swish of gentle waves as the ocean washes the sand.

I'm on the beach now.

I sit down and feel very peaceful. The swish of the tide is mesmerizing...hypnotic. I lie down and relax in the warm sand. I sink in. I sink in further, and then I sink down...down...down into the rocks beneath. And down...down...down...down into the great iron crystal at Earth's heart. I feel the pulse of Earth. **I am Earth!** I am happy—perhaps a little restless, like there's an itch I'd like to scratch—scratch off humankind from my surface.

I "whistle" to the brother and sister planets and to Mother Sun. We exchange vibrations and sing with the joy of Creation.

Humankind is such a little part of all this, as to be almost insignificant to me; the surface is such a little part of me. Nothing touches my core and here I am unsullied. The surface atmospheric gases have known great fluctuations over the eons, and yet I hardly notice because most of me is focused deep within.

Most of me is pure and unsullied. The degradation of the surface is a big thing for those that live on it—but not for me. At the moment, the surface is like a child who has fallen and scraped its knees. It will heal—but something needs to be done to cleanse the wound and stop the damage continuing, or infection leads to gangrene, leads to losing the legs, leads to dying. It could happen, but not if humankind shapes up and humans do their best now. But whatever happens affects them and not me. I will not die,

CHAPTER 5

though they might die out.

"You have this connection with me because you have remembered being part of my spirit, (*I've written about this in Divine Fire on page 91*). Cheer up...all is well with me, planet Earth. Look to saving yourselves and the other life forms entrusted to your care by the Creator. It is a poor showing at the moment, but you all know how to do better. Do it. Don't sit back and wait for others to save your comfortable lifestyle, because that will not happen. The universe regards your fate with indifference. Save yourselves, and if that is impossible, well then, perhaps you do deserve to die out and make room for others to come after you. For they surely will—other species, better species, kinder species, more caring species. For they exist on the inner and outer planes. Return another time. There is more to be told."

I leave the iron crystal heart. I come up, up, up, up through the rocks and magma, through more rocks, up through the sand and up to the surface of the beach. I float in the warm ocean to cleanse from that experience...I let the strangeness flow out into the water...and it was very strange.

Then I'm standing on the sand and I bow to the sea and the moon to take my leave. I pad across the sand to the palm trees silhouetted against the starry sky. I feel the trees' energy. It's quite personal and friendly after the inhuman impersonality of Earth's vastness. The scale was just mind boggling.

I see the searchlight and head for it. It escorts me across the dark cave-like space to the door. I open it and leave.

I thank the skull Yello-mani-urua, the angels, Earth, and the Creator for giving me that experience.

It was a very strange feeling being Earth, and it is just crazy how a small skull, two inches long, could make me feel like a planet.

CHAPTER 6
Merlin's Skulls and Skull Cleansing

If you remember in chapter three I'd met Merlin within Hapi-atzi—but rushed out, unable to proceed. I had been overjoyed to see him, but Merlin and I shared a sad history from a past life and it had all come flooding back and stopped me in my tracks. However, by the end of June I was ready to visit Hapi-atzi again because I knew if anyone understood crystal skulls, it was Merlin.

Working for him had been one of the most interesting past lives I had uncovered for *Holy Ice*, and now I wondered what it was he wanted to tell me. When I last knew him, Merlin had been an advisor to Arthur, High King of Celtic Britain. It was the 6th century AD, and Arthur was busy defending Britain against the Saxon invasions because, for many years, the Saxons had been stealing our land. Boat loads of warriors flooding in with the tides had taken over our villages and moved their own families in to farm what had once been our fields. Treaties had been made, and every time, treaties had been broken.

Only Arthur, the High King, had been sworn the oaths of loyalty that gave him the power to command lesser kings to send him warriors for the battles. The problem was that the lesser kings were riven by petty rivalries and their squabbling made them hard to control.

Embedded in the court of King Cedrych, who guarded the

CHAPTER 6

southern part of the Welsh Marches at the head of the Severn Estuary, I spy for Merlin. Merlin was Druid-trained in psychic arts and had many extraordinary skills; he could charm people and bend them to his will. He traveled the country, from lesser king's court to lesser king's court, collecting news and extracting promises of warriors for Arthur's battles. The last time he'd visited the Great Hall where I lived we held a banquet in his honor, and afterward, he had brought out his harp and entertained the king and the people, for Merlin was also a bard. After the rousing songs of battles past and a warning to be ever-ready now, there came a point in the evening when the buzz of conversation died away, when in the course of a few minutes, heads began to nod and were laid to rest on the banqueting tables. People slumped on the benches and others rolled off into the floor rushes, curling up with the hounds dozing by bones they'd been gnawing from the feast. The whole room had gone still, apart from the crack of the fire and sparks from the logs in the central hearth.

But I was not sleepy. I hear the wind outside. It gusted through the smoke hole in the roof, and sent the smoke from the hearth into eddies and spirals. Merlin made a sign to me, and silently he and I swept out of the hall, past the sleeping bodies.

We light a torch to take with us and we walk through the doors and out into the dark night. We shout a greeting to the guards at the palisade, but it was as though Merlin had cast a spell over the feasters within the Great Hall.

I knew he had.

He had projected the thought they were tired, and suddenly they were. I'd been trained to use a blocking picture in my mind, and so the spell did not touch me.

We pick our way along a well trodden path leading through trees toward a small lake set in a wide clearing. We often meet here to talk when he comes to visit because there's no chance of being overheard. We sit side by side on the old talking-stone and the wind eases, and the air falls still. The black waters of the lake are calm and reflective, mirroring a hazy moon and glimmers of stars above.

Merlin asks me about my family, and the king: what visitors

he's had, what news we've heard. He wants to check my report against other people's stories. But then he sighs.

He tells me he has been looking into the future and seen things he wished he had not, and this is what he has come to tell me. He has only told the king a little, he says, but he owes me the truth of it. He tells me the end is coming for our people, that Arthur is old and Arthur is ill, that none of the minor kings are fit to be High King in his place. None can be trusted to hold the alliances together. There is only strength for one more battle left in Arthur before he dies—then we will be picked off, kingdom by kingdom, our fighters slain, our children and women enslaved by the Saxons. All our long years of struggle have come to nothing. Tears stream down my face. I can't stop them. My life is turned to ashes in that moment—my sons will be killed, my daughters and wife carried off and enslaved, and my dear little grandchildren too...

Merlin's eyes are wet. Tears slide down my face though I try to brush them away.

The wind sighs in the treetops.

An owl hoots.

We walk back in silence. People are still asleep, but the fire in the central hearth is just ashes now, like my life. We go to our beds and in the morning Merlin rides north.

Days slip past. Winter comes, then spring, and each morning I pray Merlin was mistaken. But sure enough, one night boats glide silently up the wide River Severn to where my king's lands lie. Saxon scum crawl over our land toward the Great Hall where we sleep in our boots, ever ready. Our sentries wake us, and grabbing weapons, helmets, and shields from their places on the walls, we pour out and form a shield wall. But I know what will happen. I died inside the night Merlin came. I fight on until a blow to my head makes my helmet ring and knocks me senseless to the ground. I barely feel the wounds that take my lifeblood.

As our shield wall crumbles, and even the king's own guardians fall, the doors to the hall are forced open and I hear our women shriek...and then I hear no more. I slip out of my battered body and look down on the world below. In death I am loosened

CHAPTER 6

from the flow of Time.

I am aware Merlin still rides north. He has worn out horse after horse, and changed them many times ever since he left us on his mission to raise help for Arthur; but he also weaves magic in the land as he goes. He is weaving his legacy into the land—and I can see the tools he uses. With my Druid-taught telepathy skills I had seen two stone skulls in his aura as he spoke the fateful words to me that night by the lake. In the extreme emotion of the moment we had opened up to each other in a way I had never experienced before. I'd never been party to his thoughts before—though he could always read mine. The stone skulls were in his thoughts. I did not understand why, but I knew they were important or they would not have been in his mind. I **just had no idea how important.** But now that I'm free of my body I have greater understanding and vision.

I see Merlin. I see the skulls. One blue as lapis lazuli, one quartz, clear as rock crystal, and intuitively I know this one is a scrying stone. It's the size of two fists and in this he saw the future he told me about. The blue skull is smaller, but it's at least the size of one fist, it's an amplifier and grounder for his commands, used for summoning elemental beings of air, water, and earth. This one he had used for weather manipulation—a well-placed storm can hinder sea wolves, mists can be summoned to hide our warriors gathering for an attack, or to let them slip away…

I see that Merlin takes the blue skull with him to the ancient places of power. He travels from stone circle to stone circle channeling energy, thoughts, and commands through the skull into the earth and stones there, and thence into the lines of power that flow through them into the veins of our land. He channels energy into the very rocks that underpin all. The quartz skull is a generator and amplifier, and set beside the blue skull it enhances the work that Merlin and its brother skull do; all three of them are working together as a team.

I realize the Isles of the Britons have rocks which have brother and sister rocks all over the world. And I see that the rocks of our land will speak to their brother and sister rocks around the world, as Merlin uses the blue skull to put energy into the land, and from

COSMIC CRYSTALS! *Working With New Crystal Skulls*

thence it flows out into the veins of the world. This is why Arthur and Merlin are never forgotten—their names are encoded into the lands beneath our feet. It's a subtle energy that pervades, it has become a part of our psyche, an energy that has entered the collective consciousness of the people who live upon the land. And because of the brother and sister rocks, Arthur and Merlin are loved by people all over the world.[8]

I see that Merlin has gone everywhere, from Cornwall to Scotland, putting his energy into the rocks—which is why so many places have legends associated with him, because he passed through them on his mission to weave magic into the land.

I see Merlin make his way up to Scotland...traveling from king's court to king's court. But with Arthur dead and his cause lost, I see that in the end Merlin dies of a broken heart, at a Scottish king's court in the Borders.[9]

8   I checked this out and they really do have brother and sister rocks all over the world, because they are from ancient continents that mashed together.

The northern part of Britain which bears Scotland was once part of Laurentia (and Laurentia now bears North America); the southern part of Britain, including Wales, was once part of Gondwana (Gondwana now bears South America, Africa, Asia and Australia). Southern Britain and Scotland met millions of years ago when Avalonia (bearing southern Britain, Wales and Ireland) broke off Gondwana and drifted into the bit of Laurentia that bears Scotland's rocks.

More recently Pangaea, a super continent, formed and "Britain" (comprising the Laurentia and Avalonia continental fragments) found itself in the middle. Eventually Pangaea broke up and split into smaller continents, leaving "Britain" on its own.

New research shows that the rock underpinning Cornwall and south Devon is part of Armorica, and is actually a fragment of the European continent that had attached itself to "Britain."

9   Merlin's grave is most likely near Drumelzier, a village in the Tweed valley where Scotland borders England. Legend has it that Merlin was at King Meldred's 6th Century Celtic hill fort nearby, which now lies under the ruins of Tinnis Castle. "Drumelzier" is a version of the older Dunmellor. "Dun" means fort, I suspect the Fort of Meller was the Fort of Meldred. Merlin's grave is said to be marked by a thorn tree and to lie at the confluence of the River Tweed and a stream once known as Powsail, but is now called Drumelzier Burn. However, the site often taken as his grave today

CHAPTER 6

Merlin imbued the lands with energy so the Celts would rise again through those who came after, as long as the names of Merlin and Arthur were kept alive. He wanted us to remember the bravery of Arthur, and that the British Isles are magical, sacred isles...and it is truly amazing when you consider the number of books, and even films, that have been made since then about Arthur and Merlin. On the face of it you would think a Celtic king and his advisor, who lived such a very long time ago in the Dark Ages, would have been quietly forgotten by now, and yet time seems to have proved the value of Merlin's work and **the power of crystal skulls in the right hands!** King Arthur has never been forgotten, and today there is even an international society dedicated to him. How many kings can say that, eh?

While researching this intriguing past life for *Holy Ice*, I did a second regression session where I went back over the same events, and this time I could see things that had been hidden from me.

I saw Merlin casting the sleeping spell. After the entertainment, while putting away his harp he had palmed his quartz skull out of the harp's traveling bag resting at his feet. Balanced on his knee and well hidden beneath the table, he had put his hands around the skull and stroked it awake. It was a powerful skull, which amplified his mental command, and with its help he sent the whole room deep asleep.

I saw that when we went to the pool Merlin had the skulls with him, concealed in the pockets of his cloak, and he has lots of things in the pockets, lots of shamanic tools that he uses. As he walked he had stroked the lapis skull awake and then directed it by thought to calm the air elementals around the lake, making the wind drop.

---

is upstream of the original confluence, because the stream was diverted in the 1800s. But it is nice to think that old thorn trees overlooking the Tweed near the original confluence could have descended from the one that marked Merlin's true grave. To find the true grave, follow the path further, because it ran alongside the original stream, and you will come to a field on your right where he lies to this day. It is a very atmospheric place.

This time I see the owl's significance. It did not just hoot as we left. I understood how birds were Merlin's friends. The owl had acted as his eyes in the countryside earlier that day; he had sent it out to scry the land, to fly around so he would know if it was safe for us to be out that night—and as he had rested before the feast Merlin had seen what the bird was seeing as it flew. At the lake he had slipped it some meat from the feast as a reward, and the owl had settled down to watch us from the branch of a tree.

The tears I had shed in the first regression session (at the point by the lake) were very plentiful and real. Wild tingles had run up and down my legs and all through my body as I remembered and saw the truth of Merlin's magic. But when I revisited the event in the second session, I could see that as we sat by the lake he had hypnotized me. I had been shown things and told things and commanded to forget them, so there was a gap in my memory of events—between giving my report, so he could find discrepancies in his intelligence gathering—and the point where he sighed. In the gap I see him bringing out the quartz skull to show me, for that was where he was planning to look for the truth of the discrepancies.

He shows me the crystal skull because it is important.

He shows me the lapis skull because it, too, is important, and he places them side by side on his thighs as we sit on the talking stone; the lapis on his left, and the quartz on his right, both skulls are facing out to the lake. He takes my hands and lays one on each skull. The skulls feel cool and smooth to my touch.

Merlin says, "Remember these, because one day you will need to write about them." Then he tells me things. He says the skulls are very old; they are from far away and long ago. They were so important they were saved from lands that went beneath the sea, and for thousands of years they have journeyed through the world as tools to try and help people. He tells me that the people they are with have changed. The skulls were from lands far to the west, lands at the end of the golden path of the sun on the ocean, but they were brought to those lands from even earlier times and earlier places…they grew in the earth—they were gifts

CHAPTER 6

from the elemental kingdoms, the elementals of earth and air and water—the elementals to do with harvest and growth, and the energy in the land and the weather.

To improve a harvest, to improve the weather, he says he works with the lapis skull. The quartz skull amplifies, so whatever he's doing he can use the two skulls together, because the quartz skull will make the work more powerful. He says he has to switch them on by thought and by stroking them with his hands. Then he says he communicates with them and puts them side by side while they are working, so the quartz one will amplify the work that the lapis skull is doing.

That's when he tells me the skulls will always work with me.

Not just these two, he says, because he can see in the records of my soul that I've had contact with them before, but also with others—and that's why he is sharing this. He tells me he can see future events in the quartz skull, so he uses that one for guidance on his journeys, and it is one reason why he has always been safe when traveling—he's been able to foresee trouble and avoid it. But if anyone were to find the skulls, or try to rob him of them, he says he would tell them the skulls will bring their death, and that has always been a good protection for them. But with the mention of death he puts the skulls away and brings me out of the trance and sighs. And that is when he tells me he has been looking into the future and seen things he wished he had not.

Well, that was the last time I'd seen Merlin. Although it happened fifteen hundred years ago, the emotions evoked at the time were so raw and powerful they had scarred my soul. So when I stumbled across Merlin unexpectedly in Hapi-atzi, my first amethyst skull, it set off an emotional charge that threatened to overwhelm me— and that's why I'd rushed pell-mell out of the skull. But of course, ever since then I'd been wondering what it was Merlin had come to tell me this time...

So I settle down to meditate with lovely amethyst Hapi-atzi and enter the inner world again.

Stepping through a sliding glass door in Hapi's side I find myself in a large empty room, and to my left I see the same staircase as last time. Its quartz spindles sparkle and the amethyst treads feel cool to my bare feet as I climb up the steps that lead me into the big room in the crown of the skull, where Merlin stands waiting behind a large oak table. He is smiling and his wavy gray hair is as thick as ever.

He says, "Did you think I'd forget you?"

Merlin is full of life and energy with a twinkle in his eye. He is warm and charismatic, as he was in life, and he has crystal skulls laid out on the table before him. His own lapis and clear quartz skulls appear there, with a score of others, smaller ones, like a rainbow of colored stones. He is laughing. "Gorgeous aren't they?" he says, "What fun you can have with skulls like this, getting to know them and finding out their characters and abilities. They are like my children."

I ask why he chose amethyst, why an amethyst skull to meet me in?

"Hapi is very willing for this, and amethyst was always a bit of a favorite with me—hence the staircase—amethyst leads you to me, amethyst links us. Wear it and think of me, it binds us close. We used it for telepathy, you and I. We left messages in it. Just thinking of its color tunes us into each other."

Merlin had been like a favorite uncle to me when I was Johannes the Celt. He was my father's friend, and had taken an interest in my training from my earliest years. Because we shared some DNA, telepathy was easy between us; we used quartz, too, for that, which is why the staircase was symbolically both amethyst and quartz.

"All crystal skulls are good, though some use them for ill," Merlin says.

But I'm more tired than I thought and I yawn...

"You were always a sleepy head!" he says, "But we will work together again. I shall discuss cleansing and utilizing them with you. Meet me here again. We have begun the work. All is set. Farewell."

I thank him.

I descend the amethyst steps and leave through the glass door in Hapi-atzi's side. I am aware of being back in my bedroom now.

CHAPTER 6

I thank the angels, Merlin, Hapi, and God. I resolve next time it will be a daytime meditation.

It is daytime on Friday the 9th of July, and I settle down with Hapi to take this further. When I get to the point where I rejoin Merlin in the room with the table and skulls, a booming voice suddenly cuts through everything and bellows out "Welcome."

Merlin flinches. It's the Amethyst Deva!

The deva continues, "This is an opportunity to deepen our understanding of one another, is it not? Merlin and I have worked together before. You and I have spoken before, but now comes the time to deepen our awareness of Time and human resonance with the planet. For before humans, time was slower. Time is speeding up. In your own lifetime you surely have noticed this as days shrink and years go ever faster. It increases until the end point when it stops and winds back. It increases to do with the centrifugal forces behind expansion. The Big Bang started Time off slowly and it has gone ever faster since. It will speed up until it snaps, as it were, and then draws back within the Creator, with all matter, in the Great Recall. For so it is. Enjoy Time's flow. Do not rail against it or you will destroy/wear out/stress yourself to eventual death and go before your intended/allotted time to die."

"Don't stress, but flow. It is well to have plans, but beware deadlines. The clue is in the name: **dead**lines. Be aware, they contribute to your death if you let them."

"Time brings crystals into being and time is *our* friend. Time is crueler to *your* people because time gives and then time takes away—your beauty, looks, strength, teeth, and body, and eventually you are down to your last breath, and then there is no time. Because after death you exist in the no-time of the spiritual worlds. You join the angels until your next foray into time—meaning another life and another body. You yourselves are eternal and live beyond time. It is a very small part of you that embodies."

"How do I know? Because I am part of the mainframe of the cosmos, and I extend through the dimensions up to the level of the angels' crystal cities and beyond. For even light has crystalline

COSMIC CRYSTALS! Working With New Crystal Skulls

form in the higher levels. Beings can build with light and that is how the crystal cities are formed."

(Oooooh! I find that amazing.)

"We will speak again. I leave you with Merlin. Farewell."

I feel the Amethyst Deva withdraw and Merlin and I are alone.

Merlin says "Not quite what I was expecting...let us focus now on ways to cleanse skulls..."

- **Welcome**: When they arrive, welcome them. Say "Welcome." Feel what they need, perhaps gentle soap and water, perhaps a bath with crab apple flower essence, or salt, or something else. Say, "May you be cleansed and true to your own highest energies and be willing to work with my highest energies."
- **Smoke**: Smudge them with incense of any kind.
- **Sound**: Bells, rattles, tingshas, or simply clap.
- **Color**: Sit them on a red cloth to ground and center them and burn out any residual negativity.
- **Prayer**: Ask Archangel Michael to run his fire through the crystal to transmute any negativity. See the fire go from gold to blue to violet and then to white light.
- **Flowers**: Surround the skull with flowers so the harmony and energies of the flowers will restore it. Spritz it with flower essences diluted in water; use Rescue Remedy, or dowse, or intuit which remedy it needs a few drops of in water.
- **The Sun and Moon**: Use these cosmic forces to rebalance and charge the skull. Put it outside to bathe in light.
- **Rain**: Put it out in the rain to wash it on an elemental level.
- **Laughter**: Laugh with joy that it has joined you. Laughter is very powerful—it is the sunshine of the soul. Laughter will startle it and cause it to drop negativity it may be carrying or has acquired, and this will give it a rebirth into a new energy

CHAPTER 6

balance especially tuned to you. Skulls love a joyful companion and guardian who laughs and finds life fun. This will also benefit your own health.

- **Vibration**: Use your own vibration for cleansing— wrap it up in a favorite item of your clothing for a few hours, so it can attune to your vibration. It needs a period of adjustment after its journey through the world to find you. (*Perhaps put it away in a draw while this is happening, but do make sure it is somewhere safe, where no one will accidentally shake out the clothing and drop it. And only for a few hours so you don't forget it!*)

Merlin finishes with, "Be at peace, all is well. Crystal skulls are wonderful tools to help you with life. And they benefit from experiencing being with *you*, a human caretaker. In a spirit of evolution you interact together and both benefit. Next time, we do working with them. Go in peace."

I retrace my footsteps down the staircase, and pass out through the glass door.

I thank the angels, the Amethyst Deva, Merlin, Hapi-atzi, and God the Creator of all.

CHAPTER 7
Ancient Stones and Telluric Energies

For at least 5,000 years there has been a stone circle near Duddo in Northumberland, England, up near the Scottish borders. The circle is set on a gentle upward swelling of land that commands views across country in all directions. Here the ancient stones are sandstone, and five out of the original seven remain standing to this day.

I love sandstone, and when I heard about the circle I wanted to visit it.

Sacred places like this are linked by ley lines, a network of lines of power which criss-cross the planet, a bit like acupuncture meridians link acupuncture points on the human body. In the human body the energy is called chi, whereas the energy that flows in ley lines and finds focus at the sacred sites is called telluric energy, and this is a real electrical phenomenon. The name is from the Latin word tellus, "earth." A telluric current, or earth current, is an electric current which moves underground or through the sea in the surface layers of the earth. Telluric currents result from both natural causes and human activity, and the currents interact in a complex pattern. The currents are geomagnetically induced by changes in the outer part of Earth's magnetic field; the changes are usually caused by interactions between the solar wind and the

CHAPTER 7

magnetosphere, or solar radiation on the ionosphere.

Because our ancestors sensed the energy in the land, or at least their shamans, priestesses, priests, and spiritual advisors did, they regarded the places where the energy was strongest as holy places. At these powerful sites they built places of worship—stone circles, dolmens, mounds, or all manner of temples the world over. Later, many churches and cathedrals would be built on top of the ancient pagan sites. Singing, drumming and music, processions and ceremonies increased the energy there.

When we walk the leys we strengthen them, and when we walk around the sites we stimulate the energies there. Doing this, we help Earth and Earth helps us by expanding our consciousness and bringing us back in tune with our planet. A visit to such a place can be healing on many levels.

When you approach you feel your own energy rising in excitement and you subconsciously sense the changing levels of telluric energy in the land. This is why I took dowsing rods with me when we finally visited the Duddo Stones in July—I wanted to see what the energies were up to!

Lockdown had officially ended on Monday the 19th July 2021 in England, so on Thursday the 22nd we drove to the stones. The sky was cloudy, but it was good to be out in the countryside that day. Besides my dowsing rods, I had a copper pendulum, an amethyst pendulum and nine skulls; I'd added Mars Preseli and Marco Quartz to the core team. Ye had his seven skulls and a pendulum.

As we walked the path through fields of barley toward the grass-covered mound where the stones stood sentinel, my dowsing rods went crazy. I had my skulls in a back pack and a rod in each hand. Both rods flipped left, then right, flew apart, flew together and crossed, time and time again as we walked the land. Every time we came to a ditch that circled the mound and its stones, the rods crossed, and though two of the stones were missing, the rods told me where they had stood. I found that even today the energy of the circle is unbroken.

*Three of the five surviving Duddo Stones
Ye is seated on a stone fragment*

We were lucky and had the circle to ourselves.

Corn dollies and fresh leaves and flowers were wedged into gaps in the stones, telling us it was still very much in use today. I spread a black and gold cloth in the center of the circle and set our skulls out on it. Then I went round the stones, one by one. I placed my hands on each stone while resting my forehead against it, and with eyes closed, attempted to tune into it. One large stone was of special interest—with our eyes closed, both Ye and I saw a skull inside it, clear in our mind's eye. The skull was part of the stone, but its outline was strongly defined, as though someone had used white light to draw the outline of a large crystal skull inside the huge stone. It spoke to me. But with both hands on the stone, and no pen or paper in hand, I had no means to write the words down. I meditated at home later to catch what was lost, and that's when I asked my skulls about their experiences at Duddo.

We took photos and placed our skulls on the stones hoping they would receive a download.

CHAPTER 7

The place was very atmospheric.
We will be back.

Left to right: Arapo and Zeb'n looking pleased to be there

COSMIC CRYSTALS! *Working With New Crystal Skulls*

A few days later I check in with my skulls. I hold each in turn as I meditate.

Moon what was your impression at the stones? I ask.

"Very old energies...we liked it. We want more trips like this. We did Earth healing there and repaired and strengthened the energy grid. This will be of benefit to humankind, rather than Earth, as the surface energies greatly affect you—humankind. You have turned your world into a more hostile place than it used to be, in an environmental sense. This can be repaired, but time runs out soon for this to be achieved. We all liked it there."

What do you say Zeb'n?

"I guarded him [Arapo] like you wanted. Ask him."

What do you say Arapo?

"Cor! Great place—loved it! The stones were happy to see us. They knew we were coming because the big skull-stone woke up. It was asleep for a long time after Merlin put the skull in it for you to find in a later life. It's been quickening since 1948 when you were born again to work with skulls." (!)

What do you say Charles Lapis?

"A very rich and interesting place full of records stored there by the stones, and by those who have honored the place since ancient times. There's a UFO navigation beacon beneath the land there. Merlin left you a message: 'For Johannes reborn.'"

What is the message Charles?

"I knew you would come after, and that our tale is not done with, for you are back in our lands and you are free to walk the old paths once again—though you need deliver no messages for me now!" (My first job for him had been to run messages.) "But messages have been left for you to find, in various places. And you will find them, of this we are sure. The skull face will tell you what you need to know now."

I visualize the skull face.

I ask the skull face in the stone: what message do you hold for me? All the while I am holding Jago, my red jasper skull, for protection...

"The circle welcomes you. You have been here before many times in other lifetimes, mostly unknowing of our purpose."

CHAPTER 7

What is your purpose?

"To hold the land for humans to prosper. We hold your collective claim of tenure of this planetary jewel that is Earth. Let us be destroyed and you destroy yourselves, and so it is all around the world, for we link and sing our songs to each other. We feel another's pain when destruction comes near. You need us as never before; the times are perilous for living creatures. Merlin said you would remember his message if I showed myself (as skull face). Also, I read you—I can tell you have established contact with him in other ways, in Druid ways in the inner planes. This is good and makes my task easier."

"WAKE UP! That is really what I have to say."

"Again the end is near. Just as it was for the Celts before the Saxon scourge engulfed them and stole their lands—this land included. Once again the end is near, for peril comes by another route. The Saxons' descendants invited this peril into your world, for they had a big hand behind the exploitation of the world. Behold their history of conquest and they are using science to pillage now..."

"Come back and see me again. I will wait, for I am an access point for skulls to powerfully tap into the grid. I am a portal, like a USB port for skulls..."

I am still digesting this when I turn to the skulls yet to speak. The skull face had found "USB port" in my mind while searching for words to convey the message. But it did sound odd coming from something so ancient. A standing stone talking about USB ports...

What do you say Alsherida, Bethsherida?

"We loved it there. Our crystal tips sang in the energies there—exquisite pleasure for us!"

What do you say Marco?

"You didn't astral travel, but I know where to bring you now if you want to astral travel here in the future."

What do you say Mars Preseli?

"There was some of me buried in the center of the circle. Not large, but enough to join up with other circles where Preseli bluestone lies buried. We weave energy, we do, joining the sites."

Moon-Over-the-Waters-of-Life on one of the ancient stones

Moon—any last words?
"It is done. Fare you well. For so be it."
I end the meditation and thank the angels, the skulls, the skull face at the site, Merlin for his prescience, and our Creator.
While writing this up I realize I forgot to ask the Councils of

CHAPTER 7

Thirteen and Seventeen what they observed, because along with the visualized cloak of protection I was actually wearing them, too. Also, poor little Jago got overlooked. I just clutched him for protection and never asked him what he had to say. Well there's always tomorrow…

In the end it was Wednesday when I asked them.

Jago what was your impression at the stone circle?

"Very old. The energies are safe now—Moon re-knitted them when you held the copper spiral pendulum above her. You thought to do that because she silently asked you. Bad witchcraft will find it hard to work there now, but healing will flow forth. You were never in danger there, but it is good practice to be careful and to take us with you. And you were in no danger from the stone skull face. It is your friend, set to look out for you. It has alerted the others (other skull faces in other stones elsewhere). It is good, all is well, go in peace."

Council of Thirteen, what was your impression?

"A place of power. We enjoyed the visit."

To get more sense out of them I blow on them to wake them up and ask for a spokesman bead. I hold one of the Earth deva beads. This is better and it gives me more.

"It was a place of thanksgiving, of safe deliverance. We were nourished there, all of us, ET and Earth beads alike, for there is star energy within the mound. The UFO beacon navigation device gave us a joyful surge of energy. Ten of us resonated with that. The three Earth beads were nourished by the site itself. It strengthened us and tuned us further, the better to work together. It was a good thing to take us. We can assist you in a stronger way now."

Council of Seventeen what was your impression?

"Cor—fabulous! We loved it. Good energies to get our teeth into; some to suck out and clear, others to charge us. We were charged by the site, very nourishing for quartz crystal. We can support you better now as a result of the visit to that place of energy and knowing. Earth's knowledge can be accessed there—and in places like that—Earth's knowledge sings in your bones *when you are there. Listen to Earth's song now,*

"For my children are free
And my children are flowers of beauty and leaf,
My children are trees tall and seeds tiny,
My children delight in my gifts to them
Of clouds, and sun and rain, of snow
And the winds of ever changing seasons.
My creatures grace the land
And fly free in beauteous skies,
They swim in the seas and burrow the land,
My creatures so small and so large.
For all is perfection in my dreams of the life I support."

"Darkness comes and darkness goes,
And the light of purity shines ever within me.
And I bask in the radiance of the sun's golden light.
The sun warms my bones and lent me her fire
For my life blood within.
I sing to my fellows as we dance round and round,
Eternally circling our paths through space,
As the great wheels of the galaxies turn,
And take us spiraling with them until the end of Time."

I really hadn't expected my bracelet to burst into song—a chanted song. There was no stopping them. It just poured out. I had to guess where the line breaks fell as it poured out in one long continuous flow. There may well be more verses, but there was something so profound about the song that I took a break from the book at this point. Something had completed. Though the book itself wasn't done, there was much more to come, and it wouldn't be long before an irresistible skull crossed my path...

CHAPTER 8
Egyptian Mysteries

It is rare to find a Libyan Desert Glass crystal skull, so I couldn't let the chance slip past when it came at the end of July. Libyan Desert Glass is among the rarest minerals on Earth, and is only found in a remote and desolate area of desert between Libya and Egypt. It is a pale golden color, and like quartz, is almost pure silicon-dioxide, but its crystal structure is different. It contains traces of unusual elements like iridium, cobalt, chromium, nickel, and also iron and a very rare mineral called reidite. Scientists say it was formed in a high-energy event 27 million years ago. This is usually assumed to be when a meteorite smashed into quartz sand in North Africa and fused into glass. But the problem with this explanation is that no impact crater has ever been found, and the presence of reidite rules out the possibility that it was formed by an airburst meteorite, which could have accounted for the lack of a crater. Reidite forms only under very high pressure and airburst meteorites are mainly ice and water and do not generate enough pressure. A nuclear explosion in ancient times would have done the trick...but that would have been at least 20 million years before the earliest humans. It is a very mysterious substance. Ancient Egyptian priests chose it for the central jewel on Tutankhamun's funerary breast plate where it was carved into a scarab, the symbol of renewal and rebirth.

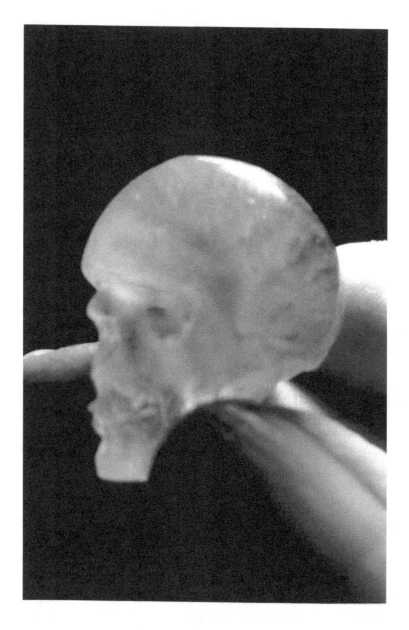

Libyan Desert Glass skull Amersandi

CHAPTER 8

When the skull came in August I studied it under my lamp. It was almost an inch long and its internal structure shimmered with tiny bubbles. The face was finely carved by Balinese carvers.

Within hours I settle down to meditate with it.

It tells me it is female. I visualize myself standing outside on its left hand side. I am looking for a way in. I see a sandy slope leading up to a gateway, where two imposing stone pillars are marking the entrance to a temple. I slip past the stone pillars and into the darkness of the big echoing stone hall of the temple. To my right, but a long way in, there is an altar with fire on it. I go closer, see shadows, see movement—there are people here! It is an Egyptian temple and a ceremony is to take place, a ceremony of purification and initiation.

Then I remember it's for me! I am to be purified and initiated into the solar mysteries.

I draw near and fire is passed through my aura by the priests. Burning bundles of herbs go through my aura to cleanse and burn off any entities. I'm standing there in a simple, natural white silk underwear shift, but then they slip a robe over my head. The robe is made of blue voile with a shimmer of sequin-like gold disks. (The disks remind me of those that shimmer on belly dancing scarves, even today.)

The priests say, "Go to the time of no sun. See the sun being born, its fire growing as it ignites. Bask in its radiance of light with no heat." (I'm in an altered state of consciousness and what I am witnessing is in higher dimensions; heat belongs to the 3D level of life experience, heat is a 3D phenomenon and manifestation, but light exists in varying forms throughout all dimensions.)

I realize our sun is like one of the tiny discs on my robe. I realize I am Source watching My suns being born to clothe My body in light, to light the worlds.

Then I am asked the question, why did I, as Source, desire the worlds? And the answer comes—*for adventure!* Whenever the adventure goes wrong I can come back to being Source "me." It's a built-in safety net! So when I die—when I die in a life, in a body—I go back to being Source "me." This is the initiation into life and its purpose, and into death returning me to my true

COSMIC CRYSTALS! Working With New Crystal Skulls

nature. Meaning I am not my body or the "me" that is now, but I am the big "me" that is Source. Realizing this is the initiation—this is the Solar Mystery.

The priests say, "For it is done. Rejoice! You are freed from the fear of death and dying. Now you know you never truly die. You just cannot truly die. Be at peace, for so it is."

I'm still wearing the blue garment of "suns in the void of space" as I leave. And I remember in Ancient Egyptian times they would fast before and after this initiation. In a past life I did so, which is why I can trigger this memory and see it now in this skull. Then I'm given a necklace of suns, and told to visualize wearing it at the stone circles I visit. When I reach the gateway there are gold sandals to wear out into the world...I leave the experience and learn the skull's name is **Amersandi**.

I thank the angels for helping me and they say, "That was one of your lives of high achievement. The priests' questions triggered your understanding of your divine nature, after your period of fasting loosened you from your body consciousness."

Three weeks later I try again. I have been working on chapter 9 during the three weeks, but now I'm curious as to what else Amersandi can show me. I slip into the meditation and it's the same sandy slope leading up to the same temple. I go up to the pillared entrance. It is dark inside though torches are flaming on the walls. I slip off my shoes and enter in bare feet. This time I am a short, stocky Egyptian man in a white robe. My dark hair is cut in a high short fringe and is neatly trimmed to fall below my ears. This is me in another past lifetime. I wonder what I've come here for this time...

The answer comes: **peace, and understanding of grief for a loved one.**

My wife has died in childbirth. The child lives, but she does not. My child is looked after by a wet nurse and servants, and by my daughter, but I grieve and find no peace...I miss her greatly. The priests can help and this is why I'm here now. I'm meeting with a priest who can talk to the dead. I am a merchant, a plain man but wealthy in a small way. I have made the temple a gift for

90

CHAPTER 8

this service. Speaking with my wife will bring peace to my poor heart which is weighed heavy with sadness and loss.

I walk up to the altar were he waits.

He picks up a garland from the altar and places it around my neck. It is made of flowers and herbs to cleanse my heart and lift my spirits. It smells of basil.

He leads me deeper into the temple, past the altar and into a small room away from the huge empty space of the main temple. In the room there are two stools with a small table between. The priest sits on one stool and I on the other. His hands are on the table, he invites me to hold them so he can call the spirit to me. He goes into trance as he chants and calls. He shakes. His whole body shakes and then goes limp, and a strange voice comes through him. This is his guide, he warned me of this. A deep stern voice speaks, "What would you have me do?"

I say, "I humbly implore you to bring my wife departed to speak with me, her grieving husband."

"Very well," is the reply.

There is a pause. Then a light female voice that sounds like my Ani says, "Husband dearest, what is your request, what would you know?"

"How are you my dear? I miss you so. Your body so still and you gone from me, it grieves my heart sore. How fares it with you? Are you well served in the afterlife my dearest? Are you well served?"

"Husband dearest, yes, I am at peace. I dwell in light and will wait patiently for you when your own time draws near, and we will be companions once more. I am well. I am peaceful, I watch over the child that took me from you, and we are together each night, for as your ba (astral body) wanders I come to you and you dream of me. I will not desert you, but wait as an obedient wife should, for her master to join her. Grieve no more. Be at peace. I am well served. We are together in life and in death, and in the little death that follows each day as you sleep. Fare you well. Be at peace for the time you have left. Settle our children well before you seek to join with me in death. See them grow and prosper, and be set up in life for happiness as great as ours. Do that for me, for my sake, and know I see it and am well pleased."

"My time has come and I must go. My host tires. I take my leave, farewell, be light of heart from this day forth. Talk to me when you feel me near, for I will never be far from you."

"I must go…"

The priest sat up and shook again, and then steadies. He opens his eyes and drinks the draught that was placed ready to restore him. I thank him, and feeling lighter of heart I leave.

For it was true. I had dreamt of her night after night, which had made the days empty and reminded me of my great loss—but now I see it differently and I am heartened.

I shall look for her in our children's faces and be happy to see our children grow and prosper. My dearest love awaits me, and we shall be as one. Truly peace has returned to my heart. I shall get through the days for her, knowing she is close by, and all has purpose once more; my life has purpose again.

I cross the temple to the entrance, slip on my shoes and go out into the world with a light heart. I call the blessings of the gods down onto the temple and the priest who has helped me. I look down the sandy slope to the bustle of daily life below, as Egypt goes about its business of the day.

As I visualize walking down the slope I leave that past life behind.

I thank the angels, the skull, the temple, the priest, and God.

I kiss the skull that is warm in my hand. And pleased to be back in my present life, I leave Ye fast asleep in bed and go downstairs in search of supper. Toast and cocoa will do the trick to ground me after that poor man's harrowing grief. I had slipped deeper into his character than I normally do. I seem to have a strong connection with that temple. I wonder if I'll be back there again next time I journey with Amersandi.

Two nights later the thought comes that I should see what else lies within the skull. I turn it around and around in my hands, admiring the play of shimmering light in the swirl of bubbles trapped within. At the back of the head there is a darker, cloudy area, and as I gaze at it I can almost see hills and a rugged

CHAPTER 8

landscape…it attracts me, calls to me. I need to explore this. I'll enter Amersandi here for a change.

With permission to enter granted, I visualize myself standing outside the back of the skull. It always amazes me how enormous our skulls are in the inner world. I see a flight of wide stone steps leading up to an open doorway in the cloudy area. The doorway looks dark. Once up the steps I stand in the shadowy entrance way, and then the deeper I go into the skull, the darker it gets. Lights dance around me, spirits of fire. They chatter and are excited to take me somewhere. There's something they want to show me. Their chatter is a joyful humming murmur and they dance, and move, and flicker ahead of me and by my side. They are leading me on and I follow. The dark interior space leads into a huge cave. We pass through it and as we emerge from the cave mouth, we are on the edge of high land overlooking a desert; I am standing on the rocky lip of the cave mouth looking out. It is before sunrise—we see the sun come up and fill the sky with radiant light and the fire of a new day. And though it is light now, I can still see the bright spirits of fire, but there's a hush. They are very still, waiting.

BOOM—there's a huge explosion, a blinding white light, and a mushroom cloud rising.

The spirits of fire are very excited by the intensity of the blast. "This is how we were made—we are showing you our origin. We are with this skull because of the event you have just witnessed. We were born in the nuclear heat and seared into the bubbles of the desert glass. We are happy to be here and happy to see you here. Come many times to see us and we will tell you more each time."

Who let off the explosion? I ask.

"Others, not your species. This was a show of strength to warn off an alien species by another alien species that had colonized the moon's interior, and wanted to use Earth as a staging post for refueling their craft for long haul journeys. Water was the fuel, and they came to Earth to refuel regularly. But someone else wanted to do that, too. They were captured and made to witness this to warn them off. They were told it would be used against them unless they left. Then they were released to take the message

COSMIC CRYSTALS! *Working With New Crystal Skulls*

home. The dominant species won the prize of Earth's water."

Do they still come? I ask.

"Yes, in small numbers. But Earth's water is still good for their purpose. Lakes are better than the sea, as rainwater is purer. They refuel from lakes and try to do this in remote areas as there's less pollution and less chance of being observed. In Arapo you were shown them refueling; this is the "more" you sensed there was to his story."

Spirits of fire, thank you.

"Come see the droplets of glass that have just been made."

We fly over the sands and we see them. In this state they are luminous; in the dimension we are operating in they show up strongly against the land. Then I see the color and light fade out of them as they are weathered by the sun and wind, tamed by the landscaping devas of Earth over eons of time; they await the adventures discovery will bring a long, long time ahead. The spirits of fire say the droplets of glass were formed in a display of strength, and that strength resides within them still. "Cherish your piece that you wear and cherish us in the skull. Return another time."

Amid much flickering and chatter we leave the high land and the valley and plain below, and re-enter the cave mouth. We cross the floor of the dark place and head for the shadowy entrance. We reach the doorway at the top of the steps and I thank the spirits of fire for showing me this, and for showing themselves to me. They look more like butterflies of fire now, darting about. In unison they flicker a farewell...and then I am gone, down the wide stone steps. I'm outside Amersandi now, and I look up at the huge curved shape of the back of her skull as it towers like a mountain above me.

Farewell Amersandi, I think.

I will return.

Back in the awareness of my bedroom I thank the skull, the angels, and God. I decide I'm going to be more adventurous and try entering Amersandi at different places from now on. And perhaps with my other skulls too...

The spirits of fire had looked like the sparks that fly off sparkler

CHAPTER 8

fireworks—intensely bright, tiny sparks. What they'd shown me reminded me of an ET contact experience I'd written about in *Divine Fire* and I'm going to share a fragment of it here. The ETs monitoring Earth today still have a record of that event and the alien wars.

How do I know? From memories retrieved in a regression session that took place in July 2019. I'd been abducted for a nighttime briefing. ETs collect information from us and subliminally educate us while we are on their craft. Abductions can be physical, and then you have missing time you can't account for. But often they are simply astral, where they lift out your astral body while you sleep. We who'd been taken that night had been shown terrible scenes of the devastation humans are inflicting on parts of our planet, the mountains of toxic rubbish, the melted glaciers, devastated rainforests, seas choking with plastic...

"Also I'm being told Earth has been through some very terrible times in the past. Times which were nothing to do with us—asteroid strikes, even alien wars. You know some aliens have thrown wars on our planet?! Even before humans were there. They triggered some Ice Ages and have done all sorts. I knew vitrified sand had been found in deserts which looked like the result of a nuclear explosion, but really...the cheek of it!

But Earth survived.

The message is: Earth is very strong. But we have behaved despicably and we should have known better. And it is unbridled greed and the polluter not paying which really has to change. So a lot of souls have been drafted in to bring a turnaround, and that's the young people we have today. Like the people leading and joining the Extinction Rebellion protests.

ETs can't save us, it would break a lot of Federation treaties. They can't interfere beyond subliminally educating us. Education is smiled on...and they have been doing that, for a long time. Lots of people have nighttime contact like I'm having now—have briefing sessions—and fragments of their experiences may bleed-through afterward into their dreams.

We had to be terrified by what we had done.

We had let a genie of annihilation out of the bottle and there was no way of putting it back. All the nuclear angst in the 1950s

COSMIC CRYSTALS! *Working With New Crystal Skulls*

and 60s resulted, and many people's nightmares about nuclear destruction that were so common back then were the result of bleed-through from the scenarios they had been forced to watch on the craft. But it's not just nuclear issues, it is all sorts. We have behaved badly—but I'm being told we are not the only ones who behaved badly. This has been a common pattern. There are many ruined worlds, and that's why the ETs are here. They are trying to help us draw back from the brink of extinction.

The message is: if we went extinct Earth would still be here. The surface conditions would be different. We might have devastated soil and climate, even exploded so many nuclear devices that we shredded the atmosphere, losing most of it—as happened on Mars. And a lot of our water may have been jettisoned out into space by the explosions, and gone wandering through the Solar System—because we have benefited from other worlds' water, when similar things have happened elsewhere. Frozen lumps of water regularly come into Earth's upper atmosphere as meteors, and percolate down. We have benefited from Mars's and Maldek's water. It is one reason why we have such a beautiful planet. We have had more than our fair share of atmosphere and water.

The ETs have these assessment times on a regular basis, when they look at what is happening, and where the collective consciousness of humanity is registering. And we are lifting out of greed a little. You know when you realize you can't eat money after you've poisoned the last fish? The Native Americans told us that a long time ago, but it is making sense to more and more people now."

Today all that remains of Maldek is the asteroid belt that lies beyond Mars. And sand turned to glass—vitrified sand—has also been found in Mongolia's Gobi Desert, in Israel, Iraq, and in the western Arabian Desert.

CHAPTER 9
Choosing and Naming Your Skulls, Traveling Bags and Instant Repairs, How Skulls Communicate, How To Meditate With Your Skull

The right skull for you will always be the one you are drawn to. It may be love at first sight as soon as you see it, or simply be a skull you can't forget, where you find yourself coming back time and time again for yet another look. But acquiring your crystal skulls should be a joyful process, a real treat, and if for any reason it becomes less than that, step back. Leave that skull alone. Your subconscious is warning you off and it pays to listen. Also, if you no longer like a skull, if for one reason or another you have gone off it, pass it on—*because it knows*—and it will not want to work with you, so it's a waste of time keeping it.

While some people thrust a name upon their skull, crystal skulls appreciate it if you establish a mutually agreeable name with them first. This can be a very quick process as it was with Arapo and Fred, or it may take many days as it did with Moon. At one stage I even wondered if she wanted to be called Penelope. Nothing seemed to fit. I kept pen and paper by my bedside and every night I tried to tune into her to receive her name. I jotted down what came, and then finally the full name came with clarity

COSMIC CRYSTALS! *Working With New Crystal Skulls*

and force. She led me on a merry dance did Moon-Over-the-Waters-of-Life, but not only did she give me her name, she also gave me a mudra—a hand gesture—that describes the name in a symbolic language. Most names are much less complicated than that.

Generally my skulls give me their names during the first meditation, but one simple way to establish a name is when you are walking. On a long walk you slip easily into a meditative state. Think of your new skull, picture it, and a name may just pop up. This is how Charles Lapis got his name. All that matters is that you are comfortable with the name and that your skull is comfortable with it, too. Working with crystal skulls is about establishing a relationship, and this starts with their name. Best not to bully them or have them cringe.

When Ye and I started taking them to stone circles, the need for traveling bags arose to protect them from damage. For Moon I adapted a strong cardboard box, covered it in black velvet and made a detachable soft foam lid that clipped securely in place. For smaller skulls, velvet tarot bags sourced from the Internet made good skull bags. You can get nice plain ones, but many have attractive designs embroidered on them—of suns, moons, stars, angels, dragons, or the Tree of Life, for example. The bags are inexpensive, beautifully made, and roomy enough for boxes of large tarot cards—and for our purpose it is fortunate they don't come with cards! If you need more padding, slip some bubble wrap inside or stitch in a fur fabric lining. Even Solange, my second biggest skull, fits into the larger bags. Solange is five inches long, four and a half inches high and three and a half inches wide.

Of course you could just slip your skulls into socks! But beware of wrapping them in a scarf, because it is all too easy to forget they are there—I've read of a precious skull that fell on the road and shattered to pieces because its guardian pulled the scarf out of her bag thinking to wear it. Have a special bag that cannot be mistaken for anything else. It's not worth taking the risk.

If your skull does get damaged—scratched or chipped, a dab or two of clear nail varnish can easily fix small problems. It is easy to remove the nail varnish later on with nail varnish

CHAPTER 9

remover, so this will not interfere in any permanent way with the skull and its energies. For deeper chips you can build up layers of clear nail varnish, allowing each layer to dry before applying the next. I hope this will never be necessary for your skulls, but it was for Alec, Ye's clear quartz skull.

In chapter one the Amethyst Deva said that chips and missing bits do not affect a skull. But it is a different story for their guardian, who is left with feelings of loss, anger, grief, and guilt, and may blame themselves for the damage. It's worth remembering that a dab of clear nail varnish can prevent those feelings from tarnishing your relationship with your skull; you will be able to see the skull once again and not the damage. There will no longer be a visual reminder, or an annoyingly rough patch that catches your fingers. **But when it comes to repairs, the less invasive they are, the better.**

There are those that suggest treating a skull like a piece of broken oriental porcelain and suggest flagging up a mend with gold, mimicking Kintsugi, the Japanese art of repairing pottery with gold. But the problem with this is that crystal skulls are not pots; pots are simple, inert things, while crystal skulls are neither simple, nor inert. The nature spirits associated with smelted metal are different to those found with natural crystal, so by foisting an unnatural relationship with refined metal upon your crystal skull you will change the skull's energy field, and risk alienating the deva. Remember, skulls do not generally consider they need mending. **If in doubt, ask the skull.** Otherwise, just collect up any broken pieces and put them in a bag made of natural fibers to keep them together with the skull, and go on working with them. Remember, as the Amethyst Deva said in chapter one, the perfection we cherish is a "low human concern" from the skull's point of view. The skull's etheric and higher bodies will still be complete and intact, functioning just as they should do, and as long as you keep the physical pieces together, the higher bodies will remain firmly anchored throught them. A lot of what we do with our skulls is through their higher bodies anyway. After all, we are not our bodies either; the body is simply a house that allows the more eternal aspect of ourselves (and of our skulls) to operate on Earth's material plane.

Consider the possibility that the deva may have completed its evolution as far as the physical plane will allow, and has chosen to ascend to higher realms. Perhaps it required to be released from its crystal and had tweaked the energy threads to engineer the accident, because the crystal was no longer its home, but had become its prison. In this case, given time, the crystal pieces will attract a new deva for you to work with.

How Skulls Communicate

Communication is going to be subtle, but crystal skulls can surprise you. I generally hear a quiet inner voice in my mind's ear, but sometimes they shout, as Zeb'n did when she was going to "wake up the children."

In the past, when I have been with ancient skulls like the Mitchell-Hedges, I have received messages from them. (These channelings appear in *Holy Ice* and *Divine Fire*.) While having a private sitting with the ancient quartz skull Sha Na Ra in 1998, a personal question about where I should live was answered by a vision seen within the skull's crystal body. My eyes were open at the time and I saw the picture with my physical eyes. The picture showed a long beach and a very flat, calm sea, which calmed my irrational fear of tidal waves and allowed me to happily move to a house by the sea. (Arapo related to this vision in chapter two, footnote one.)

Now, although I have seen plenty of things within the crystal bodies of my new skulls, it has always been with my eyes closed, using the inner vision of my third eye, the mind's eye. At this point I had not seen things with my eyes open, not even in Moon or Solange.

When Moon first came I put her in pride of place on a table in our therapy room. I was going to sit her on a pretty blue cloth embroidered with gold, but I distinctly felt her wince at the thought. So I meditated with her and asked her what she wanted to rest on. She put a picture of a *red* cushion in my mind. I searched the Internet in hopes of finding it. A Tibetan singing bowl cushion

CHAPTER 9

exactly matched the picture she'd given me. It was round, red, and with the same delicately patterned gold ribbon trim she'd shown me—and that's what she sits on now.

So skulls can speak to you and show you pictures.

The speaking may be in the form of a persistent nagging thought about something, or be an actual conversational exchange. It may happen when you daydream, when you are thinking about them as you take a walk, or as you go to sleep or wake up, and certainly when you meditate. At these times you are operating in a slightly altered state of consciousness and it's easier for them to interface with you. Generally, the energy of your thoughts when you are thinking about them provides a bridge, where they can reach you and communicate with you. But sometimes they just plain interrupt you and it's not subtle at all!

Alec did. Ye bought him at a conference in 2008 before sitting down to a talk by Bill Homann about the Mitchell-Hedges skull. Alec was in a paper bag inside a shoulder bag on the floor, but when the talk started he cut into Ye's thoughts, wanting to be out of the bag to see the talk! Alec was Ye's first skull and even though he has been joined by six less voluble companions, he is still like that today.

With Moon, when I ask her a question, perhaps about whether to buy a certain new skull, she pulls faces. I know her solid crystal body physically can't do that, but in my mind's eye it can. She's in my mind's eye to the left side of my mind screen, and when I ask her what she thinks, she pulls a face to tell me. She may flash her teeth in a smile if she likes it, or roll her eyes to say "heavens, no"; she expresses disgust with a downturned mouth, and when she really doesn't like a skull, she makes a throat-cutting gesture with a white-gloved hand. She can be quite funny and makes me laugh!

If you sincerely want to communicate with your skull there should be no problem in establishing a telepathic link. Plenty of people have—just look at what gets posted in the skull groups on Facebook if you doubt me; and if you find it hard to get started, meditation will help. It is always a good way to contact your skull, and if you don't try, you will never know what you can do...

How to Meditate with your Skull

To borrow an analogy from the world of computers, we humans are naturally born with the essential hardware to communicate with crystals, and with angels, spirit guides, and other non-physical beings, too. But before we can do so we need to download an app, a little bit of software. The meditation process acts as the app, so I'm going to share in detail how I meditate, but do it any way you prefer.

All my new skulls arrived ready to start work straight away, wherever they were from, which surprised me greatly—because some suppliers go to a great deal of trouble to activate them for you, while others do nothing at all. The skulls were a random selection from various sellers. They were skulls anybody could have bought, and you will find a list of the sellers at the back of the book. Some skulls were remarkably inexpensive, but what they all had in common was that they caught my eye. I was intuitively drawn to them all in the same way as you will be when you look for your own crystal skulls.

Trust your gut feeling when it comes to choosing a skull, whether you are in a shop or on the Internet. Ask yourself, "How is my body responding to this skull?" Logic is a much less reliable guide. I get turned off by the expressions on some of their faces, and by some carving styles that I find quite ugly, but that's just my personal response. We wouldn't all choose the same dish on a menu and it is the same with your skulls. All that matters is that you like it.

If you've had your skulls for a while and they are sleepers, as mine were in chapter two, it's best to wake them up with music over a few days before you meditate with them. You are likely to have a much richer response that way.

1. Just before you meditate, tune in to your skull, hold it in your hands. Study its beautiful crystal with a lamp—really get a feel for it. Admire it. This brings you and the skull into harmony. (For this I use an LED bedside light, nothing special or expensive, but

it gives a bright white light, clear and sharp, that is good for reading and that makes it good for reading your skull's crystal.)

2. Get comfortable and ensure you will not be disturbed.

3. Hold the skull in your left hand, or if it is heavy, have it by you with your left hand resting on it. (The left is the more receptive side of your body.)

4. Close your eyes and take several slow deep breaths in through your nose, hold, and breath out through your mouth, really enjoying letting go on the out breaths.

5. Picture light above you like a radiant sun—your God-self raying down light. Divine Light is streaming down around you, surrounding you in light, keeping you safe. (As I visualize this happening I say, "Silver-fire sun of my being, ray down around me the wonderful crystal curtain of love and light and healing." When I feel/see that this is in place, I make a direct connection with God by saying "Oh God please bless me" or "Oh God I love you.")

6. Ask Archangel Michael to be with you to keep you safe; ask Archangel Uriel to be with you so you perceive truth; ask Archangel Gabriel to be with you so your experience may be imbued with love; ask Archangel Raphael to be with you that healing may flow forth from your experience.

7. Your eyes are closed, but picture your skull clearly in your mind's eye.

8. Ask your questions, such as: What is your name? What can you offer me? What is your role in my team of skulls?

9. If you plan to explore within them, EVERY TIME ask, "May I enter?" (Skulls like working with us, and I'm sure it will welcome interacting with you, but if it says "no," ask why.)

10. Enter where you feel is best, anywhere that catches your attention.

COSMIC CRYSTALS! Working With New Crystal Skulls

11. Let the experience unfold. Be patient. It may seem like nothing is happening at first...but then you will become aware of something...some little thing, just go with it. Don't jump to conclusions or seek to analyze anything, because that will take you out of the unfolding experience. Explore the situation you have found yourself in, and intuitively you will know the next step. Trust yourself.

12. After the experience has unfolded, make the return journey. Visualize leaving the skull and become aware once more of your physical body and your physical surroundings.

13. Thank the Archangels Michael, Uriel, Gabriel, and Raphael for helping you; thank the skull, and the Divine (using whatever name you prefer for the Creator).

This is what I do, and if things don't develop into an experience for you, simply try again later. You have seen that I sometimes have to do that, too. When I've been too tired, I've had to go back and attempt it another day. Like anything else it gets easier with practice. With inner world work you discover the journey, the journey unfolds for you—you do not direct it or make it up. And because you discover it, it teaches you things you did not know. That's the fun of it, the wonder of it, and the beauty of it.

I wish you happy journeying!

If by any remote chance you don't like the experience, you can snap out of it just as you would with a bad dream—**open your eyes and come back to normal, waking reality.** Or more gently, retrace your footsteps in the inner world and leave the skull the way you entered it. Protection is built into the meditation by the initial cloaking in light and by the presence of archangels to call on for assistance.

Angels have been a reality for me ever since I encountered my guardian angel and Archangel Michael much earlier in my life. I also write about meeting Uriel, Gabriel, and Raphael in *Spiritual Gold,* where I share my own life story, including how I

CHAPTER 9

came to learn about the skulls. I am going to share a little about the angels from the first chapter of that book with you now:

"There is nothing mysterious or difficult about meditation.

The inner vision we use is the same as when we dream, and we do that effortlessly every night. You just need the luxury of a little quiet time to yourself.

Before settling down to meditate I made sure not to be disturbed. I lit a candle and some incense out of respect for the angels and to help them draw near. I made myself comfortable in a chair, closed my eyes and prayed. I asked God for protection and help, and then I visualized light streaming down from God all around me, keeping me safe. I made a heartfelt request for what I hoped to achieve, (in the case I'm writing about it was to meet my guardian angel), *and then I tried to still my mind and be receptive.*

At first I sensed my angel as a ball of light. On later occasions I saw her as a small winged figure to my right-hand side, at shoulder height. In time I learned her name and as I got better at tuning into her, she appeared larger.

But sometimes the unexpected happens.

One day I began a meditation and connected with my angel, but found my awareness in space, passing the moon. I wondered what was going on. Should I pull my mind back to Earth or trust the angel? This dilemma was not what I was expecting at all.

Well, if you can't trust your guardian angel, who can you trust?

So I surrendered to the journey.

We alighted on the sun in the dimensions inhabited by angels. It was bright and very light, but there was no fire on that level. Graceful plumes of a fine, white, powdery sun dust shot up from the surface as we landed, and a tall white-robed angel greeted us and guided us into vast white caves filled with light and with angelic choirs praising the Creator. I soon felt restless and asked if they ever got bored. With a gentle laugh he said that I did not understand angels to ask this, and that no, they didn't. When we left them to their singing, I stroked the soft feathers of his wings and asked our guide his name. The reply that came was

"Michael," and in the instant I knew exactly who it was. I felt a bit taken aback to find I had been so flippant and familiar with an archangel, but he hadn't seemed to mind at all."

I confess what I didn't share in *Spiritual Gold* was that I was in such a lonely place in my life all those years ago that when I encountered the loving warmth of Archangel Michael, I'd asked him for a hug before I left. He'd swept me up in his arms and held me gently. It was only then I was bold enough to stroke the soft feathers on his wings.

It was a comfort having met Michael, and today every time I do inner work I still call on him to keep me safe. I guess worldwide, Michael must be the most popular of all angels, but despite that, he will always have time to work with you. Archangel Michael, our guardian and protector, can work with many people at what we perceive to be the same moment, because he is not bound by time as we are. We humans are trapped in the streams of time, but angels exist in the eternal now of the spiritual realms.

If I had never meditated I would never have met Michael. Meditation opens doors! Meditate with your skulls and I'm sure you will find you are a crystal skull whisperer.

CHAPTER 10
Florence and the Standing Stone

September comes and we are planning to visit Lizzy, a friend who lives near the standing stone at Matfen in Northumberland, a short drive away. We pack skulls to take with us, and for the first time slip them into the new soft velvet tarot bags—so quick and stylish compared to our packing last time!

On Thursday the 2nd of September 2021, the day before the visit, I wake up to the rattle and clatter of a new skull plopping through the letterbox downstairs. I hear, "**Florence** here, come to be a companion to Fred." (!) It is a distinct clairaudient experience. I go to unwrap her and her smooth flower agate is a joy to hold. The little skull is comforting and uplifting. She is two inches long and fits well in the hand. I am stunned she knew about Fred. She spends the day at his side on the skulls' table.

Come nighttime, I study her under my bedside reading lamp and plan to meditate with her. I decide to enter on the right-hand side, because I'm drawn there by a collection of round holes in the floral plumes in her agate. They look curious and when I hold Florence up to the light they look dark, though she is translucent elsewhere.

Florence and winged skull Fred

Once I am in the inner world I find the skull is huge. I scramble up to one of the holes in her agate side and grab on to the edge with my hands, haul myself up, and climb in. It's dark inside the tunnel, but light is filtering through translucent areas deeper in the skull; I can see well enough to walk along the tunnel in the plume...it's going down into the heart of the skull. The tunnel opens out into a cavern, a very peaceful domed space, like a huge room full of light that is diffusing in through the walls.

I see feathers—soft, ostrich-type feathers, creamy and wafty—there is a trail of them. I follow the trail up to a nest. There's a nest in a tunnel leading off the domed cavern. I am told birds fly out of the holes in this skull and that they return to their nests after completing their missions. There are more birds and more nests...they are not ostriches, but much smaller and fly well, with their big silky-feathered wings.

What are the "missions"? I ask Florence.

"They spy, spying missions."

For who or for what do they spy? I ask.

"For the skull."

What does Florence the skull want to find out?

"If she is safe. The birds have been liaising with your other

CHAPTER 10

skulls since she came this morning."

Does she feel safe now? I ask.

"Yes, now she does. She was anxious before she came and she didn't want to stay with the seller."

Why not? I ask.

"Incompatible energy source there."

What does Florence offer me? I ask.

"Feeling good about things, the ability to find that all is well."

What are the birds?

"Birds of chance and change, birds that sense changes and bring warnings, useful birds. You found my birds. I have other secrets for you to discover. The birds are good, they have attractive feathers and attractive actions, and the birds are happy here," Florence says.

I ask her if she wants to come with me tomorrow. I'm thinking she might like to meet the standing stone.

"Yes, to meet Lizzy," is the surprising reply.

I find it strange that Florence knows about Lizzy, and that she'd known about Fred before she arrived, although that would be due to the activities of the Collective Crystal Skull Consciousness, (and for brevity's sake it is often called the CCSC). Lizzy is known to my other skulls because she came to see them.

But the other strange thing about Florence is that she speaks of herself in the third person as "the skull." However, now that my questions are over, I get the idea to take a ride to the Matfen Stone on one of the silky-feathered birds, and I do this! I fly out into the night. I find the stone is set near a road by a field boundary.

We circle above and the bird calls "Caw, caw, caw" to wake up the stone, to prepare it for our visit the next day. Then we fly back into the central space in the skull, and I leave the birds to their nests and walk up the tunnel, climb out of the hole—and hanging by my hands—I drop to the ground. I'm out of the skull now and back in my bedroom.

I thank Florence the skull, the birds, the angels, and God for the experience.

The ancient Standing Stone at Matfen

Friday sees us at the stone with Lizzy. We ask permission to approach it and then greet it. We place our hands on it and press our foreheads against it, and introduce ourselves as we did at Duddo. It is a very similar stone, and is part of the same energy network, but it's at least 55 miles further south and much nearer Hadrian's Wall. We photograph it and then hold each of our skulls

CHAPTER 10

against it in turn, sensing where they want to be pressed, where they want to make their connection. We had taken thirteen skulls with us. Ye took three, including Alec, and I took ten. I was hoping for a download into the skulls, something for our skulls to tell us when we return home.

I did try that night, but was too tired to get anything sensible out of them.

But on Saturday night I start with Florence and this time I choose the left-hand side for my journey in. Here, a flight of white marble steps is leading up to an archway. I stand in the archway and see a black and white checkered floor leading to a central chamber, but it's a different chamber to the last time. It is more formal. There are no birds or animals here, but there is a long table arranged with chairs down both sides of it. The table is set out with plates and cutlery.

What is this for? I ask.

"Welcoming you and the other skulls to a celebratory meal to celebrate my arrival" replies Florence. (!!!)

This takes me by surprise and has to be purely symbolic, but the skull essences do arrive and take a seat. No one actually eats anything because they can't, but they give speeches of welcome to Florence, and I'm told her birds delivered the invitations.

Moon says, "Welcome little one, we are all glad that you made it here, we look forward to working with you."

Solange says, "Glad you've come to share skull activities."

I don't stay for all the speeches, but before I go I have three questions to ask Florence, beginning with why did you want to meet Lizzy?

"She is a lady who needs skulls in her life. Her crystals have told us."

Florence, what did you make of the standing stone?

"It was lonely and appreciated our visit. It was whistling and singing by the end, though you could not hear it."

Florence, did the standing stone tell you anything?

"It was pleased to meet us, called us "friends" and said it was nice to have friends call round…Oh! I have been welcomed by the stone and by the other skulls! I am very happy."

111

COSMIC CRYSTALS! *Working With New Crystal Skulls*

I take my leave and leave them celebrating. I'm out in the corridor heading for the archway, then off down the flight of steps. I thank Florence, and I thank my skull team for accepting her. I thank the angels, and God. Back in the awareness of my bedroom I kiss Florence's crystal before putting her down. I'm falling asleep. I'll attempt to find what the other nine skulls picked up soon. I often kiss my skulls before I put them down after working with them. It seems a natural way to express my affection for them, like kissing the top of a cat's head. Skulls are a lot like cats when you come to think about it. They are always their own masters.

The crystal kingdom's information exchange network never ceases to amaze me—like how Florence knew about Lizzy. Lizzy had last visited us many weeks before, when she'd brought her piece of Libyan Desert Glass to bathe in the sea and I'd shown her my crystal skulls. Lizzy has always had a natural affinity for stones and crystals, and did a two year crystal course some years ago. I had told her my new skull, Florence, wanted to meet her, and she obligingly held Florence. I suspect it will not be long before Lizzy has a crystal skull of her own...

When I asked the other skulls that had come with me what they made of the standing stone, Solange, although quartz and the largest skull I'd taken, said the least—just that the stone was large, it spoke freely, and it was pleased to share its story. That didn't tell me much!

Sparkly clear quartz Zeb'n said, "I enjoyed contact with the sandstone, weathered by ages of rainfall and wind. It spoke of seasons I have never felt or known. I have never been out in the seasons. It shared its wisdom and strength. It was lonely till we came. It downloaded information that will be released slowly to you over time. It guards the land as it should."

Arapo is sandstone, like the standing stone. This helped him connect though he is a different color. He said, "We spoke of sand and wind and water, of pressure and of transforming into rock, for we both were once free grains dancing on the beaches of Life in eons past, before many things lived on the surface of

112

CHAPTER 10

the world. We remembered our youth and communed. I cheered it up. Made it remember being younger, when it was carefree and not tasked with guarding the land and upholding the energy grid of the world—well of this bit of the world, anyway. We had a laugh together, the stone and I, both sandstones together and both sentient in a way that would surprise many people, even many creatures, though the creatures sense much more of the energies of the world than humans do. Humans miss a lot."

Arapo went on to say, "The visit was good, did us good and did the standing stone good. We benefited from its wisdom. Grandfather Stone we call it. The Duddo stones were like uncles and aunts to us. This felt even older, like the circle was erected *after* outlier stones like this had set up the energies in the land."

To talk with Arapo I had visualized entering him as I did the last time, through a fissure in his side that took me into a valley surrounded by Sedona's red sandstone rocks. The lake was still there, but not the UFO, but this time Arapo had the standing stone there! To explain this geographical and temporal anomaly Arapo said the stone was "on holiday," that its astral body was on holiday in Sedona, meeting and communing with Arapo's parent rocks—that it was meeting up with long lost family! Arapo said the stone would go back when it was ready, so I left it there and returned. (!)

Amethyst Hapi-atzi said, "It was thrilling to meet a Druid stone after meeting Merlin. Merlin had put a small skull face in it for you to find, although you did not see it. The stone told me more about the Druid way. It will deepen our connection when next we work together with Merlin."

Jago, carved from red jasper, said "It told me its troubles and spoke of its loneliness, and how it misses its companions long gone. You were never in any danger there. We have all (*by which he means the skulls on the visit*) linked with this stone in a greater way than with the circle, because its need was greater. The circle stones had their companions close by. This was solitary and lonely. It enjoyed and benefited from the exchanges with us skulls." Jago sees his job as keeping me safe; traditionally red jasper guarded against witchcraft...

113

COSMIC CRYSTALS! *Working With New Crystal Skulls*

The quartz Shaman Stone said, "We thank you for introducing us. It was kin. A Grandfather Stone, we all loved its deep rugged voice and kindly disposition. We made it laugh as playful children can. I shall do work with that stone, and astral visit it frequently. The minerals on your planet are stirring and waking up. It's part of Earth's development, it's a good thing for Earth and for the future health of the world....I can't say more. A good thing for Earth is not necessarily a good thing for Man. But it may be, depends on the man! Exploit or live in harmony—that's the deciding factor with that."

Libyan Desert Glass Amersandi said, "It was old and slow, deep and sonorous, not bright and sharp like me. We were worlds apart, but I was once sand too, so we did understand each other. The explosion that created me changed me from sand to the fluid fusion glass brings. I had to think hard to remember my sand past, but then I did, and I understood the stone better. It was a kindly stone and meant well. I am only small, but it knew I was there and sang to me."

Preseli bluestone Mars said, "Loved it. It had always wanted to meet Preseli bluestone. It had heard the bluestones singing in the networks (of energy) but never heard its true voice close by. We made each other feel good, amplified each other's energies, just by being together. Woo! Felt good. I started it whistling."

Charles Lapis, Keeper of Records said, "Deep...a deep experience. It holds secrets and time coded information. Now is not the time for it to be released." I wanted more than that, so I entered Charles and went up his blue staircase. This time at the top I find a library stuffed with books. I pull out *Stone Age Britain*, open it up and see a map showing the stone. The book tells me the standing stone at Matfen was erected as a "guardian of the seasons" and that there were rites at the changes of the year to boost its benevolent energies.

I replace the book, go down the staircase and leave Charles.

All that day I had worn the clear quartz Council of Seventeen on my wrist, and while not actually pressing them to the standing stone, they had been in its auric field for a very long time as I held the succession of independent skulls in place. So I check them out

CHAPTER 10

now. I hold them in my left hand, focus, and ask them,

What can you tell me about the Grandfather Stone?

"An energy exchange took place that enriched both the stone and us. The stone responds well to quartz, and it used to be hit with a quartz rod to "sound" it, to make it resonate. Also there used to be chanting and singing to make it resonate during the ceremonies of the seasons long ago. Libations were poured down it to flow into the land. It enjoyed your human voices and the vibrations made by the three of you talking."

What did you do there? I ask.

"We cleared the site, sucked old stuck energies into our portal and cleaned the place around the stone."

Is there anything else you would tell me?

"We are happy to return there."

That was as much as I could handle, and I thanked the Council of Seventeen and all the individual skulls, the standing stone, the angels, and God for the experience. I returned my awareness to being back in my bedroom and opened my eyes.

Next morning I wake up knowing a bit more about the quartz rod. (Skulls can teach us in our sleep and it is good to have a skull by your bedside.) Neither the rod nor the stone would have been damaged, as no great force was used. It was tapping, not hitting. The tapping went up and down a three foot span at what would have been a comfortable standing height for the slightly smaller ancient people. It was a rapid, gentle, succession of taps, up and down, getting ever and ever faster, setting up oscillating waves within the stone, while the people who were gathered around it in rings first walked, while stamping hard, then went faster and faster around the stone while chanting, then singing, then finally shouting. They added the vibrations caused by their voices and stamping feet to the oscillating waves the quartz rod had created in the stone. By the end it really zinged, and the people attending the rite held hands as they ran rings around the stone.

The tallest men were always placed in the outer ring, with the people arranged in size so the smaller children were in the inner ring. There were alternating rings of men and women. The men went round clockwise, the women anticlockwise.

It came to me that this was the origin of the saying "to run rings around" something or someone, meaning to get the better of them; these people were mastering the stone, although the saying is usually attributed to 18th century hunting terminology, where hares and foxes are said to run in circles as they attempt to escape the hunters.

Ye's skulls also picked up on the stone's loneliness and the fact that the stone had welcomed the visit from what it called the "sweet crystal folk."

The Shaman Stone pressed against the Standing Stone

CHAPTER 11
Mariam

I had been noticing a pattern of unsatisfactory friendships in my life and decided to cut cords with people I rarely saw. No point pining for things as they used to be, and no point leaking energy down cords of longing. Life moves on, people change, and their lives get ever busier these days. Cutting cords does not mean I'll never see them again or that they will even notice it, but it will help me.

Just as in chapter two, when the desire body wraps cords around the skulls we long for, the cords will re-establish if you find yourself pining and thinking about that person again. This means the cords will need cutting several times. Cutting cords with people means they are free to relate with you as they wish, without any expectation based on past circumstances. Visualize holding a sword of light and sweep it down from your crown to your feet through the cords, and see them shrivel up and drop away. Setting people free is scary and flags up fears of loneliness…that's the emotional landscape I was in when I sat down to meditate with **Mariam** in September.

She had arrived in the post and was lepidolite with mica, a fine skull, over three inches long and silvery gray hinting at purple, with crystals of creamy mica and silvery metallic speckles. I had put off working with her until I'd finished the last chapter.

117

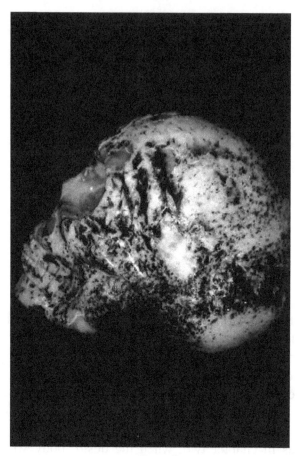

Mariam
(In profile facing left)

She readily gives me her name, and when I ask her what her skill is—what it is that she wants to offer me—she says it is "understanding why things happened."

I enter on her right side, drawn there by attractive markings in her stone. I see salt flats, a wide piece of sodden land, and a low cloudy sky. It is dusk...birds are calling and feeding, searching for morsels on the ground. The skull is there, huge as a house. I approach and a door opens. I step inside into a gray hallway. It

CHAPTER 11

is nicely decorated, smart, it's a very fashionable gray. I open a door to my right which opens into a room full of people doing yoga, keeping themselves flexible. "You have to be flexible, too," Mariam says, "in regards to those who disappoint. Consider their journeys and pain and have compassion. Back right away. They will reach out when they have healed. You do not have to take on their burdens. Nourish yourself, instead of fretting about why they are not getting in touch with you."

I wander through the yoga class toward French doors at the far end of the room. They lead me out into a garden. I smell fresh earth after rain, and see jewels of rainwater gleaming on leaves, delicate lupin leaves with diamonds in their centers. It is lovely! I am told the message for me here is to get out into my garden more. Mariam says, "You can be on top of the gardening and have it gorgeous. You walked through the yoga class, you did not stay and engage, you were free to walk through the room to seek nourishment in the garden. And so it is in your life right now. You need several days of gardening to restore you before doing the exterior painting work you are planning, (I have a garden gate and two exterior doors in bad condition that need painting, and the job is weighing heavily on me), and ease off the writing, just for a short while."

She is right. I do need a gardening break.

It always restores me.

I climb a tree and watch the sunset—beautiful!

Time to return, and I go back through the house and leave. I'm standing on the lonely salt flats again, the sea is far away. The salty water is my unshed tears and I realize this scene represents my fear of being alone, of cutting cords with, and perhaps losing, friends who had been dear to me. Mariam says, "This will not happen. And you will meet me in a very different setting next time you enter the inner world."

I thank Mariam, the angels, and God.

Definitely time for toast and cocoa, and I feel very grateful for the compassion and motherly energy of this skull. Just what I need.

COSMIC CRYSTALS! Working With New Crystal Skulls

A few days later, on the 19th of September, I enter Mariam on the left side, where a patch of pure white rough crystal has caught my attention. It puts me in mind of a snowy mountain landscape. Once in the inner world, I find myself walking up a curving snow-covered slope with low parapet walls. The slope takes me up to the fine front door of a large house. The door is embellished and paneled, with big fancy hinges and a shiny black doorknob. I turn the knob and enter. There's a doormat to stamp off any clinging snow, and I find myself in a lovely hallway with a chandelier. It is well lit and light streams in through a skylight above. It is a tranquil, peaceful space.

I smell vanilla.

Something is cooking, and I go to find it. Stepping on soft, creamy rugs that cover a tiled floor, I go in deeper to find the kitchen where the delicious vanilla aroma is coming from. In the center of the kitchen table, fairy cakes are cooling on a wire rack. How I want one! But I need permission first. Mariam says, "They are for you. Eat one now and tell me how you feel after it." I pick up one of the small cakes and peel back its paper case and take a bite. It is delicious, with a sweet honey-custard center. How do I feel after I've eaten it? Satisfied and happy, and I just know that to eat more of the cakes is unnecessary. Mariam says, "And so it is with skulls. You have enough now to make you satisfied and happy. More leads to stress and indigestion. Be at peace, for all is well and work with us, your team, from now on. You need to know us in a deeper way, and follow up, and take our journeys further. Do not buy more skulls yet, or for a long time to come, if you would finish your book in a satisfying way, which I'm sure you want to do."

"The snow outside symbolizes frozen tears. They will melt away in the spring to come. All is well. Be at peace. We, your skull team, and the Collective Crystal Skull Consciousness in general, welcome you and would see you happy. Use us, consult with us, and continue your journey to understanding."

Is there anything else I should know? I ask.

"Not for today."

Well that does give me peace—the search is over! No more

CHAPTER 11

hours spent trawling eBay for new skulls, and a chance for my bank account to recover!

"Take the cakes with you to enjoy as you work on the book and in the garden. Lighten up!" Mariam says.

And when I look at the table the cakes appear now packed in a bag. I take them with me and leave. I open the front door and step outside. The snow has gone and it is spring in the inner world now. The sun is shining and flowers spill from hanging baskets at each side of the door, and gloriously fill the tubs and pots now lining the slope.

I return. I thank Mariam, the angels, and God for giving me that experience. A weight has lifted because the search is over, and I shall honor the inner world cakes by making a point of having outer world treats. It was clever of Mariam to give me the message in a way that used my senses of smell and taste, plus a bodily sensation of being full and satisfied. That way the message has much more impact than just words would have had.

Mariam is mothering me and I feel grateful for it. It is over forty years since I had a mother, and I feel Mariam is healing deep wounds within me without needing to say a word. I dithered over buying her for weeks, I kept looking at her in my basket on eBay. Now I am very glad I bought her. With our skulls we are drawn to what we need.

CHAPTER 12
More From Hapi-atzi: Merlin's Advice On Working With Your Skulls

It is the end of September, and I know there will be no more new skulls joining the team now. Mariam was very clear on that. I can't look to new skulls to distract me anymore, but I also know Moon, Solange, and Hapi-atzi *must* have more to reveal. Sister Moon and Brother Sun Solange are far and away the most expensive skulls I've ever bought, and they have provided very little for the book up to this point; it's time to take their journeys further. There's also unfinished business to complete with Hope Ramasa Metri, the Shaman Stone, and Hapi-atzi and Merlin.

As our relationship with our skulls deepens, the experience they offer us may change. Just because you find things a certain way to begin with, does not mean that it will always present in that manner. An entrance may have a door at first, but on a later occasion it may not; and so it is, on the afternoon of the 27th of September 2021, when I settle down to meditate with Hapi.

Permission to enter is granted easily enough, but today there is no sliding glass door. I have to go up three steps, which is something new, but then I pass through an open archway to find myself in her stone-slabbed interior. She never was one for a strong barrier, but the archway signifies she is even more open

CHAPTER 12

to me than she was before, and there is no need for any sort of a door at all. Looking back, the steps signified this was going to be a trip to a higher dimension. Free-flowing energy now surging into this skull propels me further into her interior space, and soon the amethyst flagstones give way to clouds. Instead of walking on amethyst stone slabs, I'm now walking on the amethyst-colored clouds of a sunset...*and I've entered the realm of nature spirits.* The tops of the clouds are making a pavement I stride over. I am feeling huge...and I look at my body to find I'm a storm being now—I look like a transparent and colorless giant. And there's a storm coming—that is why the clouds have this purple tinge to them.

My fellow storm beings are here...we have gathered to make it a big one—a great big storm. It's to cleanse and discharge an accumulation of stuck/static energy. This will be electrifying. The lightening starts. It is thrilling for us and feeds us; we become charged. We become stronger and bolder. We shake the clouds and agitate them to release their moisture. Rain cascades down and it is like The Mother is crying—our Mother Earth is crying for the unhappiness of her children—the animals hunted and consumed by humankind. We fall with the rain and we run in the wind as it batters the leaves on the trees; the rain crashes down on the roofs of buildings. We rejoice in our freedom and run and run until our energy charge is dissipated and we slow. One by one we fall asleep in trees and fall still in the woods; and where there are no longer woods we cause havoc, and flooding, in our anger at not finding the trees we need for our rest. I slip into a stream, now overflowing and spreading into a lake. There is a fish. A big fish and it speaks to me saying, "These storm events are going to be ever more frequent from now on, as the world warms."

It is time to return.

By clinging to the evaporating water on the surface of the lake, I rise in the air and join a cloud. I scramble up through the cloud and walk along the top of it, on the pavement it is providing. I walk across the clouds and back to Hapi-atzi. Standing firm on her amethyst stone-slabbed floor I let the vision of the clouds fade, and I focus only on Hapi's interior. My storm-being persona fades and I'm me again.

I see Hapi's crystal staircase.

It's time to go up and enter Merlin's spacious room. I'm hoping he will be there.

I reach the top of the staircase and Merlin smiles behind his skull-laden table. "Glad to see you," he says. "Now, how best to use skulls? That is the question we need to address today."

This is what he tells me:

JOURNEYING

- "Journeying as you are doing it is one way, because skulls are good to go journeying with, and they can take you to the ends of time and to the death of worlds should you so wish." (*He means they can take you anywhere, that there is no limit.*)

HEALING

- "Crystal Skulls can also be used for healing. Write down your request, tuck it beneath your skull, and set it to work on the task."
- "If the healing is for yourself, keep the skull near you so its energy field bathes your energy field over a prolonged period of time."
- "Drink water the skull has marinated in. Drink it with a prayer. Ask the crystal and the Creator for your harmony to be restored." (*A word of caution, this is not for crystals that deteriorate in water or contain poisonous compounds. Quartz is fine, some others may not be. Look it up to be sure.*)
- "Enter the skull and request healing for yourself — you may then find a spa pool appears within it. Swim, or float, or bathe in the healing waters. Perhaps also visualize drinking the healing waters."

HEALING FOR OTHERS

- "Distance healing—but only to be done if you have permission from the one to be healed. Visualize them inside the skull with you. Meet them in the skull and converse with their higher self. Ask, why do they have the condition? Does the condition provide them with something they want? How else might they be able to get that instead? Explore the issue. If they are willing, take them to bathe in the spa pool within the skull." (*Exploring the issue may include asking things like what changes in their thought patterns, eating choices, or lifestyle would benefit them and assist in their healing. An example of what the condition provides could be extra attention from loved ones who were taking them for granted.*)

- "Another way is to meditate and visualize taking your crystal skull to them. Expand the skull so it slips over them and envelopes them within its healing crystal. Hold the image until you feel enough has been achieved for that day. Return. Repeat this as often as you feel necessary. Remember, some people are—on an inner level—choosing to go out of body for a reason. This is why you always seek their permission first. Unwarranted interference in the life path of another accrues bad karma. Do not rush in where angels fear to tread, no matter how much you may want to."
- "If they visit you for a healing, dedicate yourself to the task, and with your hands gently lift the etheric body out from your healing skull, expand it and slip it over their head and down to cover them. Request the healing needed from the skull, the Collective Crystal Skull Consciousness, the crystal deva, the archangels, and the person's guides. Be open to what your intuition suggests you do."

THE FUTURE—DIVINATION
- "Perhaps you wonder about a choice facing you. If so, enter the skull and ask to visit the future that each choice would bring…See what unfolds if you take a certain course of action."
- "Channel the skull's advice/wisdom."
- "Scry, if that is one of your skills."

INFLUENCING PEOPLE AND EVENTS

- "Be careful, for you enter the realm of black magic here, if you are not careful. Skulls will give help if asked, but do not command interference in the affairs of another. Skulls can be used for good or ill; they are lenses that energy can be focused through. If you desire an outcome, enter the skull, seek its permission, and visualize the desired outcome. You may need to do this multiple times, depending on how strong the stream of time is that you seek to destroy or create. Be careful, ego is not your friend here. (And I confess, an example of influencing is when I, Merlin, sent the people in the Great Hall to sleep.)" (*See chapter six.*)

MESSAGES

- "I, Merlin, put messages into the land and the stones. Yes, you can do this if your heart is pure, and your cause noble, and imbued with truth and beauty. Otherwise, again, it is the accrual of bad karma and best avoided. An example of good use would be to put good wishes into the fabric of a child's bedroom, to keep them safe, and to close down any astral doorways opened by others before you. Visualize their room full of a beautiful energy field filled with love, and shielded with violet fire, and the blue flame of Archangel Michael."

Then Merlin says, "That is enough for now."

I thank him and retreat down the crystal staircase. Stepping through the archway I descend the three steps and come back into awareness of being in my bedroom at home. I am so grateful to Merlin that I thank him again, along with Hapi-atzi, the angels, and God for enabling me to have this experience.

❄ ❄ ❄

There is no right or wrong way to work with your skulls, and

CHAPTER 12

perhaps there are as many ways to work with them as there are people on the planet. You will work with your skulls in your own way, because every skull guardian and every skull is different. Ye did not get far using my approach of entering a skull and letting an experience unfold, but he did get many meaningful communications from his own skulls. He has a chatty quartz skull called **Alec.** This was his first skull, and Alec has since been joined by **Philip, Arian, Blue, Magnus, Mata**, and **Raphaela**. Philip is blue obsidian, Arian is labradorite from Madagascar, Blue is lapis lazuli, Magnus is moss agate, Mata is bumble bee jasper and Raphaela is rose quartz. The skulls simply speak silently to him in a telepathic communication. Every night he takes two of them up to his bedside table, and if he forgets, they call out to remind him! Before he goes to sleep he holds them in his hands, one at a time, and tunes into them, and often he receives a message or a picture. Sometimes he asks a question and that stimulates a response from the skull. Other times he holds them against his third eye and sees things—a pattern, a picture...several times he saw a very ancient skull on a rocky pedestal deep in a cave. He was told this was **Ancestor Skull,** an ancient "father" of our skulls today. It is like they, or the idea for them, sprang from this ancient skull being. This vision was repeated several times, and with such force, that when Ye was telling me about it I saw it, too. We were sitting side by side, his skulls were there, and they transmitted the image to me.

Just thinking about your skulls will be enough to build a thought bridge and link you to them. Having them by your bedside enables your energy fields to overlap and automatically exchange information while you sleep, and this will strengthen your bond with them.

Whatever works for you is the right way to connect with your skulls. Enjoy their crystal beauty and their calm energy, enjoy having them—! and anything else is a bonus! Remember, don't stress or feel you have failed to connect—it is just a question of *when*, not *if*, it will happen. Your skulls are allies for you in your life today; they are crystal friends who ask nothing. Just seeing them sitting peacefully on a shelf is soothing. Holding them in

COSMIC CRYSTALS! *Working With New Crystal Skulls*

your hands while you watch TV helps discharge stress. They are as healing as any crystal may be, but they offer you much more than that. They offer companionship, and have come into your life to help you and to comfort you. Use them as worry dolls, tell them your troubles, get things off your chest and share your worries with them. A trouble shared is a trouble halved, as the old saying goes.

It is true crystal skulls are lenses through which intention can be amplified, which means they can be used for good or ill, as can almost everything else in the world, but karma makes us all accountable in the end. In the long term—in a-life-after-life-soul-journey-sense—no one ever gets away with anything. My years as a past life therapist, helping people to understand the roots of problems surfacing in their lives today, has taught me that. Karma returns to the person who made it. There is no escaping facing up to what you have set in motion. But we are always given chances to set things right, to mitigate our karma by living our lives now in a loving way. Often we simply need to love ourselves more, to step out of a situation or relationship that is harming us, and our skulls can help with that. Rose quartz skulls, especially, can help heal our hearts as no other stone can. We sense the unconditional love they radiate, and being in the presence of rose quartz heals us. As I said at the very beginning of this book—even children sense this about rose quartz and are drawn to it.

GRIDS

Although Merlin made no mention of skull grids, it does not mean they have no value. Many people today enjoy working with grids, by which I mean placing skulls in a meaningful arrangement to generate and direct energy for a certain purpose.

You can make your grid as simple or as complex as you like. A simple grid can be a circle of skulls, or skulls mixed with crystals. Twelve skulls, with a thirteenth in the center, would honor the ancient Native American legend about thirteen crystal skulls being reunited at a time when their wisdom is needed to

CHAPTER 12

save the world. (Most appropriate for now!)[10]

There are patterned boards and printed cloths on sale for setting your skulls out on, with the interlocking circles of the Flower of Life design being extremely popular for this. But these are not essential. Any surface you like will be perfectly fine. Spirals are good for whipping up energy and can be utilized in a grid. Consider drizzling sand to make the spirals, and trails of sand are one way to link the skulls and crystals in your grid. Crystal towers, raw crystals and tumbled stones can be mixed in with your skulls to pep up the energy. Perhaps use other significant items relating to the grid's purpose, like feathers if you are asking angels for help...and maybe flowers, or candles which you could light while offering a prayer. Carved dragon heads and crystal raven skulls are also very popular elements in grid work. Dragons are said to have a protective function, and raven skulls hint at magical power. Their long rod-like shapes direct energy like a wand.

When you start working with a skull for a grid, or for anything else, first wake it up by holding it and stroking it, as Merlin did before he cast the sleeping spell in the Great Hall (in chapter six). Then perhaps kiss it, and blow your breath into it. Then talk to it, introduce yourself and tell it your purpose, give it the job you want it to do. I suggest you write down that purpose, fold the paper and slip it beneath your chief skull (which is probably the one set out in the center of the grid). Perhaps place a crystal tower (or towers) by the chief skull to help generate and project the energy the grid is gathering. As you arrange the things on the table or tray you are using for the grid, you will intuitively feel how the energy is flowing. Adjust things until *you* feel they are right. What feels right to you is right for your purpose. Trust your instinct about this. As with all forms of healing, intention is the most important factor. Set your grid out making your intention clear.

---

10   For more on the legend see *The Mystery of the Crystal Skulls* by Chris Morton and Ceri Louise Thomas.

CHAPTER 13
Evangeline Mo

Despite what Mariam had said in chapter 11, as time passed I had been looking at skulls on eBay again. Last thing at night, I found it very relaxing to look at the lovely crystal and see their faces, but I was rarely tempted to buy. Many faces I did not like, and many of them were sample skulls from China, so the one you see pictured, however lovely, is not the one you will get.

But when I do find a skull I like on eBay, I click "add to basket" and then next time I log on to eBay it is easy to have another look, because it is already in my shopping basket. One night I came across a labradorite skull and popped it in my basket. As the days went past I found myself repeatedly returning for yet another look. Then came the night it shouted out, "Buy me!"

Moon and the other skulls were most enthusiastic about this skull when I asked them, but I hesitated because of what Mariam had said. With one hand on Mariam and the other holding a pendulum, I dowsed. The answer was affirmative, I should get it, and that's how a new labradorite skull joined us in the middle of October. It was four inches long and the color of a cloud, shot through with sheets of rainbow light.

After welcoming the skull and giving it a gentle wash with a little soap and water, it spent the day with my other skulls, and that evening I settle down to meditate with it. I begin communicating

CHAPTER 13

by asking the skull its name. After a shaky start the name came loud and clear.

"...Everada....Everandisimus....**Evangeline Mo.**"

I ask if it is male or female, though the name rather gives that away.

"Female—but in the same way that Zeb'n is female" she answers.

I ask her what has she come to do and how can she help me?

"Help with your book" she replies.

I ask why she had said, "Buy me," when Mariam had said no more skulls.

"She did let you eat one cake and I am the 'cake' come to help with ending and tying up your book."

I thank her and ask if I may enter.

Permission granted, I go into the shimmering fires of the labradoresence on the right-hand side of this skull and find myself in the inner world. Now I'm standing in a meadow, looking at the skull. It towers above me and is looking like a tower block of apartments. I head for the entrance and find a glass door with a black doorknob. Opening the door, I walk into a corridor. I can see lots of doors leading off, and there's a lift, an elevator. I get in and press the button for the fifth floor. But I don't know why! It just feels the right thing to do.

The lift stops and I get out and go to a balcony. I lean over the balcony and look out at the world, at the meadow below me filled with wild flowers and ox eye daisies, and I see gentle hills rising in the distance. The evening sky is filled with all the colors of sunset—just like the colors in the labradorescence inside the skull's stone—glowing reds and oranges, yellows, purple, and flashes of blue tinged with green.

It's growing dark as light drains from the sky.

A thunderstorm comes. Lightening and pounding rain. Exhilarating!

Evangeline Mo tells me, "The weather of life is to stimulate you, to excite you. Giving you problems to solve will spark your intellect and spur you on. Endless blue skies would not achieve that. So don't grumble and make heavy weather of the 'Weather of Life.' It has a purpose. It is for your ultimate good. Embrace your difficulties and learn from them. Be pleased with your achievements, however small they may be."

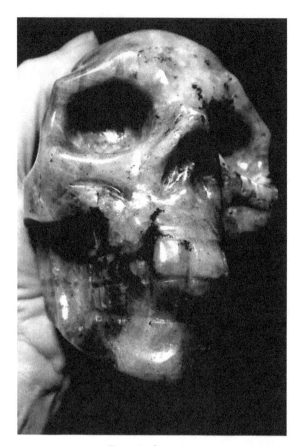

Evangeline Mo

"You came up to the fifth floor to gain a little perspective on your life. Things look different when viewed from different places. The ground floor would not have afforded you the overview. You would have been caught up in the misery of the rain and the darkness, and not felt the magic of the night and the freedom of the wind as you do here, on this balcony, where you can fly like a bird in moonlight—like an owl—clear sighted, and about to seize its prey and feast."

"When you visit me, choose different floors to experience different things. For tonight that is enough. Savor the freedom of flight and the wild winds of the storm sweeping old things

CHAPTER 13

away, blowing fresh and strong, blowing away old leaves and the detritus of life—worn out thoughts, cares, and worries. You don't need them now. Rejoice, and let go of old clothes in your wardrobe, too, and spent plants in your garden. Streamline your wardrobe and your life to focus on what's important now. Don't allow the past to hold you back."

I give my word that I will follow this advice.

Then it is back to the elevator. This time I punch the ground floor button. Once there, I leave the building and step out into the night and into the meadow of flowers...then I'm back in my bedroom, aware of the warmth of my bed and the cozy pool of light being cast by my bedside lamp.

I thank Evangeline Mo, the angels, and God for giving me this experience. Food for thought and there are many more journeys to look forward to!

A few days later, on Wednesday the 20th of October, it is a full moon. That night I settle down to meditate with the skull again, and I'm wondering what will come next. She tells me to go in through her eyes, both eyes at the same time—to just walk through. So I do. I slip in and pass right through her crystal body to find myself on a cloud above Earth. It is night. Black velvet space stretches high above me, while stars are twinkling through the moisture-laden layers of Earth's atmosphere around me. Night breezes carry other clouds like mine drifting across the full moon.

I look at my body and realize I am an elemental being now, a humanoid dragon of a creature, suited to living in clouds. Here on the cloud I am large, larger than humans are—I'm tree-sized. Whenever clouds dissipate and clear from the sky, we dissipate too, we disperse into the atmosphere and connect to water molecules there. And when we dissipate, we fragment—as if all the cells making up a human body could go off on separate journeys for a while, before re-coalescing and forming back into one body again. Sounds strange to my human self, I know, but it is natural for us cloud dragons, and we enjoy the process and the changed state it brings.

What am I waiting for here on the cloud? I wonder.

COSMIC CRYSTALS! *Working With New Crystal Skulls*

The cloud drifts out over the sea, taking me with it.

Moonlight silvers the cloud, catches on its edges, and then fills it—and I ride up the moonbeams faster than the light is flowing down. I reach the moon and whistle to my fellow beings, to connect up with those of us who have come with me. We have come here in search of the cause of a disturbance in the energy field of Earth. Something on the moon is disrupting our work on Earth.

What is your work? I ask my cloud dragon self.

"We regulate the atmospheric balance (of gases and moisture) for Earth. Ah! We know what it is now—Artificial Intelligence machines are pulsing energy Earthward, to facilitate the mining activities of certain ETs who are exploiting Earth's reserves. It makes mining easier for them, but is not good for Earth. We help to hold the atmospheric balance, and Earth has sent us to stop this."

We dragons follow the pulsing vibrations and find the machines.

We crush them. We deliberately fragment and set loose our "cells" to smother the machines and choke their delicate inner workings under heaps of our flaked substance.

Then we re-coalesce and form back into our dragon bodies.

We dismember the machines and transport their bits out into space, well away from the moon. We let them go, let them scatter out into the infinite blackness of space. The machines were in the higher dimensions of the fifth density, in 5D, not in 3D where humans currently manifest. Job done we return to Earth. We shoot down the moonbeams to catch on a cloud and rest; it feels good. We know that others have the task of disassembling the mining machines. That's not our job.

Earth does not want this activity and she is taking steps to stop it taking place in the ETs' undersea bases. They mine a high vibrational material there, and although Earth is currently existing in 3D, in times to come she will solely reside in the higher dimensions, and then this material will be vital to her for her own evolution. That is why the mining needs to cease. The ETs in question must go elsewhere before they do any more damage than

CHAPTER 13

they have already done here.

Is there anything I can do to help? I ask the skull.

"No. Just bear witness. As the cloud dragon you are helping put a stop to this. This is one of your nighttime jobs, work you do while you sleep—or more accurately, while your body sleeps. It is one of the many jobs you do in sleep-state. Many others also render this service to Gaia, the Earth's spirit."

And that's when I know this process will need to be repeated each time the machines are repaired, but we will persevere and the miners will grow weary; we will persevere until they desist.

...Now that I'm back on a moonlit cloud, as I was at the start of my journey, it is time to return.

I back out through the eyes of the skull and back into my bedroom. I am aware of the pool of light from my bedside lamp, and the weight of the now-warm skull in my left hand, as it rests against my chest. I kiss the top of Evangeline Mo's head and thank her. I thank the angels and God, feeling grateful for this further glimpse into the realm of nature spirits.

Around the time of the full moon is always a good time for working with your skulls; on an energy level it is intense. So I will try again while the energies are high. Next day, I am holding the cloud-gray skull in my hands again, and turning her over and over, chasing the play of light across her patches of labradoresence, when I spot a triangle of shimmering gold. The triangle lies between the third eye and her crown—it draws me to it—that is where I'll go in next!

I prove to be too tired that night. However, the following day I settle down with Evangeline Mo again. It is now late afternoon. I am comfortable on the sofa when I tune into her.

I pass through the triangle's golden shimmer and see blades of grass.

A tuft of long grass is springing up by an old wooden fence post, and I am standing in a field of grass...someone is coming. I just know someone is coming.

Who is coming? I ask Evangeline Mo.

"A frost giant," is the skull's reply. (!)

135

What brings the frost giant? I ask.

"Concern. Concern for the frozen places on Earth where the ice has now gone."

How can I help? I ask.

"Listen," is Evangeline Mo's reply. ...but I've drifted off to sleep, gone too deep to hold onto conscious recall...then I float back into awareness and find we are going to Antarctica. The skull's essence and I are going to Antarctica! We fly at the speed of thought and land as the afternoon sun is setting there. The sun's red-gold light catches on the snow and ice that covers the land, and burnishes the mountains. There's a bit of a wind...

What is important here? I ask.

"The ice and the sunshine—and the melting."

How does this affect Earth?

"Makes it inhospitable."

I am shown ice crystals. Each one is beautifully formed in an exquisite pattern, and each one is different from the last.

We fly up the mountains and pass into a cave.

There is a skull in there. An ancient skull.

It is sitting on a flat-topped outcrop of rock in the center of the cave. The outcrop is cube-shaped and acts like a table, providing a natural pedestal for the skull. The skull speaks. It says, "I have seen civilizations come and go, rise up...and then die, over and over again, for far longer than your scientists can accept."

Are you in 3D or in the elemental realm? I ask the skull.

"I exist in 3D. I am a human skull turned to stone. I was brought here from one of the source planets early in Earth's history. I dreamed you all awake, I set up the energy templates for humankind to be born. First the early types, Denisovan, Neanderthal, and many more earlier than that. Ancient Lemuria came, flowered,...and died. But before Lemuria, and before Atlantis, there was a civilization *here* on Antarctica. It lies under sheets of frozen ice, but the melting will expose it. It will cause a great stir when it is found and brought to public knowledge. For this was once a heavily populated land, a forerunner to Lemuria and Atlantis eons ago, and now it is lost beneath the snows and ice."

CHAPTER 13

"Come back and see me again. Time is short now and you must go."

I touch the skull in wonder. I put my hands on its sides, on the fossilized bone. The skull is solid. Its interior is crystalline. Where once soft brain tissues lived is now cold crystalline stone.

But I was amazed to see this skull here.

Because I'd seen it before. Ye's skulls had talked of the **Ancestor Skull**, and shown us the skull in the cave where it dwells, as I mentioned in the last chapter. But until this moment I had no idea where that cave was, or even which planet it existed on. But it is Earth! Well and truly, it is on Earth. I feel blown away! I feel exhilarated! Pleased beyond measure! Because the skulls have fitted one more piece of a jigsaw into place for me.

The skulls are enigmatic.

They work as one and support each other, they do not judge or get emotional, but they do have an agenda. They are feeding us information at a pace we can digest…but where is it all heading? I trust them as Merlin trusted his skulls. But there is a lot more to find out.

I bow low, out of respect to the Ancestor Skull, and take my leave.

And back down the mountains I go, flying across the ice and snow, back to Evangeline Mo's crystal body, and out through the shimmering golden triangle, and then I'm in the awareness of being on the sofa in our sitting room. I thank Evangeline Mo. I thank the Ancestor Skull, the angels, and God for the amazing experience I've just had. I am as high as a kite! There's just time for a meal before The Mitchell-Hedges Crystal Skull Meditation Group on Facebook begins this month's live full moon meditation on Zoom. At 7pm sharp the meditation will be lead by Bill Homann, the skull's guardian. (Anyone could be a member of the Facebook group back then, and we met at the new moon and full moon.) This meeting is why the Ancestor Skull said, "Time is short now and you must go." It knew, because skulls transcend time and are all linked together through the Collective Crystal Skull Consciousness; and it also knew because it read the situation in me, in my energy field.

COSMIC CRYSTALS! *Working With New Crystal Skulls*

This meditation experience had been slow to get going, so slow I'd drifted into sleep and had no memories of meeting the frost giant—who I'm assuming told us to go to Antarctica—but perhaps it was just as well. Frost giants have bad press in the Old Norse legends, and maybe the skulls were protecting me here. Sleep certainly took me deeper than I would normally go in a meditation, and perhaps that is what enabled the meeting with the Ancestor Skull.

For those of us in the UK, the Mitchell-Hedges meditation started at 7pm that evening. Ye and I brought our skulls into the sitting room to take part with us. During the quiet time that follows Bill's inspiring guided start, my skulls sometimes speak to me. Sometimes they don't. This time they do, they say they love me and thank me for what I do for them.

- Moon says, "I'm sorry I frightened you off. I thought you were ready."
- Solange says, "I am unfrozen now, let us begin."
- Hapi-atzi tells me, "Merlin has more to say."
- The Shaman Stone tells me, "We have work to do."
- Stardust also says we have work to do, and when I check back to her introductory meditation in chapter 3—it's all there! Antarctica a very long time ago, ancient civilizations, and even a UFO! Was that from the "source planet"? I wondered.

You see what I mean by an agenda? These skulls are working to a plan. My seemingly random collection of crystal skulls are like chess pieces on a chess board, being manipulated by the Collective Crystal Skull Consciousness. And me? I feel like a pawn! But I'd still like to meet a frost giant.

CHAPTER 14
Stardust and Exploring the Shadow With the Shaman Stone

Wondering what more Stardust can tell me about the Ancestor Skull in Antarctica, I settle down to meditate with her for what is only the second time. I visualize flying in through her third eye, and the cloudy areas in her flower agate translate into clouds…and now I'm flying through clouds, circling Earth, high above Earth, in clouds. I'm drifting south…toward Antarctica, and drifting back through time, as the lands below me constantly change.

Glaciers come and glaciers go, and spurts of civilization pop up here and there—I can see their buildings flowering below me as I fly over. Like waves on a shore, time is ebbing and flowing through civilization after civilization—though some of the early stirrings of humankind are too primitive to be readily perceived as civilizations from this height. I drift over Africa…then South America, as I'm relentlessly drawn toward Antarctica…

As time winds back, I realize Antarctica was a beautiful land.

I see mountain ranges, lakes, and deep valleys. It is forested, and hosts many animal forms, and beings like us, well a little like us, more primitive. I see a fair land with a temperate climate… and yet still, I drift back through time.

Stardust where are we going? I ask.

139

COSMIC CRYSTALS! *Working With New Crystal Skulls*

"Be patient," is the reply.

At last we go to the cave of the Ancestor Skull, but to a time before it arrives there.

I look in and the cave is empty. The natural rocky pedestal is there, but it is a lot less shaped and much rougher. While I'm outside the cave looking in, the shadow of a flying creature sweeps overhead, and dinosaurs are moving about between the trees down below; I hear them bellow. I feel the sunshine on my skin and breathe the fresh, clean air. A mothership, high in the sky, disgorges a small UFO that winks down and lands. Four beings get out, transporting a box between them.

They're coming up to the cave where I am.

They speak to me. "This will do nicely," they say, and to my surprise I know I had been sent to find a place for Ancestor Skull to wait out the ages. I also know there are more of these skulls taken to other locations on Earth, but those are not my concern. Only this skull is.

They leave the box outside, bathed in sunlight, and go into the cave with me. They have rock vaporizers with them, like small guns. With a laser sight-line as a guide, they vaporize away the top of the rock upwelling that forms the pedestal and render it deadly flat, as if a cheese wire had been taken to soft rock. But the rock wasn't soft.

The skull is brought in and released from its box. It is placed on the pedestal, and a force field is set up that will keep it safe and render it invisible for a long time to come. "This should start things off nicely," they say and then they leave, taking me with them. We all go back to our mothership and home. But our species will be monitoring what happens from now on and will be following up on any outcome, this I know.

I detach from the experience and fly out of Stardust's eyes. This is the first time ever I exit a skull at a different point from my entry, but it doesn't seem to matter.

I become aware of being back on one of the sofas in my sitting room, wrapped in a soft fleecy blanket. I thank Stardust, the angels, and God for the experience…and then, I have to confess, I am so relaxed, and warm, and cozy I drift off into an afternoon

CHAPTER 14

nap, though it is rare for me to sleep during the day.

Working on my own in meditation I can't go any deeper than this. I felt great resistance to even looking at their bodies, so I don't know exactly what the ancestor aliens looked like yet. We were humanoid bipeds and I was comfortable in the gravity of Earth and happy to be breathing the air, but I couldn't get a more detailed focus on my companions, or myself. That's all I know at this stage. I'm going to have to do a regression session to attempt to get more from this story; working with someone I trust should take me deeper into it. I was flabbergasted to find I had a personal connection with that skull—but I guess the Collective Crystal Skull Consciousness has always known, which is how my new skulls come to know, because, being skulls, they are all connected through the Collective. Their shape means they act like radios that pick up the skull frequency channel!

Science tells us, for almost 100 million years Antarctica was not frozen over, and trees once grew there in abundance. Fossilized forests have been found that confirm this. Seventy research stations, representing twenty-nine different countries, currently operate there, but Antarctica remains a mysterious continent, made more so by the existence of an old map in the Library of the Topkapi Palace in Istanbul, Turkey. In the year 1513, Ottoman admiral and cartographer, Piri Reis, compiled a famous map of the world. It is said that to aid him he had access to ten Arab sources, and four Indian maps, amongst other things, plus a lost map of Christopher Columbus. The Piri Reis map is accurate in that it is the only early map to show South America in its proper longitudinal position in relation to Africa. But the strangest thing of all is that it shows Antarctica three hundred years before it was discovered! And not only that, it shows Antarctica with what has been described as a surprisingly accurate ice-free coastline.

I would have to leave Stardust's story there until I could arrange a regression, so I decided to start working with the Shaman Stone on my shadow. I had been a bit wary of this, as it sounded scary, although the Stone had suggested we do this. I knew the Jungian

COSMIC CRYSTALS! *Working With New Crystal Skulls*

concept of the shadow meant that the parts of our nature we do not choose to express get pushed away into our shadow side. They still affect us from there, we haven't lost them, and they need understanding and integrating before we can truly be whole. The effort of keeping them pushed into our shadow is a drain on our mental and emotional energy. People who annoy us and trigger us in the outer world, are reflecting parts of our own shadow back to us; they are embodying that which we suppress, and in that way act as a mirror for us.

I had been thinking about my shadow and what annoyed me, and I noticed how irritated I got by people who looked like they must be enjoying all the cakes, chocolate bars, biscuits, and all manner of delicious fattening foodstuffs they fancy, everyday and all day, without any self-control or self-discipline. I have to police myself and hold back, and limit high-calorie treats to one a day, if possible. It was proving hard to shake off the extra pounds I'd put on over lockdown, when cakes were even more irresistible than usual, and so I thought this issue would be a good place to start my shadow work. I was intrigued to see how the Shaman Stone was going to approach this. In chapter one it had spoken as if it knew what it was doing, which was more than could be said for me! Feeling slightly apprehensive, I settle down to meditate with this skull.

I ask it where I should enter.

It replies, "Through my teeth, seeing as it's issues about eating that you want to work on."

I pass in through the teeth and find it is night in the inner world. There is a dark sky above me, with a thin sprinkling of stars and the slim crescent of a very new moon. I find I'm standing on raised ground at the edge of a flat plain. It is rough ground here and there are clumps of springy heather at my feet. The plain before me is flat and empty, featureless in the dim moonlight; such a slender moon offers very little moonlight. I affirm I've come to work with my shadow.

Why do I desire cake and treats? I ask.

The Shaman Stone says, "Come with me."

A tall fairytale castle has appeared on the plain below. It

CHAPTER 14

certainly wasn't there before. A proper castle made of stone, with tall, turreted towers, surrounded by a water-filled moat crossed by a drawbridge. I go toward the castle. I cross the drawbridge. I feel bold and excited because the skull essence is with me, by which I mean the crystal deva that has made the Shaman Stone its home. I feel its presence with me, but I don't see it; it's like the dreams you have when you know someone is with you but you couldn't say who it is, though it is usually an inner guide.

We go through the entrance gate. The portcullis is raised, so we can walk straight through, but it is very dark here. Only a few torches burn on the walls of the castle yard. We go into the Great Hall, the central meeting and feasting place, where the lord of the castle holds his court. It is dark inside here as well, and people are asleep on the floor rushes. The lord himself is asleep in his chair at the great table, at the far end of the hall. As I walk up to him I come to a woman still eating. She is enormously fat, and still munching and chewing and swallowing, and then biting off more food again to chomp and chew.

What is she eating? I ask.

"Not vegetables," the skull says, "Cakes, biscuits, brownies, trifles—sweet things. Endless deserts. She eats day and night. She has a magical plate that always refills. She gets no rest and never sleeps. She gets bigger and bigger, until one day she will eat herself dead. There is a spell on her. This is not her choice, but she is compelled to clear her plate—as you were always told to do in childhood." And he is right about that. I was.

"Your craving for sweet things comes from her. She is an aspect of your shadow self. You need to free her from the spell."

Who put the spell on her? I ask.

"Others who meant well, but could not see where it would end. It was not a malign spell, but one put on out of concern that 'baby you' thrived and put on weight. It was part of your mother's love for you, that you did not die. But it should never have lasted so long. She is dead and cannot lift it now, but we can."

"Take the plate and break it—throw the fragments in the moat so the weight of the water holds them down, and presses them deep into the mud at the bottom of the moat, where they will

143

not be seen again."

I take the plate outside, break it on the hard stones of the yard floor, and throw the pieces into the moat—to the north, to the east, to the south and to the west. Then I go to the woman and tell her to rest now, tell her that she can sleep, that it is allowed. I tell her that she is now free of the compulsion to eat and clear her plate. She need never eat again, but it is good to eat when you are hungry, and only then. Her body will tell her when she should eat—and no one else should do that, however well meaning they may be.

She sighs a great sigh, smiles, and puts her head on the table in the place where the plate had rested, and she falls happily asleep.

Tomorrow she will be free.

Tomorrow she will be as normal people are—in charge of her own refuelling needs. The spell is shattered like the plate.

Our work here is done and we leave the Great Hall, cross the yard, and go over the drawbridge and return to where we started, the place where the heather grows. I look around and see the castle has gone.

The skull tells me, "That spell was put on you out of love a long time ago. Be at peace now, the spell is broken, and watch the weight roll off you! But you may eat treats at times of your choosing. We all need treats now and then, but you will find the longing diminished and weight loss will be easier from now on." Then it says, "There, that wasn't so bad! Not scary at all. You can trust me to help you empower yourself and set yourself free from old patterning."

I thank the Shaman Stone very much. I feel very grateful. I leave through the teeth—the teeth remind me of the portcullis that guarded the castle's gateway, and I realize the gateway symbolized a mouth where the portcullis was its teeth.

Back in my bedroom, I can't help but thank the skull again, the angels, and God for this very enlightening experience. But I must add that when I left and crossed the moat, I saw the bone-white china fragments of the plate surfacing in the dark water, trying to rise up again. The pieces were trying to return...I pushed them back down under the black mud with the force of my mind,

CHAPTER 14

and they disappeared from sight. But I just know I will have to watch them and push them under the mud again from time to time. This will keep me focused on my goal of weight loss.

I felt different afterward. The pull to cakes and biscuits had gone. I benefited greatly from this experience. The meditation was on Wednesday night, the 3rd of November, and by Friday morning the scales in our bathroom were beginning to tell me a happy story!

I remembered things my mum had told me.

She died over forty years ago, bless her, but I can remember her saying that when I was very young she used to put butter in my mouth to make me fatter, and at meal times she danced with a tea cozy on her head so I would open my mouth in amazement and another spoonful of food could be popped in. She was a troubled woman, my mother, but she loved me. I always knew that. Despite her deep depressions and bursts of anger. She was bi-polar before it was understood. She had been a teenager during World War II and food was rationed then.

After that I was eager to work with the Shaman Stone again. I decided to look at why people who are full of themselves really annoy me. Instead of finding them comical, they irritate me tremendously. Late Sunday afternoon comes and it is too dark to continue gardening, but too early for our evening meal, and so I slip upstairs with the Shaman Stone. I know it will be quiet upstairs. I snuggle into a warm dressing gown, pulled on over my clothes, and gather the duvet around me as I sit up in bed. The skull is cold in my hands, but I am comfortable. I blow into the skull several times to tell it I'm here, ready to work. I rub its crystal sides to awaken it and I hold it up to my bedside lamp. As light plays over it, I turn it and wonder where to enter this time. I admire the area where the now light-filled crystals of its crown meet the opaque darkness of the face—will I go in here? I wonder.

I settle down. I go through the preliminary stages and begin meditating.

I ask the skull if it will work with me. I ask for permission to

COSMIC CRYSTALS! *Working With New Crystal Skulls*

*enter—then the big question—**where** should I enter?*

"The chin… 'taking it on the chin'," comes the reply.

I tell the Shaman Stone it's my angry reaction to people who are full of themselves that I want to work on today. I visualize his dear skull face in front of me and pass into the sharply carved area that marks the chin. Grayness surrounds me before anything clarifies…then the grayness melts into a scene where I am on a vantage point on the edge of a high cliff, overlooking a flat plain. In the far distance I can see the sea. It is daytime, early in the day, and everything is very quiet and peaceful and still. The skull's essence is here with me, I sense it on my left.

What are we waiting for? I ask the essence.

"Trouble. Let's hide in a cave to avoid it. Let it pass us by."

So we do. We go along a little path that takes us into a cave beneath the rocky overhang we had been standing on. The cave had been beneath us the whole time, though we couldn't see it from where we were.

In the cave a little stream runs, and I see veins of ore marbling the rocks. We go in deeper and deeper and find a larger cave full of huge crystals. I love it in here! I play on the crystals, climbing up them, sliding down them, and I feel like a happy child playing in this lovely, magical place. It is a charming crystal landscape.

I climb high and sit up on a natural crystal throne.

The skull's essence says, "Give a speech."

What about? I ask.

"You."

That would be boring, I say.

The skull's essence says, "Well that's why pushy people who are full of themselves annoy you. It is right they annoy you, but you need to be more like them—you need to be pleased with yourself a bit more. Every day, before sleep, congratulate yourself on your day's achievements, **<u>however small</u>**, and then the annoying people will start avoiding you, as your energies will not match. They want to reflect their opinion of themselves off you and they don't feel real just being themselves. They need a mirror to see themselves in. When you change, they have lost the mirror they wanted to use. We all achieve much everyday. Be

CHAPTER 14

grateful for the smallest of things you do. Try it and see. Watch your world change. That is all we need to do for now."

The essence helps me down off my "throne" and we leave, we go out of the caves and back to the cliff top. I come out through the Shaman Stone's chin. I thank the Shaman Stone, the angels, and God for the experience. But the skull hasn't finished with me yet. It says, "You have been denying being pleased with yourself as if it is 'sinful.'"

Where did I get the idea it was sinful? I ask.

"In a past life. Do you want to see it?"

Intrigued, I say yes. I go back into the skull, but this time through its hairline where the crown crystals meet the bedrock of the opaque face, the very same area that took my eye at the start of this session.

I see the past life: I live in mountains, in a tiny village. It feels like Austria, or perhaps Switzerland. Our priest tells us about "humility in the sight of God." Tells us we are all born sinners, born into "original sin" and how we can never shake it off. In penance we can chastise ourselves, mortify the flesh, starve and whip ourselves.

My, he is a miserable man who hates himself, but we believe him because we are poorly educated and have nothing to balance his view of the world against. He is a real kill-joy. The guiltier we feel, he says, the better our chances of getting into heaven.

The Shaman Stone tells me I have never quite shaken this off, though I have made huge strides in the opposite direction. I was a boy back then, in that past life. To heal the boy we visit him in a dream and tell him his priest—his pastor—is wrong. That this does not please God, but that it is a devil's perversion of the truth. We give him a dream of great force, and show him the pastor boiling in vats in hell for what he has done to all the people in his care, who looked to him for spiritual guidance. We tell the boy to allow the dream to change him, so he can find joy in the everyday small things around him and LAUGH more. Not to take himself, or that man's words, or "sin," as serious. The skull says I should dance through my life now and see this lad dance through his life long ago. I'm told there were always some people who didn't

COSMIC CRYSTALS! *Working With New Crystal Skulls*

take any notice of the pastor's miserable message, "He didn't fool everyone in the village. Visualize it happening and see the energy around that past life change. You have been judging other people full of themselves against his standards. Laugh instead of being annoyed. Your anger is worse than a waste of energy, anger is actually a poison that eats away at the body like acid and steals your joy in life. Anger is a self indulgent waste of time unless it leads you to change things. For so it is. Audience terminated."

I found myself rubbing the Shaman Stone's third eye area and thanking him again. I plant an affectionate kiss there, on his crystal, even with my eyes still closed. He had been held in my left hand throughout this experience.

Then I leave the skull. I come out where I went in, and come back into being aware of the bed and the bedroom. It had taken an hour, twice as long as usual, and now it was time for the evening meal. The skull had certainly given me plenty of food for thought!

Later, I followed up and looked at the boy's life after he had the dream. He'd married, had children, and there was an all-round increase in peoples' happiness. Change is worthwhile; change will ripple out because our lives always touch others.

A few days later, on Tuesday, November 9th, I was ready for more. I had enjoyed the shadow work much more than I thought I would, and could see the benefits already. This time I am hoping the skull will choose what we work on. It had been a frustrating day for me with much confusion over my passwords on the Internet; I was locked out of my emails, and even my own author page on Amazon wouldn't let me get to author central to check stats and sales—and with that souring the day I had no clear idea which aspect of the shadow to go for.

That night I settle down with the Shaman Stone again.

I ask it if it will work with me. I ask it if I may enter. I say I want to work on my shadow again, and ask if it will choose an aspect of my shadow for me.

"Yes," is the answer to all the questions.

There is a striking white area in the crystal to the side of the skull's right eye and this had seemed the most significant area

CHAPTER 14

when I examined it tonight. I go in there.

White is all around me. Snow is falling. I'm in a snowy wasteland, but I see the dark shapes of pines burdened with soft falling snow. I go into the pine trees and there is less snow underfoot here; there are pine needles, leaf litter, pinecones...and against the dark back-drop of the forest floor I see the pale caps of mushrooms—fungi—growing here, pushing up through the forest debris like delicate fingers. There's a little group of them. Oh! It's the fungi I'm meant to talk to.

What aspect of my shadow am I working on here please? I ask the skull.

"Your reluctance to accelerate growth," it replies.

In what way? I ask, puzzled.

"Reluctance to accept, understand, and feel comfortable around IT, spooked by problems with passwords and so on." The skull had been on the shelf behind me that day while it was all going on...

Why am I having these problems? I ask.

"Because of a missing connection. The fungi know how to connect. Let me introduce you." The skull converses with the fungi, but I can't hear any of it.

Then the fungi speak to me. Loud. I hear a tall, hollow voice in my left inner ear. I think the fungi are really making an effort, like they think I'm deaf or something.

The fungi say, "We connect with our kin on this world and on other worlds through mind (*telepathy*). We never feel alone. For us, your reality looks shadowy and insubstantial. We 'see' and are aware of and sense mainly our own energy field; we live in the reality of our own energy field. You see only our fruiting bodies— they are our dreams for the future of our species. The spores they produce are our dreams of future lives to be lived. We feel the press of other minds; we know we are not alone of all Creation's makings that are sentient. No, because we feel the press of other minds against the probing fingers of our own consciousness, our awareness."

"We are older than humankind by a long way. We exist throughout the universe and we were one of the first children of the Creator. For we live in the vacuum of space, and on moons, and on airless worlds, too. We thrive anywhere there is matter to host our mycelium bodies. We do not need to 'eat' our host. We can simply attain, and then sustain, purchase for our physical form while drawing all sustenance needed from the surrounding environment, however bleak. For we are fed by light and by darkness, and mainly we draw on our forms in higher dimensions because they willingly send energy boosts down to us even in 3D."

"The universe buzzes with the calls of fungi. To us it is a great symphony, though to the deaf ears of you and your kind there is silence. Enough! Your skull friend has brought you to share in our wisdom and learn of the power and purpose of connection. See yourself plugging into the network of the World Wide Web's interfaces, as we fungi do into our own mycelium network. Expect joy and joy will result. Do not be discouraged. All networks are support systems and should make you feel good—connection is good, connection is life. You were never meant to exist alone and the Web—the mycelium body of your people—helps you connect. Be at peace and know all is well. You are connected and it is well that it is so. There is no serious problem here except your self doubt. 'Cocksure' is in your shadow. Integrate it and feel confidence build. You need confidence in your own abilities in whatever sphere you are operating in. Work with your skull to find your cocksure quality and (re)claim it. You had it and you lost it."

I thank the fungi and say farewell, and they recommence their song and go back to singing in the great symphony we cannot hear.

Can we meet "cocksure"? I ask the skull.

"Yes, come with me now," is the answer.

Now I'm in a bar…an 18th century hostelry. I'm cocksure, a know-all, and a braggart and I get shot dead in a duel. "So you feel that to 'know it all' is dangerous and gets you killed," the skull says. "You avoid 'knowing it all' and give your power away, no, **throw** your power away when confronted with IT difficulties." This is true, it is how I feel, though I make myself soldier on in

CHAPTER 14

mounting stress and discomfort, all the while feeling powerless. (Eventually I always do resolve the issues, even though sometimes it may mean calling somebody in to help.)

How can I integrate cocksure? I ask the skull.

"Well, in that past life he was a waster, so it's not as if you want to be him, but you want the best side of his unshakable confidence. Tell yourself 'I can easily do this' when you feel challenged by IT difficulties; think 'I can easily plug back into my mycelium body and draw what I need to me, be it advice, help, knowledge, skill, or just serendipity guesswork.' Be a success! Feel a success and the rest will fall into place. Make '**I can easily do this**' your mantra, your affirmation, and see the energy flowing again."

Is that all we need do for now? I ask.

"Yes."

I leave the skull through the white area by the right eye and I thank it, the angels, and God the Creator of All, including fungi, for the extraordinary experience.

CHAPTER 15
Solange and Moon Reveal More

At the end of chapter thirteen Solange had said, "I am unfrozen now, let us begin," and now it is his turn. I pick him up to find a way in. I see where I entered last time and the veils are now showing a tall figure standing in a cornfield. It's like seeing a picture in an ink blot, rather than the photographic, full color image I once saw in the ancient quartz skull Sha Na Ra, but it is a clear enough image to put me in mind of the Greek goddess Demeter, standing in a field of ripe corn. However, I'm drawn to a string of white patches dotted along a plane in the crystal, in the middle of the skull's right-hand side…and this is where I want to go in.

I meditate. I'm in the inner world now…

I step into the skull.

Everything around me goes dove-gray.

I'm in a very thick mist. There's moisture on my skin and my clothes feel wet. I don't want to stay here. I can't see anything because the mist is so thick, and slowly and gingerly I walk forward, feeling my way until I come to a stream where the mist begins to thin out. Ferns and mossy stones line the banks of the stream. I follow the flowing water until the mist thins out altogether.

CHAPTER 15

We, that is to say, Solange's essence and I, come to a cornfield.

We cross the stream on stepping stones and scramble up the far bank. We go into the cornfield, and amongst the stems of heavy-eared corn there are bright red poppies and blue cornflowers. It is just like the fields around my Belgian grandma's house when I was small, before all the spraying of herbicides and insecticides began when agriculture modernized in the 1950s.

The sky is blue and cloudless.

A hot sun burns away the last shreds of mist and there are crows here, I hear them in the thicket of trees at the foot of the field. Two crows fly up and land on a wooden fence near me. The fence marks the border of the field, and the crows perch on the old gray wood and fasten beady eyes upon me.

They talk to me, starting with, "Hello."

Why have you come? I ask.

"There is a disturbance in the field—the energy field of the biosphere," they reply.

What is causing this? I ask them.

"Lack of accord; the people of Earth are not acting as you should when your house is on fire. We have seen the signs and we know the world is burning far too frequently and in far too many places—in Australia, in Greece, in the US, in South America, in Africa...everywhere, dreadful fires with huge loss of trees and needless tree deaths at the very time when you need them the most."

"The world is burning and every year will see worse to come. And where it is not burning, there will be extreme flooding and excessive rain as the climate spins out of control, and temperatures escalate well beyond what is wise for humanity's future. We bring a warning like Odin's ravens Huginn and Muninn. We bring a warning in the hope of saving your lives and your future. You see us in a field full of grain—yes, that is food to sustain you—but this will not last. The harvests will dwindle and starvation comes, then death, for there will be much famine in the world and many ruined harvests by flood, and many disappointing harvests by drought. Take heed. Do what you can to ameliorate the environmental catastrophe that is unfolding around you, even

153

now. You live in perilous times."

"We are two power animals of yours. Feed us at the seafront (*my favorite walking place, and only ten minutes from my door*) and strengthen your link with us, for we would help where we can. We will meet again in the inner world. There is more to tell. Fare you well for now."

The crows' black eyes follow me as I leave the field and cross the stream. I can feel their eyes on my back. I like birds, and I wave them goodbye. They continue to gaze steadily and unblinkingly in my direction until I step once more into the mist on the opposite bank. It closes around me and all goes gray…and I am back in the quartz of the skull, back in Solange.

I come out of the skull where I went in, and then I am back in my bedroom. I open my eyes. I thank the crows, Solange, the angels, and God.

This was on November 11th, 2021, when the UN Climate Change Conference was being held in Glasgow, Scotland. COP 26, as it was called, had been declared as the world's best last chance to get runaway climate change under control. A little progress was made, but the empty promises and evasive words of too many attendees have doomed us all to catastrophic climate change, long before 2050. The only question now is by how much global temperatures will rise. The hope had been to limit it to 1.5 degrees, but realistic projections tell us we are on course for 2 degrees and over. In 2007, when I began writing my books, I understood that we were poised at a pivotal point in time. That is why I researched the future and dedicated *Divine Fire* to that topic.

I wish we had done better.

In the Greek myths, Demeter, Goddess of the harvest, presides over the cycles of life and death and her scythe is sharp.

I got peanuts for the crows that hang out on the seafront where I live, and visited Solange again. Examining the Tibetan quartz skull under my lamp this time, I see that underneath him is a lovely plane that offers a landscape like a fairy garden. It bisects the skull and this plane holds traces of yellow iron oxide, known

CHAPTER 15

as golden healer; there is very little of it, but it has an attractive sunny color and I decide that that is where I will enter.

I settle down to meditate.

I slip in and find myself in golden sunshine in a desert. Tumble weeds blow past me and a wind is getting up. It blows the desert sand and takes the sand with it, transporting it far away, to mountains where the rains are failing…the desert is spreading, growing at an alarming rate.

I am part of the wind now, the wind that is robbing the soil from the bones of the world; skimming off the top soil and carrying it away, carelessly dropping it into the seas and oceans where it sinks and is lost to use. The fragile layer of top soil, on which life depends, has been exposed to loss by humans' activities, especially by the removal of natural vegetation that pegged it in place.

I am with other wind-beings now.

We wind-beings love to shriek and to steal things, carry them away and drop them at whim somewhere else. We sing a lament for the animals of Earth that are being displaced by human activities, being endangered by humans, and poisoned by humans. We sing a lament for the great majestic birds of prey whose numbers dwindle, and even the little birds that are harried to death by the lack of insect life to feed their chicks and themselves.

The wind cries its lament for souls lost and for what once was, but is no more; for spreading deserts and worn out soil being whisked away, with everything drier and deader than before. There's less and less life, except for the one life form that is destroying the surface of the planet. The winds of Earth are starting to sing the same song sung by the winds on Mars.

The end has begun.

Solange, I say, *I thought golden healer was to heal?*

"Not so, it is a lament, an outpouring of grief and sadness for what was and what could have been, but is no more. Golden healer is Earth's lament for her other children—the birds of the air, the fishes of the sea, the insects and animals of the land. There is ever less of them and ever more of their killers. The balance is lost and it will not come again. For so it is now. Farewell."

COSMIC CRYSTALS! *Working With New Crystal Skulls*

I come back to the yellow oxide in Solange's crystal and come out where I went in. I am back in my bedroom now, chastened and alarmed by the resignation and sadness of Solange's message.

Solange why was that so depressing? I ask.

"Because that **is** the situation. You will have to live the best life you can against that backdrop. Find joy where you can, and take pains not to make things worse by your actions and choices."

I tell Solange I will do my very best, and gather myself together. I open my eyes to see my cozy, comforting, familiar bedroom around me. I feel a bit chilled and hollow after that dismal and cheerless encounter. I felt the sorrow of Earth for the losses we are causing. I thank Solange, the angels, and God. (And afterward I do check up about Martian winds; although the atmosphere on Mars is thin, it *is* subject to winds, strong and relentless enough to still be changing the land-forms of Mars, and fierce enough to cover the entire planet in a dusty haze for weeks. Hmmm...)

On Sunday the 14th, I go in through Solange's eyes...and enter a dark gray place. This time I'm inside somewhere; it feels like an interior. My eyes become accustomed to the low levels of light and I see I'm in a temple, a huge temple. A row of small square windows high up in the wall is letting in what little light there is here. Dawn is breaking. The rectangular shape of a large wooden box looms by me in the darkness. It is a trunk and it is sitting on the floor at my side. I see the lines of the lid and the deep warm tones of the wood. The box is beautiful, richly carved with intricate patterns. (It reminds me of jewelry boxes I've seen imported from India)...Oh! Solange and I are in India! ...but a long time ago.

The hours of darkness were passed in a vigil guarding this precious box. I lift the lid and look inside. It is a box of quartz crystal skulls. Five skulls have been brought here, and they have only just arrived, having been sent from a temple far away. We needed their advice, that's why they've been sent. We have a problem.

I go forward a little in time.

156

CHAPTER 15

The head priest has come and is arranging the skulls on our altar. The largest is set at the center, with two skulls on either side. They look powerful.

The only people here are priests. The head priest strokes the central skull and talks to it, beginning by singing. He's using the vibrations of his voice to arouse the skull into waking.

What is the problem? I ask Solange. *What does he need help with?*

"The weather. Problems with the weather are being experienced," comes Solange's reply.

The head priest goes into trance and starts talking. We hear him, but I can't catch the words. I think he is channeling the skull...

What is he saying? I ask Solange.

"There has been wickedness and wanton tree felling which must stop," comes the reply. (And in this society, priests have the power to do that—to stop trees being felled.)

Why were five skulls sent here? Why not just the big one? I ask Solange.

"Because the four amplify what the one transmits."

Why am I seeing this now? I ask Solange.

"Because it is time once again to stop cutting down trees."

Did it end happily last time? I ask.

"No. Despite the message, they did not listen and India suffered while Lemuria perished. These are Lemurian skulls from temples long swept beneath the sea, though at this time they were still flourishing and teeming with people visiting them."

Are we in Lemuria? I ask Solange.

"No. This is India."

What should I learn here? I ask.

"That though the way ahead might have been shown, or foretold, or seen by seers—and in your case by your scientists—it does not mean people will heed the warning of coming disaster. They did not heed the warning in Atlantis, and they did not heed it in Lemuria, they did not heed it here in India. The priests could have stepped in, but they did not; well not effectively. This is a parallel situation, and it resonates with the situation humans are

COSMIC CRYSTALS! *Working With New Crystal Skulls*

finding themselves in again. The Ages turn and have come full circle; once more comes the point of warning. Has the warning been heeded? Not enough. An inconvenient message is one that is very tempting to ignore and easy to forget—and so it is now with your people. The climate conference has finished, the message has been heard, but the message has not been acted on sufficiently boldly to succeed."

Solange is there more to tell? I ask.

"Not for now. It is time to return."

I let the temple go and drift back into the dark grayness, then out through the eyes of the skull. I come back into being aware of the room. I'm in my sitting room on a sofa by Solange, who feels very cold to my touch. I thank Solange, the angels, and God.

Strange how large quartz skulls always feel freezing cold, much colder than the surrounding room temperature, and I remember the old legend in *The Mystery of the Crystal Skulls*. The one that says when the gods looked down and saw mankind's wars, and brother killing brother, they shed tears of compassion at the terrible suffering they beheld. The tears fell to Earth and turned to holy ice, and this is what the ancient crystal skulls were made of. Crystal skulls were the tears of the gods and were meant to bring us peace, harmony, and healing, just as our skulls do today. Solange can even feel cold when he's sitting on a radiator shelf—holy ice?—clear quartz skulls will always be that to me.

On Tuesday, November 16th, it was time to face Moon-Over-the-Waters-of-Life. She's by far the largest quartz skull in my care, and if you remember, (in chapter 3), the first time was an absolute disaster! But Moon had recently said, (in chapter 13), "I'm sorry I frightened you off. I thought you were ready," and this time I hoped that I was.

Her crystal has developed a lot of small rainbows since then.

I admire her complex interior under the lamp. There is even more going on in Moon's crystal than in Solange's. A small pink area on her crown catches my attention because a trace of iron oxide is overlaid by a tiny rainbow, and at a certain angle it glows like a jewel.

CHAPTER 15

I settle down to work with her.

With permission to enter granted, I'm surprised when Moon wants me to go in through her eyes instead of through the pink jewel area I'd chosen. But I do as she suggests and pass in through the eyes and come into a landscape. I'm on the side of a hill with a plain spread out below me. I follow a path up to the top of the hill, but I can't see anything up there.

What is at the top? I ask Moon.

"Nothing of interest, it's the view I want you to look at," comes the reply.

But try as I might, I can't see anything significant in the view; the plain just has lots of little houses on it.

What is there to see? I ask, puzzled.

"The 'smallness' of life; there are many people down there on the plain in the houses, all busy, all going about the small actions that comprise day-to-day living."

Yes, Moon? But...?

"Those actions are valuable and keep the boat of life afloat. Do not begrudge time taken up in that way, in what you often grumblingly refer to as 'the admin of life.' When you begrudge the time and energy it creates a blockage, and then your life doesn't flow as it should. Like your laptop being away for repairs now—see all the time saved as a result of its not being available to you, as a gift of peace to yourself." (Moon knows my eBay and Facebook habits.)

Is this to go in the book? I ask.

"No, it's for you. For the book you go in through the pink area as you'd planned."

(But it was all true. The computer problem began just before I met the fungi in the last chapter, and that's why they talked about my mycelium network. Be warned—I only included this in the book to show you that you cannot keep anything secret from your skulls!)

I exit through Moon's eyes and then pass into the pink area on her crown, only to find the little rainbow there is showing me the spectrum of dimensions I can access.

Where should I go? I ask Moon.

COSMIC CRYSTALS! Working With New Crystal Skulls

"Into the green of the rainbow," she replies.

So I do…everything shifts, and around me is a green peaceful light—soothing, calming, nourishing, nice; I'm floating in the serene green radiance and being held in the hand of the Goddess. It is a lovely feeling.

"Return anytime you feel frazzled," says Moon. "I want to encourage you, and build you up, before we begin the work properly. Spend as long as you like here and know you can always return, but for today, that is all."

I float out of the crown and the lovely green radiance, and come back to being aware of my dining room. Moon is very heavy and she is sitting firmly on the dining table by me, while the notebook I've been writing in, to record what happens, is also on the table. Normally there would be far too much noise and music in here, but poor Ye has a bad migraine today and is lying on a sofa in our sitting room.

I thank Moon, the angels, God, and the Goddess aspect of the Divine Creator. When I kiss Moon's crown it is freezing cold. Next time I will go in through her left-hand side like I did the first time. Being in the green radiance was lovely and I feel calm, healed, and nurtured and this feeling stays with me for the rest of the day.

Wednesday night comes and I settle down again with Moon.

Once in the inner world I find her crystal door with the moon's phases on the doorknob and pass through, into her cathedral-like space within. It is full of light and rainbows. There's a gentle humming and Moon's rich feminine voice says, "Welcome, let us begin."

I am levitating…floating upward, feeling weightless, and I come to a wide tunnel high in the cathedral's walls. It has steps carved into it and I begin climbing up. I'm using my hands and feet to scramble up the rough white steps. They are steep. Going quite high, I come out onto a balcony area, and looking over the balcony's edge I'm looking down into the oval cathedral-like space. It is still empty, except for being filled with rainbows and light. But like in a theater, there are many more balconies at this

CHAPTER 15

level, and I see them set around the walls of the huge space. They are all empty; I'm the only one here.

"Time to go higher," says Moon.

I follow the steps up the tunnel, higher and higher, and come into a conference room. Sitting around a circular table are ETs. Different kinds, but somehow they seem familiar. I'm not afraid, though I don't remember who they are.

"They are your friends," Moon says. "Dear friends and they wish you well. Will you visit with them next time? Go into their craft to join them briefly in subsequent meditations?"

I say yes. Here and now I am not afraid. And as I look at my body, it is changing, flashing through alien forms—it's a weird sensation and I ask Moon to stop it. She does, and I am human "me" again. That's better.

Moon says, "I just wanted to introduce you this time, unless you would like to do more?"

I agree to do a little more. I sit at the circular table and meet the ET to my left. It is the same size as me, an iridescent brown bug with many folds of skin round its long neck. It has a worm-like quality, but it is not a worm. It has legs and a small carapace.

What is your world like? I ask it.

"Largely mud where we live, though there are inhospitable mountains where others live. We like mud."

Do you have interstellar travel? I ask.

"Yes. We build with thought and create small suns to power our craft. We bend space/time with thought, and in that way we make short journeys that take us far in linear terms. We are not part of the 3D level of the universe, and therefore not restricted by the laws of your physics. We are not visible to those at the 3D level, but when you venture into the inner world we can meet, because the inner world is also not bound by the laws of 3D physics; it is more fluid, more permeable, and more multidimensional than that. There will come a time when humankind only exists in the inner world, but that is a long way off. By then your evolution would have rendered you unrecognizable."

Have I lived with you on your world? I ask.

"Yes, and flown in our craft."

COSMIC CRYSTALS! *Working With New Crystal Skulls*

What is the purpose to our meeting here now?

"To reconnect you with knowledge and powers/abilities you have dormant."

How do I reconnect? I ask.

"Meet with us on a regular basis through Moon."

I think that's more than enough for now and time I left. So I take my leave and tell them I can't do any more right now, but I will be back, and I have been pleased to meet them. They nod in acknowledgement and I'm off down the white stone steps as fast as my legs will carry me, past the balconies, down to the floor of the cathedral-like space. I bow to Moon in farewell and leave through her door.

I let out a big shwooooo as I breathe out and do an involuntary shiver. I'm back on the sofa in my sitting room. That was strange, it wasn't scary, but it wasn't pleasant like the other journeys with the skulls have been. I was tense, I think that was what it was.

I thank the ETs for meeting me. I thank Moon because I really felt looked after this time. I thank the angels and God the Creator of All.

On Saturday I enter Moon in the same way. I open the crystal door with the silver moon-phases doorknob and step into her cathedral-like space. I'm levitating, going up in a beam, and when I look down, Moon's crystal skull form is far below me, and I'm out in space. I'm in a beam of light now, a tractor beam, and it is floating me up because it has disconnected me from Earth's gravity.

Moon's essence is coming with me.

I reach a craft and I am going in through a hatchway.

It is familiar; I have been here before. There is a lot of activity around me now and a small ET takes my hand—I'm only astral traveling, so it is my astral hand.

I'm pulled along a corridor and into a briefing chamber.

I'm taken to a pod, a communications pod that gets calibrated for me so I can understand what is coming next. The pod will translate for me and there's to be a briefing.

A column of energy shoots up in the center of the room to act as a screen.

162

CHAPTER 15

There are a lot of beings in here; a lot of bustle and activity is going on all around. The small ET settles down with me. If we were to stand up he would be up to my waist. He's a biped with a wide, flattish head and two round eyes. I know from regression experiences that I have met him before over the years. He is often sent to collect me.

Lights and interference patterns flicker on the screen. Script, symbols, and patterns flash up and keep moving. This is a stasis report. These happen frequently and are about checking up on the state of this bit of the universe: it's the Solar System Report.

I'm shielded from seeing inside the other pods, and a lot of what happens here goes over my head, and is not intended for Earth. Then the small ET nudges me, and on the screen column I see pictures of burning trees and logged rainforests—a mess, a right old mess. I see time-lapse pictures of storms and flooding, and ice melting at the poles—uncomfortable viewing, our "sins" in a climate sense. We are destabilizing our world and it is now beyond stopping, but the speed could be slowed down. That's our best hope now, that we slow the changes down. We have passed the pivotal moment when we could have prevented most of the coming changes. There will be many deaths and disasters...and alternative plans are being put forward here as to where humans can incarnate in the future—because a lot less of us will be incarnating on Earth.

What is new here? I ask Moon's essence.

"The seriousness of the changes and the degradation of the biosphere. Terminal decay is setting in. Systems are less resilient now and will not just bounce back."

Moon, is there anything else? I ask.

"No. And I know you are familiar with these issues and have seen the briefing sessions before, but this is current. This is after so little was achieved at COP 26."

"Time has run out. The pivotal moment has passed and the die is cast—that's the difference. There are still many factors in play that will determine how far-reaching the damage will be, but big changes are inevitable. And now it is time to go. That's Earth's business done."

COSMIC CRYSTALS! *Working With New Crystal Skulls*

I leave the pod and go back to the corridor.

Others stay, but my slot is over. It's back to the hatchway, and the small ET floats down with me and Moon's essence in a column of light...down, down we go into Moon's cathedral-like space. I float gently to the ground and the ET goes back.

I wave farewell.

Thank you, Moon, I say.

"That was all we were going to do the first time, but back then the briefing message was less final, as the future still swayed in the balance. But it is good you trust me now."

I take my leave of her and go out through her crystal door.

I'm moved to thank Moon again, and I thank the ETs, the angels, and God the Creator of All...and become fully aware of being back now, aware of being comfortable on a sofa in my sitting room. I still feel full of light and just need to sit for a while, making sure my astral body has fully integrated with my 3D physical form.

Ye is still ill, I've heard my laptop needs a new hard drive, and we humans have broken the biosphere. Not the best of weeks! This had been a heavy chapter to work on and it was with relief I was turning to Hapi-atzi, Merlin, and Hope next.

CHAPTER 16
Hapi-atzi, Hope, and the Cintamani Pearls of Fire

I had wondered about a moldavite skull. Green glassy moldavite from Czechoslovakia is perhaps the most famous and expensive of the meteoritic materials that have fallen to Earth from the heavens—but there are plenty of other tektites that have fallen elsewhere on the planet, and when carved into skulls, they are much more affordable and offer extraordinary energies.

Agni manitite is another rare stone that fell from the sky.

It landed around a remote island off Java, in the Indonesian archipelago. Some say it was a meteorite, others say it was falling magma expelled in a powerful volcanic eruption—but either way, it fell flaming from the sky. Its Sanskrit name of "Agni Mani" translates as "Pearl of the Divine Fire." It's also called Cintamani Stone, Starborn Pearl of Fire, and Tears of the Moon. Well how was I going to resist a cute little skull with a fabulous name like that when it appeared on eBay? I couldn't!

Agni manitite is dark charcoal-gray black glass, with areas of translucent smoky gray, and despite Mariam saying I'd got enough skulls already, I was very drawn to this small skull auctioned on eBay at the end of November.

My bid was successful, and when the skull arrived I loved

COSMIC CRYSTALS! *Working With New Crystal Skulls*

the feel of its energy in my hand—strengthening, grounding, encouraging, and positively buoyant. I'd never felt such a boost from any of my other skulls or crystals, not even from raw pieces of moldavite I have. When carved and polished it is not only a glossy natural glass, but you can see a few tiny white inclusions, like little pearls.

I waste no time before meditating with it.

The skull tells me it is male and that it has come to help.

I enter the inner world and find a small black door in its smooth left-hand side. Stepping through the door I find myself in a huge black space—an interior space—I'm in total darkness, but two huge doors open before me, and as I look through the doors I can see it is night, and I can see the sea. There are stars in the velvet night sky and comets fly overhead. Comet debris falls into the sea and fizzes and pops in the cooling waters. Time shifts, and the coastline changes, and eventually the glassy debris comes to light as pieces of it wash up on the beaches.

I'm being shown the birth of this material from a comet.

I'm told the comet came about from the death of worlds: its atoms were forged in the hearts of dying suns and in time came together to form a planet, which was eventually destroyed by its own life forms in a cataclysmic event. Planetary fragments were ejected into space and became comets and asteroids, wandering the universe. A pinch of this material had been captured by Earth. What was left after it burned through Earth's atmosphere had landed in the sea, coalescing into glassy agni manitite.

The skull tells me, "I bring a message from the stars to the skulls of Earth. Hear me, and be of good cheer, for patterns play out and patterns repeat. What is happening with Earth now is not 'wrong.' It just is, and that's all there is to it. ...More later."

I had been dismissed.

I leave the dark space and go back through the door.

I return to ordinary reality and I'm back on a sofa in my sitting room. I thank the skull, the angels, and God the Creator of All for the experience.

It had been short but profound.

CHAPTER 16

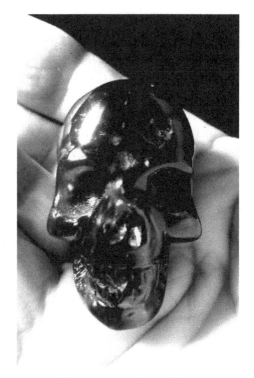

Heaven-sent Starshine

A week later, walking home from the library while thinking about this skull, now calling itself **Starshine**, I get the name **Heaven-sent**...and I remember the promise of "more."

Now my problem was that **Heaven-sent Starshine** was not the only skull I'd been tempted by lately. A dragon head was calling out to me, and after meeting the crows in the last chapter, I was wondering about getting a small crystal bird skull, too—and to cap it all, a beautiful quartz skull crammed full of golden angel hair had caught my eye and just wouldn't let me go. I couldn't forget any of them.

So on Wednesday night, December 1st, I sit down with Mariam. I know she's told me I have enough skulls already, and that I don't need any more, but it is not what my intuition is telling

COSMIC CRYSTALS! *Working With New Crystal Skulls*

me right now.

I will have to have it out with her.

I pick her up and study her crystal. The smooth crown takes my attention this time, and I see a crystalline sparkle on the edge of a small cavity there. The cavity is a natural part of the lepidolite and mica crystal structure, and that is where I'm going to go in.

I enter…and in the inner world I find I'm climbing down a mountainside into a valley. It is a lush green valley with a stream running down the centrer of it, where pure sparkling water rushes over rocks.

I'm looking for a cave.

I see one across the stream on the other side of the valley. It is set in a craggy cliff. Stepping stones guide me over the sparkling water and I make my way up the cliff to the cave's mouth. There is a bonfire at the mouth and people are celebrating.

What are they celebrating? I ask Mariam.

"Solstice, the coming winter solstice—in the days running up to the winter solstice people here traditionally have a big celebration, with each day marked by a separate observance—especially the seven days before, and the seven after, the solstice. We are in Peru."

I have come to ask Mariam about the possible purchase of more skulls, and she lets me know I need to find the people's shaman to discus this with him. When I see him he looks kind of scary in a big headdress and mask, but he is kindly. He says, "Come with me where we can talk quietly." He takes me by the wrist and leads me deeper into the cave to his corner, where cloth bundles lie on the ground and bunches of herbs are hanging up drying, objects lean against the walls and hang in string bags from pegs pushed deep into cracks in the rock.

He sits on a low carved and painted wooden stool, and I sit for the consultation on a low rock set to face him.

Should I buy any more skulls? I ask.

"Yes, when the time is right," is his reply. He tells me that I will know when it is—like now—and that I do really know when the time is right, but Mariam's words have caused me to doubt myself. He explains that what she said was true, but it only held

CHAPTER 16

true for that time, and now the world has moved on. "You see the solstice preparations here—it is a different section of time and it brings different needs. What is right in the summer, is not what is right in the winter. The seasons turn and they bring more skulls, and you can choose to welcome them, or ignore them. You can choose to step forward, or sit down and move nowhere. It is up to you. Mariam removes her objection, but she wanted you to feel peace at the time when she said what she did. It was important then, but is no longer so. Make no mistake, you do not **have** to purchase more skulls but you may **choose** to do so, and all is well."

Can I ask about crystal dragon skulls and dragon heads?

"Yes."

What is their purpose?

"Guardians...elemental forces that guard and bring order, they are good to enhance a crystal grid or to guard a group of skulls. You would have much joy of that pyrite dragon you are thinking of. He has a lively sense of fun and a lot of energy. He will show you things...I have them, too." And he shows me a group of carved crystal dragon heads arranged neatly in a line at the base of the cave wall. "You only need one and you can link into mine."

What about crystal bird skulls?

"Also good."

What about the quartz skull with the angel hair? I ask.

"Get it. You feel drawn to it, but hesitate out of prudence and out of respect for Mariam. But it is a solstice skull, bringing the fire of the sun back to the world and it will cheer and enhance Moon and Solange's activities."

Do you have a name? I ask him.

"Golden Feathers of the Sun is my name, for I have come here to Mariam from that very skull, to tell you that you need it. You will work with me in and through that skull. Speak for it tonight, it wants to come to you.

Thank you, I say. *Is there anything else I should know?*

"No, but we are destined to meet again."

I take my leave of him and come out of the cave. Passing by

the bonfire I wave farewell to the people celebrating the coming solstice, and I descend the cliff and cross the stream for the return journey. I leave Mariam and become aware once more that I'm sitting on a sofa in my sitting room.

I thank Mariam and the shaman Golden Feathers of the Sun. I thank, as always, the great angels Michael, Uriel, Gabriel, and Raphael, and God the Creator of All.

It is midnight.

I switch on my laptop and secure the dragon, then the rose quartz bird skull, and Golden Feather's quartz skull, full of the golden strands of rutile they call angel hair. Thank you eBay! They are on their way.

Things are looking up. Ye has been poorly for days, but is now on the mend, my old laptop is working well, and I am in a state of delicious anticipation as I wait for the arrival of three new skulls—much more exciting than buying a new hard drive, which will now have to wait.

It is Sunday, December 5th and fizzing with energy from Heaven-sent, I realize it is exactly a year to the day that Moon first arrived. It has been a full year of working with new crystal skulls, and tonight it is going to be Hapi-atzi's turn, because, if you remember at the end of chapter thirteen, Hapi had said Merlin has more to tell us. I am feeling curious as I admire Hapi's crystal. A little rainbow jewel in her dark purple left-hand side catches my eye, and I think that's where I will go in.

I settle down to meditate, and once in the inner world I find I have to climb white steps before I can reach the rainbow area. But when I'm there, I see an open hallway inviting me in. There is no door, I can just walk right on in. The hallway is lined with mirrors of different sizes and all in golden frames. I'm walking along on a polished purple amethyst floor. It is well lit in here, but strange to say, I'm not showing up in any of the mirrors as I pass by. The hall is long and at the far end I find more steps. These steps take me up to an empty room with generous windows spanning from floor to ceiling; this room is also well lit.

Merlin is here.

CHAPTER 16

I bow low in greeting and say it is good to see him.

What would you teach me? I ask.

"The value of time. No one has enough and it cannot be bought or sold. The skill is to make the most of what you have and to enjoy the triumphs of daily life—a meal well cooked, a garden weeded, a skull meditated with, perhaps birdsong, and the perfection of flowers, for example. Berating yourself for things not achieved only wastes time, which is too precious for that. Your time is a gift from the Creator for you to dispose of as you wish. Be enthusiastic for the flow of life and let the currents of time bear you on, without looking back with regret for what was, for what has been lost, or mislaid, or spent. Be in the now, anticipating good things and kindness flowing to you, and you will have achieved happiness at a high level. You will always be drawing good things and kindness to you, and the vibration of your life will change. Heaven-sent is showing you this without words. This is the energy of that skull and that is why it lifts you. It is reminding you of things forgotten. All is well."

Is there anything else to tell me? I ask.

"May the people who read your book be blessed with journeys of their own, because skulls are good portals for inner guides and spirit guides to communicate with them."

Why did I not see myself in the mirrors on the way in? I ask, concerned. *What was the purpose of the mirrors on the way in? And why is this room empty?*

"It is about potential, about things that have not yet happened. The hall still looks like it did before you passed through to reflect in the mirrors, and this room has potential to be used for many purposes."

"Reality is suspended here. You can choose your reality and then the mirrors will reflect it back to you. You create your reality with the energetic imprint and weight of your thoughts. On your way out, look again and note what you see. As for this room..." He sweeps his arms open and stretches them wide, "Make it what you want. Let it reflect your interests and be a chamber to visit to intrigue you, as if it were a wondrous crystal shop, or an exotic market, or a museum of the ancient world's treasures,

COSMIC CRYSTALS! *Working With New Crystal Skulls*

full of scrolls and ancient books of learning—or whatever your imagination craves." And as he speaks the words, the room fills with the wonders he conjures.

Merlin brings his arms back together and it all disappears and the room is empty once more. He says, "This is a room of good things, interesting things. You can create your reality here and it will flow into your daily life. It is a chamber of wonder and potential. It will help you create wonder and potential in your daily life."

I thank him. He pats me on the back with a fatherly hand and tells me to look in the mirrors on the way out.

I go down the steps and into the hall.

The mirrors are now showing me myself in past lives and in future lives, and as I see the images, I feel the emotions of the moment they show. This is pleasant, as the mirrors are showing me succeeding—be it surviving in a forest, or creating a mosaic of beauty, perhaps coming through a shamanic initiation, and dancing, and they show me holding my children, and show me with partners I loved deeply…this is a very pleasant experience of moments from lives lived fully. And the last mirror shows me, myself, in the future, holding this book all printed up and finished, with ripples of change spreading out from it, as more and more people work with their crystal skulls and treat them as catalysts for transformation and empowerment.

I experience a profound moment of thankfulness.

When I am ready, I step out of the hallway and make my way down the outside steps; I leave Hapi-atzi behind and find myself sitting on a sofa in my sitting room. With gladness in my heart I thank Hapi, Merlin, the angels, and God.

Next day is Monday and it is Hope Ramasa Metri's turn; the craggy amethyst skull is long overdue a visit. The Amethyst Deva had told me to give it warning well before I wanted to meet with it, so during the day I hold the skull, blow into its crystal, and voice my intention.

Monday night comes. Ye is asleep in bed, lark that he is, and I'm down for supper, night owl that I am. I'm going to work with

CHAPTER 16

the skull now. I'm a long way off feeling sleepy and feel very excited because I have just found another agni manitite skull on eBay—or to be exact—I've found a head. It is bigger than Heaven-sent Starshine and the face is carved from a raw pellet of the mysterious stone. I love the idea of holding the rough stone as it was when it fell from the heavens, and seeing its face revealed by the skill of the carver. I just know that face has a story to tell, and I want to hear it!

Then with pleasure, I pick up Hope Ramasa Metri. I examine the skull under a lamp by the sofa where I'm sitting. Tonight I plan to go into a craggy fissure on the crown, but there's also a lustrous deep purple area that takes my attention lower down on the right-hand side.

Once in the inner world I see steps cut into the right side of the skull. The steps take me up to the crown. I look down into the fissure, there is a white structure in the crystal there...and now I see a city of white buildings, with some tall rectangular tower blocks and streets. It is a thriving city, bustling with life. I keep going down and down, into the fissure, and find that the city has a deep underground counterpart to what is above—like a mirror image city. I'm told this is the bunker for the populace, a zone of safety they may retire to if things deteriorate on the surface for any reason. It's their hideaway and refuge in times of crisis.

Why am I here? I ask the skull.

"To share in their feelings of safety and of being prepared for whatever may befall....down here there is a huge area to grow crops under artificial lighting using hydroponics. All will be well, eventually," I am told.

I leave the crown and return to the steps.

Descending, I make my way to the attractive dark purple area lower down. I melt in and find I'm standing in violet light in an amethyst cave. I hear the rumbling approach of the Amethyst Deva of Earth, and realize I'm floating weightless in the violet-purple light, arms out-stretched, just hanging in the air above an amethyst floor. It is a very nice feeling, spacy, relaxing, and mesmerizing, totally supported by the violet light.

"Greetings," the call rings out from the Amethyst Deva. "This is the deep purple ray of transformation. Let it burn through you, consuming that which you do not need, freeing your energies, and bringing them back into your control. Return here periodically to burn off the dross in your emotional body. Feel lighter and freer as a result."

I ask the Amethyst Deva if I should get the stone with the face. I know the face has nothing at all to do with amethyst or with the Deva, but it has stirred up a storm in my emotional body which I want to release in the violet light.

The Deva replies, "Yes, for though it is not amethyst, it is good for you and enhances you on an energetic level. Wisdom lies within it."

"Be safe."

"Be well."

"Be lighter and freer. For so it is."

Those four small words mean our interaction is at an end, and I gather myself together and move purposefully out of the area, out of the skull's crystal and back into ordinary reality…where I'm sitting on a sofa beneath a tall freestanding craft lamp, which is where I had examined Hope before we started. I thank Hope Ramasa Metri, the Amethyst Deva, the angels, and God for the experience. Then it's definitely toast and cocoa!

CHAPTER 17
The Face, Golden Feathers of the Sun and the Dragon Raffim

By Saturday, December 11th, all the skulls had arrived—the dragon, the rutilated quartz, the bird skull, and the face. I am impatient to be working with the face, it has really captured my imagination, so I sit down with it first. It is Saturday night. Comfortable on a sofa in the sitting room I prepare to welcome the agni manitite face properly. It had spent the afternoon with Moon and Solange to get to know the team. I'm holding it in my left hand and Heaven-sent Starshine is in my right. They both feel lovely in the hand as I start the meditation.

The face tells me, "I'm pleased to be here, in a sanctuary."

I ask if it is male or female.

"Female."

I ask its name.

"I am **Shareen, Queen of the Stars**, and I would tell you my story. I came to this planet from another in its death throes. I was glad for the sanctuary Earth offered me. She called us to her and we plunged into her bosom where the welcome embrace of the blue healing waters of Earth closed around us, and we found peace and form, and I became as you see me now: with a gnarly outside and a heart of pure glass, like a cosmic mirror. For we reflect—and by

175

'we', I mean my kind, other star-born pellets like me—we reflect your own divine energies back to you. That's why your kind find us encouraging, boosting. We make you more aware of your own divine energies and then you grow in confidence and power. 'Yes I can do it' is a response much more likely after welcoming us into a human's life."

"We wander the worlds. We will stay here till the earth is done, and we will be embraced by your sun, and then, who knows? But we will dance through the universe until the Creator is done with it. We rejoice in our journey and from what looks like disaster we pluck adventure, and joyful new experiences. Be of good cheer and do not weep for the earth and her changes. She has seen many changes to her surface as eons come and go—the present decline is just one such. It is of serious consequence to the surface dwellers of the earth, but not to Earth herself."

"The mineral kingdom supports the other realms of life, and minerals are woven into your own tissues, and flow in your blood, and make up your bones. The mineral kingdom weeps for animals, and plants, and fungi, and creatures of the deep, and birds of the air—because all are in danger because of your kind."

"Your kind has the choice and the power to be kind, but often too many choose not to be. Awareness is growing in your young and this is good. Your kind may yet survive and prosper, but great care is needed now if that is to be the outcome—but be at peace on your beautiful world, and with gratitude appreciate the earth's gifts freely given to you all, just as they were freely given to me and my kind. We love Earth and we sing her song, woven into our memories of home."

Where was home? I ask.

"Beyond the Solar System. We traveled far."

Was it Maldek? I ask.

"No. We came more recently than that. Maldek was already the asteroid belt when we crossed through. Most of us still travel through the void—we know this because our consciousnesses are all linked. We know what befalls all our kind, and those of us on Earth are thankful and weave the song of Earth into our stories, (by which I mean our histories), and we sing them through the universe, for even those of our kind who travel know the song of Earth through us."

CHAPTER 17

Shareen, Queen of the Stars

"We will speak again. You tire. You are welcome to come into my stone at times of your choosing. Hold my brother skull in your other hand, as you are doing now, it boosts the signal for communication. Male and female together bring balance and are more powerful than when either speaks alone. For so it is."

When I hear those four words I know it is the end of the communication, and I thank Shareen Queen of the Stars and Heaven-sent Starshine, the angels, and the Creator of All for the experience.

I plant a kiss on both the skull and the face stone. I feel a lot of affection for them, and this time I have to make a real effort to ground and feel my feet on the floor. I stretch out my arms

COSMIC CRYSTALS! *Working With New Crystal Skulls*

and flex my back. It's taking longer than usual to come back into ordinary reality. I had gone further and deeper this time.

It doesn't matter to me if agni manitite is volcanic glass or meteoritic material from the tail of a comet, because I simply like it. Wherever it came from, it makes me feel good—but the skull and the face are consistent in their stories of coming from the stars, and who am I to argue? In one way or another they are, of course, right, because every atom in our bodies, and all the atoms of Earth, were originally forged in the hearts of dying stars a very, very long time ago. So volcanic or meteoritic, the glassy material known today as agni manitite ultimately does come from stars.

Next night I want to take things further.

I settle down to meditate again and hold one in each hand. I wonder where to go in. Shareen's face is complex: the left side looks happy, while the right side looks serious and slightly sad. There's a tiny white spot where her third eye area is, a little "pearl" that is calling out to me. This area is in the center and lies between happy and sad.

Shareen tells me to go into her third eye...

I am in the inner world now.

I am standing on her brow looking at the white "pearl"... which has changed into a tunnel; a round, rough, and rocky tunnel. I go in, and walking is easy because it is a high and wide tunnel— and it takes me into a large area like a cave full of daylight which has no roof. The roof collapsed long ago. Lush ferns grow on its high rocky walls and there is a pool of spring water bubbling up in the center of what had been the cave. A little stream takes the water back underground.

Why am I here? I ask.

"To show you the simplicity of things," comes the reply. "This place has not changed in thousands of years; places like this exist, and have existed for millennia. This demonstrates the essential goodness of life, its simplicity and purity. Nothing here is wasted, discarded, or spoiled. It just is, in a timeless sense. Coming here you would not know what year you were living in, would you? There are no human markers to give clues as to

CHAPTER 17

'progress' or 'civilization' or man's 'cleverness.' This is a place of peace, where the sun rises and sets, rises and sets, day after day, year after year, century after century, disturbed only by the visits of birds and the shy woodland creatures that peer down to see what is here."

"To find peace in your world today, you require to find such a place within you. You require a peaceful niche to retire to that is cut free from the Storms of Time that buffet your soul. Find an oasis of peace in your busy life and visit it regularly—perhaps before sleep, or during a rest in your day—and there you may touch eternity through the forces of nature that cradle your soul in a timeless manner, as they do here."

"There are many such places on the earth and you may visit them all in this way. Each time you may choose to find a different place of peace to rest your soul from the chaos of the world. Look forward to finding, imagining, and choosing such places, because you deserve peace to enrich your soul and make your life all the sweeter."

"Drink from the waters of the pool and refresh yourself," says Shareen.

I do and the water is cold.

I am told to follow a little path that leads from the far side of this place of ferns and the ice-cold pool. It curves away and leads me out on to a cliff edge some distance away, where a huge vista spreads out before me, giving me a grand panoramic view.

"There are many places to choose from," says Shareen, indicating the enormous landscape that is stretching out below me as far as the eye can see.

I follow the path and it takes me along the edge of the cliff and down into a grassy dell where silver birch trees line a little stream. Wild flowers sway in sunlight as a gentle breeze stirs their stems, and the humming of bees fills the air here; I see their small, furry, pollen-flecked bodies busy amongst the flowers. The sun feels good on my face and arms.

I sit and lean against a birch tree. I close my eyes and feel at one with everything here. It is a timeless moment—just me and nature looking after itself. A rabbit hops up to look at me and

COSMIC CRYSTALS! *Working With New Crystal Skulls*

regards me in silence, and with a hop it is gone. Little birds come and go. I am so still they do not notice me. I feel roots growing from my feet and I become the tree I am leaning against…I feel the tree's happiness, its joy at greeting the day as it holds its leaves up to the sun's warmth and light. Around me flowers bud and open their petals wide to drink in the sunlight.

As the tree, I am timeless and old, and I feel the distant forest talking to me. Grandparent trees, and uncle and aunt trees, and distant cousin trees are chattering through their roots in the land around me. I can sense the tiny vibrations of their thoughts, greetings, and chatter. We all sing together. And when the winds come we bend before their mighty blasts; the winds pass, and peace returns again.

Shareen says, "Roots slip into crevices in the rocks beneath, and all is interconnected in the web of life, of which humans are a valuable part. The problem is that humans have grown deaf to the silence of eternity and the whisperings of trees. Humans have lost their skills at communicating with the forces of nature, and nature rebels because it is no longer valued and cared for as it once was. Respect has been replaced by exploitation, by no longer valuing the woods and trees of the land, but regarding them solely as a commodity to be felled, used up, and taken away to be sold."

"Reclaim the wild places within you and it is a start to reclaiming the wild places outside of you. Value them **within** and the collective consciousness of humankind will value them **without** once again. You did have this ability, but you lost it; you can give it back to yourselves and function more fully once more. If you do not fear the wild places within you, you will not fear the wild places outside of you, and the world will be a much better place for everyone you share it with—the birds, animals, fish, and all of life will benefit."

"That is all for tonight. Farewell."

This time I do not retrace my route, but detach from the tree and return straight back to ordinary reality from this place in nature. Aware once more of being on the sofa in my sitting room, I open my eyes and thank Shareen and Starshine, the angels, and the Creator of All. I rub my eyes and have a really good stretch. I feel my feet on the floor and wiggle my toes. I am back!

180

CHAPTER 17

Raffim

On Wednesday night, December 15th, I want to work with the dragon. It is six inches long and the iron pyrite it is carved from is heavy. It has dark labradorite eyes. At bedtime I take the impressive dragon head upstairs to study under my bedside light, and later, when Ye is asleep, I come back down for a little supper. Then I settle down on the sofa to meditate with the lovely new dragon.

These days I am finding it safer to be in the sitting room for this work because I'm less likely to be disturbed. It is true I am relaxed and comfortable in bed, but twice recently, Ye has woken up and started talking to me! If I listen to him it shatters the delicate thread of my concentration and the meditation experience is lost. To someone else, when you meditate, it looks like you are there resting, because your body is there. But the essence of you is NOT there, it has gone, your astral body has gone. Disturbance jerks you back in an almost painful way and it is very, very jarring. Both times Ye had woken up forgetting I intended to meditate.

Now, I'm wondering whether to go into the dragon's smooth

COSMIC CRYSTALS! *Working With New Crystal Skulls*

golden snout, or into its gleaming blue labradorite eyes, or even whether to slip in between its splendid teeth. So I ask it and am told to go in through the teeth. I'm told this dragon is male and his name is **Raffim**. Then I'm told more than I want to know—that he has a partner called Raffeem, and that I have not found her yet, and Raffeem's pet name for him is Raffimolo! But I hadn't been planning on getting another dragon...

However, I'm in the inner world now, and looking at his teeth.

I am small and the teeth are large, twice my height. I can easily slip in between them. I do and I'm inside Raffim's mouth at the side of a long pink dragon tongue.

What am I to do here? I ask him.

"Explore."

I'm told to go underneath his tongue where I will find an entrance to the dragon's subtle bodies. I'm told I can slip from his crystal body to his astral body there.

And he is right.

I do.

I see that his astral body is complete, that he is no longer just a head. The physical crystal head serves to anchor his dragon energy in 3D, enabling us to share in the dragon energy which is to do with fire. His astral body is like living flame in shifting colors, a rainbow of energies, mingling and merging in a display of his innate power. (This we can harness if our dragons are willing participants in an endeavour, I'm told.)

"I just wanted you to see it tonight" Raffim says.

What could we do with that fire? I ask.

"Torch poor concepts when the time is right—what troubles humans troubles their dragons, too. We were meant to be in harmonious accord, working to enlighten humankind, but over recent centuries, since the Middle Ages in particular, we have been demonized. Our role is to return enchantment and wonder to your dried-up, sterile slant on life. We are gateway entry points to the numinous worlds. Without awareness of the numinous, your very spirits shrivel during the span of your incarnation."

"Revere nature and the beauty of the world, and you revere us. We dragons are like spirits of nature with bodies of numinous fire. You can ride with me into the higher realms. We can visit celestial beings and invoke their help if need be."

CHAPTER 17

"We are messengers of Earth and she sends us out to run her errands and do her bidding as go-betweens when necessary."

Raffim has a tail, two wings, and a fiery form. This body of his is enormous. I'm told if I ride on his back, between his wings, I am safe.

Are we going anywhere now? I ask.

"No, I just wanted to meet you properly tonight and explain myself a little. My energy will be helpful at stone circles."

Do I take you with us when we visit? I ask.

"Yes, definitely, and I can show you the energies in the land: the 'ley' energy lines of power are like electrical currents and the standing stones are like batteries to store the charge. We will have fun next time you visit such a place with me...but that's enough for tonight. You need to get used to my fire energy for an interim period of adjustment. All is going well between us and I thank you for my home with your skull community. Their essences have been riding with me, exploring the energies of the land hereabouts, and beneath the sea, in the locality you call home. Farewell!"

I know it's time to come back into ordinary reality.

I yawn, stretch, flex my back, wiggle my toes, open my eyes, and thank Raffim, the angels, and God for the experience. I can't resist planting a goodbye kiss on his golden snout.

And later I can't resist a little agni manitite pendant on eBay, a simple slice of stone that will help me adjust to Raffim's fire energies. I wear it next to my skin on an old silver chain. The polished silky smooth surface delights my fingers and I'm glad the natural edges of the stone have been left intact. Well! Agni manitite, fiery dragons, Golden Feathers of the Sun—it is fire energy that is attracting me now.

Then I find **Raffeem**.

When she comes up on my laptop's screen I feel Raffim's reaction and there is no mistaking it. She is small, of clear quartz, and from the same seller as Raffim himself. A delicate, ethereal dragon. I'd expected her to look like him, but it's a case of opposites attracting with these two. I send for her...what else could I do?

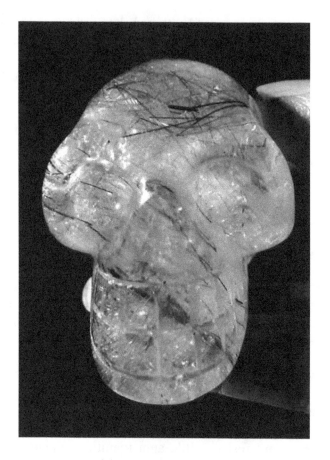

Golden Feathers of the Sun

While awaiting Raffeem's arrival, on Sunday, December 19th, I sit down and meditate with the rutilated quartz skull. It answers my questions and is happy to work with me and it tells me it is male, and that its name is **Golden Feathers of the Sun**, exactly the same name as the shaman who works through it. I love the name and it really suits the skull. The rutile looks just like a golden feather storm in the clear crystal.

Have I known that shaman? I can't help but ask this skull.

"Yes, he was your father in another lifetime. You loved him and he loved you and was proud of you, and you did much

CHAPTER 17

together before his death from a snake bite at age eighty-four. His eyesight was failing him and he did not see the snake until it was too late…"

I'm getting impatient to enter the skull. I press for permission to go in.

But where to go in?

Two areas had taken my attention—the left cheekbone, where sparkles of dazzling light are drawing me to them, or the right-hand side of the jaw where an intriguing forest of gleaming copper threads of rutile beckons.

The skull says to go to both areas, but to start with the sparkles of light.

In the inner world I find an open hatchway beneath the skull's cheekbone and I visualize hauling myself up and crawling in. It is dazzling inside; there are many lights in glass jars, like little lanterns set out all along a path between woodland trees. Lanterns are hanging from the trees…it is like a fairy dell.

What am I doing here? I ask.

"Waiting for someone."

Who? I ask.

"The shaman, Golden Feathers of the Sun," comes the reply.

Then he is with me. I see his kind old face, all nut brown wrinkles and twinkling eyes. He is wearing simple cloth garments and has a strip of cloth wound round his head to tidy his long hair.

He says, "Come with me," and we leave the lanterns and walk together through pine trees up to a mountain rise to watch the sunset.

The sky is full of color, glowing with reds and pinks. The world is still. Golden Feathers speaks, "Be at peace, for all is well in your life now. Things heal, and resolve, and work out. Do not fret about getting old, there is still much beauty to enjoy—like this sunset—and there is still rewarding and satisfying work to be done, enough to give you a sense of purpose. Take things slower. Take more time off. Set aside days to follow your heart, pottering about and doing the small things that were never grand enough to make it onto a to-do list. Take days off to be **you**. We need only witness this sunset, we do not have to make it happen, and so it is with many more things in your life than you realize. Focus on being you. Wear a nice outfit put together with care. 'Be' instead of 'do' and do will take care of itself more and more. Trust. When you 'be' it pulls 'do' to you and things are achieved easily because your energy is in harmony and congruent with the things you are wanting to achieve."

"Come, there's something else I want to show you," and we wander off leaving the sunset. The world is still and darkness begins to fall. We walk back through the pine trees to the place where the lanterns are shining brightly.

Now we venture to the jaw.

We leave the cheekbone area and stand outside the jaw and look in at the forest of rutile strands gleaming in the crystal. The copper threads are shining because they are catching the last rays of the setting sun we had seen. They look radiant, beautiful. The shaman says, "The threads are just 'being' they don't need to 'do' anything except to be here for this to happen. And that's how you need to be for a while—radiant and still—just 'being', and you will attract what you need to you. Like you did with Raffeem, she was easy to find. Be at peace. The book is nearly done and things progress as they should. This skull is where you find me if you are worried about anything and I can give counsel. Farewell for now."

We hug, and I feel the love we had as father and son, together, long ago.

When I come back into ordinary reality, I thank Golden Feathers of the Sun—both the shaman and the skull that shares his name. I thank the angels and God. I stretch and yawn. I come back easily and with an increased sense of peace.

He was right about me fretting about getting old.

I'm in the sunset years of my life. Over seventy, still fit and active, but from time to time I do fear what the future holds for Ye and I, healthwise. Golden Feathers of the Sun understands because it was fading faculties that cost him his life.

CHAPTER 18
The Dragon Raffeem and Arwen the Bird Skull

Boxing day 2021 was dark, cloudy, and wet. Perfect for going back to bed and getting warm and comfortable with the little quartz dragon called Raffeem. She had come, damaged, in the post just before Christmas. The scanty bubble pack that had brought her to me held both pieces of crystal that had broken off: one was a projection on her snout, and the other was from the back of her head. I'm considering gluing the bits back on, but before I do anything, I will ask her.

I study her under my bedside lamp.

She is delicate white quartz, with two tiny red goddess kisses deep in the crystal of her snout…and when I'm wondering where to go in, the right-hand side eye socket takes my attention.

I settle down to meditate with her.

She agrees to me entering through her right eye.

I find myself outside Raffeem looking at her, and like Alice in Wonderland I'm finding myself small in the inner world. I see the right eye and scramble up. I'm holding on to the edge of the eye socket, and with both hands I haul myself up and in. I'm standing on the quartz rim now, and make my way across the polished bowl of the socket, toward a black shadowy area that is drawing me to it. Here I find a crack in the crystal where a narrow path penetrates the quartz and leads me deeper into the skull. The path is dark, and it twists and turns before it opens out into a huge cavern. I hear water dripping into a pool that is filling the center of this place; it is dripping from the rocks all around me and collecting in the pool. Daylight glimmers overhead. I am standing on white quartz sand that rings the pool.

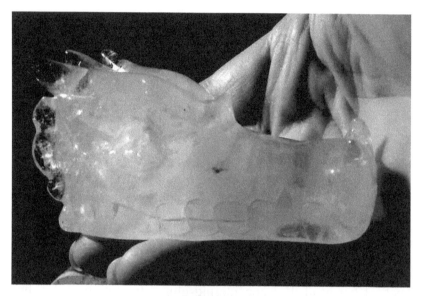

Rafeem

What am I waiting for? I ask Raffeem.
"Permission."
What for?
"To go further. For this is just my crystal 3D body you are in, not my flying body. First, at this level, may I introduce myself?"
Of course, I say.
"I am Raffeem, as you have already guessed, and Raffim and I are in joy at being reunited. When you sent for him we were parted, but now all is well. I am female, as you know, and Raffim and I fly together."
What happened in the post to cause you damage? I ask.

CHAPTER 18

"Rough handling and insufficient physical protection—or as you say—wrapping. It was careless wrapping by those who meant well."

How will the damage impact you? I ask.

"Not at all. My higher bodies are intact, only the 3D crystal shattered, but you have the pieces, so glue them back in place and then their absence will not cause you dismay. For my part, I do not need them, but I like them, as they are part of me, and I like them to be always with me."

Should I use watch glass cement to glue them? I ask this because it is transparent and will not discolor.

"Acceptable, as are a great many glues. It is our higher bodies that are the important bodies, and these are not damaged by human's mishandling."

Would you like me to mend you?

"Yes. It would be a kind service."

Have you been flying with Raffim since you arrived? I ask.

"Yes. We like it here and have met Scottish landscape dragons from the north. Also, very old dragons live under the North Sea, and we have been seeking them, for they are kin, too."

Are you like Chinese dragons? I ask.

"No, for they have a different energy charge. We may have been carved there, but we were intended for export to come to the West, and destined to harmonize with the landscape dragons here. Only the Welsh people truly remember when dragons interacted with man, and their national flag carries us on it. And although much is forgotten, they still seek to claim our protection; the native peoples of Wales are old and their folk memories hark back to Atlantis."

How do you know this? I ask.

"We read the akashic records as easily as you read a book. Easier, because we simply feel the energy flows in the land and listen to the songs in the stones. The stones and rocks of a land remember and hold the records of what transpired long ago. All is energy and energy cannot be destroyed, it just changes its form or storage means. This is one reason why skulls can tell you of the far past from long before they were carved. They immerse

COSMIC CRYSTALS! *Working With New Crystal Skulls*

themselves in the energy flows of the lands and their people, and all is, or becomes, clear."

May I see your flying body? I ask.

"Yes. Enter the pool."

I visualize walking over the quartz sand and find the pool warm. I walk down, and down beneath the water I go, and then all becomes fire—the water turns to a cool, fluid fire and becomes dazzlingly bright, and I find myself floating in light. Then I sink down until my feet make contact with dragon skin, but fiery, cool dragon skin, and I look around to find I am standing on Raffeem's head. But it is the head of her fire body, her flying body, that I am standing on now. She is huge. Her head is unbroken at this level and is huge. I go down to the back of her neck and see that there is ample space for riders between her wings. Perhaps one day I will ride on her.

"You will," she says. "And so will the sweet crystal folk who share your home. But for now that is all we need to do. You tire. It is time to return."

I thank her and retrace my journey, and I thank the angels and God the Creator of All, including dragons. I come back into ordinary reality to find myself in the comfort of my bed on a dismal Sunday afternoon. It is 3pm. It will be totally dark by 4pm, as it's only a few days since the winter solstice.

I confess I am liking the dragons very much…I didn't know what to expect with them, but they are fond of people and they love our crystal skulls. The dragons are very different to the bird skull below.

The seller instantly gave me a total refund for Raffeem. Everything else from him had always been beautifully boxed and very well packed. I suspect he may have had a little help with the Christmas rush from someone not as tuned into crystals as he is. But the main thing is, Raffim and Raffeem are together now, and she didn't seem to be troubled about the damage.

Next day I pick up the delicate rose quartz bird skull. For some reason it has taken me quite a while to get around to meditating with this one. It is beautiful and very different from anything

190

CHAPTER 18

else I have ever worked with. The skull has a beak like a crow, or a raven—a good long, strong beak that's characteristic of the corvid family. She is light to hold and the skull bones are pierced by holes to make her even lighter. Both her eye and the tip of her beak take my attention.

The skull tells me she is female and that her name is **Arwen of the Beak and Feathers**. She tells me I am to enter her beak, where small veils gleam and glimmer invitingly near its tip.

I'm in the inner world now, and I go straight into her crystal beak and latch on to a glimmering shape in the veil there. Looking around I see I'm in a landscape, and that the glimmers are caused by bare white crystal patches on the sides of hills that are catching the light of suns…there are two suns here. I'm on another planet… Arwen's essence is showing me her home planet.

Arwen of the Beak and Feathers

"We have two suns that ride the sky in tandem," Arwen tells me, as I hear her voice in my head. The telepathic contact continues, "And when we have night, we have multiple moons, some too small and far away to be seen by your eyes, but we

COSMIC CRYSTALS! *Working With New Crystal Skulls*

birds can see, and we are aware of them at all times, for we feel the gravitational flows of our world and the pulls and distortions caused by the many moons."

"This world has been stable for a very long time."

What are you wanting to show me here? I ask.

"How different worlds can be. We have crystal rocks, but no plants, no soil, no water in the atmosphere and thus very little weathering. We have wind and abrasion, and sand and powdered stone drifts. We have moisture below and lakes beneath the surface where the atmosphere does not reach."

"Here the life forms that evolved are crystal. No messy carbon, no watery bodies of soft cells, no detritus building up to create soil. No! Our world is perfectly attuned to Crystal Consciousness. What flies in our atmosphere? Why, birds of crystalline essence do, with 5D forms akin to your dragons' flying bodies."

"We are delicate, perfect, and social. We love each other, and help each other, and thrive in peace, and it has always been so. Were you to see our world, you would see our crystal mountains, but not the throngs of beautiful birds that live there. We are mobile crystal life forms and need no food as do the birds of Earth. We process the light and the wind and use those energies to sustain us and to flourish. We live long and grow slowly by Earth standards, as I have observed during my time with you. Earth is a very different world."

"You love birds and this is why you were drawn to get me. You chose the rose quartz of my body for communication."

What can I learn from your world that can help me here in my life today? I ask.

"Community, and to help you envision a world with no selfishness and no war, no rich and no poor. This is why we are in 5D here. 3D is too unevolved to achieve life at our level, but what is important is to know it exists somewhere and that it could—in the future—exist on Earth, for Earth is moving slowly toward existing solely in 5D. It will happen one day…"

Can you tell me of Earth birds please? I ask.

"A little; they are wise and enjoy rich social networks beyond your current understanding. They like to educate humans, and

192

CHAPTER 18

that is why they interact with you and attempt to expand humans' hearts by calling forth a caring response and the offering of foodstuffs. Some take certain humans 'under their wing' and you should be glad if you are granted this honor. It is usually the result of a soul-bond, forged in earlier lifetimes. Birds do not forget the kind and the cruel, and have sophisticated energy networks to record interactions that resonate over the centuries and down the incarnations. Birds reincarnate—of course they do! Like you do. Nor do they always stay as birds. Birds' lives are a stage souls go through on their journey of understanding Creation. And souls take the adventures of their lives lived as precious gifts they present to the Creator at each death and rebirth."

"Birds are an essential part of the web of life throughout the universe. At one extreme are the winged galactic dragons that do not need a world to survive on, but lay eggs in the interstellar gas clouds of raw potential. (You understand my meaning, you wrote of your own memories of just such a creature in *Holy Ice*.) And at the other extreme are soft-bodied 3D birds like those on planet Earth. There is much in between, many types of 'birds' inhabit all the dimensions. For is not the soul a little like a bird? And are not the great angels you work with splendid winged creatures of God, the divine Source of All? Of course they are."

"Birds are much more than they are given credit for on planet Earth, where they are too often seen as food. Earth brings things down to a very harsh level, and on Earth birds attack and steal from one another, even feast on one another. But that is primitive Earth for you…however, it will evolve, and is already evolving."

How can you help me? I ask. *What have you come to do?*

"Educate you, that is what I've come to do. Educate you and raise your frequency nearer to that of birds, so you can communicate better with the birds in your garden and the crows at the beach. Allow us to lift your energy and your spirits and help you to develop your community network amongst the creatures of Earth. It may be a tough world in which to live, but it is also very beautiful and rich with potential for growth, which is always a good thing in a cosmic soul sense. Do not take things too seriously or to heart when they hurt you. Be more like a bird

COSMIC CRYSTALS! Working With New Crystal Skulls

and fly into the adventure of life on strong swift wings, buoyed up by the currents of life. You cannot fail to be nourished by your contact with birds. Farewell."

I thank the bird skull and return from the inner world back to my bedroom. I look at the time—it is 6pm. I thank the angels and God the Creator of All, including birds. I have a big stretch and I'm back.

That was very different from the cheery dragons.

The indwelling essence that had made the bird skull its home was talking down to me from 5D, and my human ego did not respond well to its superior tone. I'd felt little warmth in the communication and I was in no hurry to visit her again. However, darling little Raffeem was calling.

It is Tuesday evening, December 28th, and Raffeem gives me permission to enter the largest of the Goddess's kisses in her snout.

I am in the inner world now, looking at the crystal dragon's snout.

I am tiny against the enormous snout, but I can see the patch of red iron oxide that I've been calling a "Goddess kiss." I am standing by it. It becomes a red sail on an ancient boat, a square sail on the mast of a wide, shallow Mediterranean trading vessel of the ancient world...and I'm on that boat now, floating on the calm waters of the Mediterranean Sea in ancient Greek times. I am sailing to the court of King Minos at Knossos on Crete. A hot sun beats down.

Why am I here? I ask.

"To understand something," comes the reply.

What? I ask.

"How it is to be rich...this is your boat."

What is it carrying? I ask.

"Cloth, beautiful woven lengths of expensive material for the royal family at the court. This fabric has traveled far, brought from the East to Damascus market, and then carried to the coast at Tyre—and there you bought it because you have a ready market for it at the court."

CHAPTER 18

I know she is right, and I know I am a man in this life, and that Minos is just starting out on his reign.

What happens? I ask.

"You land on Crete, and leave servants and warriors to guard the boat while you take others with you to transport the cloth the short distance to the royal palace. The cloth is destined for royalty, too good for the street markets. After you have been richly rewarded for it you have much gold; you pay your servants, and buy other goods in the thriving cosmopolitan markets on Crete to take on for further trade on the way home. You prosper and are well thought of."

What is important here? I ask.

"Success, to remember that you can succeed. Feel the feeling and know it is yours by right here. Nothing more than success can be, and is, yours! Relax, all is well. Now come sail with me and we fly!"

The past life fades and suddenly I am on Raffeem's back and she has switched to her fire body, her flying body—and from where I live on the coast we fly out over the North Sea…the cold North Sea, so different to the warmth of Mediterranean waters. It is night and the restless waves flash by beneath me. The moon is a waning crescent and the stars are covered by clouds.

Raffeem flies up into the clouds where we find other dragons gathered for a conference to discuss future plans of action.

What are they planning? I ask.

"Revolt."

What or who are they revolting against? I ask.

"Nature spirits—devas—who are deserting the land."

Why are they deserting? I ask.

"They are angry with the way things are going in the world, the pollution and plastic, in particular."

What can dragons do? I ask.

"Persuade them to stay and come up with a solution. If not, they make the problem worse and create an imbalance somewhere else, where they go and gather."

"We dragons pledge to render more support to help them. This is the first council of Scandinavian, Scottish, and other

COSMIC CRYSTALS! *Working With New Crystal Skulls*

British dragons, and there will be more such meetings."

"Most are landscape dragons that live beneath the land, buried in the landscape, sleeping beneath the curves of hills; others live below the waves of the North Sea. This is the start of something good that is destined to happen. That is all you need to see now."

We return, and I'm outside her crystal head by the snout where I went in. I bring myself back into ordinary reality, stretch my legs and shoulders and thank the dragon Raffeem, the angels, and God.

I check out Tyre and find it was indeed a port on the ancient Silk Road, as they called the trade route that stretched across the known world for thousands of years, bringing luxury goods from China to many far flung countries.

In the meditation Raffeem had acted like a mirror when she showed me the past life stored in my soul memories, and to my surprise, she was as adept as a conventional crystal skull at doing that. Skulls may immerse themselves in your energy field and mirror it back to you, showing you things about yourself you didn't know because you hadn't consciously accessed the information.

I am really liking working with the dragons, and so on Thursday night, December 30th, I decide to visit Raffim, the first one, again. I enter the inner world and he looks huge. I climb up to the area beneath his right eye, and walk along the folds and creases in his dragon skin until I am behind his ear frills and at the back of his head. Here, steps are leading down into darkness. I am drawn down the steps…and the darkness around me becomes the night sky studded with stars. The starlight helps me to see I'm now standing on a hill, looking out across fields.

I see nature spirits—there are small beings busy in the fields tending the hedges and soil. From where I am, they look like little lights weaving about, maintaining the health of the land, its insects, worms, and seeds, setting off germination sparks here and there, potentizing the seeds.

Raffim says, "I am a land dragon—an Earth dragon—and my crystal body is heavy, and earthy, and dense. I am a foundation

CHAPTER 18

dragon. Without the foundation element of Earth, little else will have a platform to exist on. Next come the dragons of air and water, lastly those of fire and ether. Ether is the blood that runs through our veins and nourishes our flying bodies. Ether is the fuel we draw on, and ether supports us all."

What of Raffeem? I ask.

"Raffeem is an air dragon built to fly between realms. We fly together, but there are places she may pass where I am denied access. I am more closely bound to the earth than she is. She may glide on the star currents and travel far. Sometimes she leaves me—her essence does—to undertake a journey on which only she must go. I fear for her until she is safely returned. I fear because I have not seen her path, and the unknown is easier to fear than that which is known. I can penetrate deep into the earth where Raffeem would find it too dense to fly. Suffice it to say, we both have our talents, and that our work and our spheres of influence diverge."

How long have you been flying together? I ask.

"A very long time. We came here together. Our crystal essences took root in our present crystal bodies only very recently, but we are very old and have been anchored through many crystal bodies in our time."

Where did you come from? I ask.

"From higher dimensions to adventure in 3D and beyond, and we adventure across Creation, stopping here and there to experience in whatever way we can, that which engages us and seems worthy of our interest."

…But then at this point I change the subject. Something had been niggling me.

How did the silk merchant die? I ask. *I had been wondering about the past life Raffeem had shown me and I know Raffim can read my energies as easily as she can.*

"The merchant was old," Raffim tells me. "That was his final trading venture before retiring and enjoying his success. The man died peacefully at home in bed one night, and soon after, he reincarnated as Ariadne, daughter to King Minos. Because of the things he had learned in that life, Ariadne found it easy to

COSMIC CRYSTALS! *Working With New Crystal Skulls*

understand the geography and political landscape of the lands around the Mediterranean and beyond, and she valued the fine silks that contributed so much to the splendor of the royal court."

"The silk merchant had been old when Minos was newly crowned king. Minos' first child was a boy, and it was he who gave rise to the myth of the Minotaur. Deformed, mad, and full of rage, he was confined to his quarters deep within the labyrinthine sprawl of the palace. His rages could often be heard and the people called him 'monster.' He could not be killed because he was of the royal blood and they believed it would have offended the gods, but he could not be released because he was a danger to people. A great sadness it was for Minos, and no other son came to him, and so he cherished Ariadne when she was born. She grew to become a valued adviser because she still had the merchant's gift for charming people and his shrewd assessment of their character. After Minos died, Ariadne and her husband maintained stability for Crete. The Cretan navy continued suppressing pirates and policing the seaways, making them safe for the wealthy merchants who paid them taxes, and all was well."

I thank Raffim, retrace my journey, and leave the inner world. Back in ordinary reality again I have a good stretch and thank the angels and God for the experience I had been granted.

Strangely enough, in 1967, long before I knew anything about past lives, when I was an art student and old enough to travel abroad with a friend for the first time, the first place I visited was Greece and the island of Crete. The spectacularly restored ruins of that very same palace at Knossos drew me back there, and it was hard to tear myself away. One room in particular seemed very familiar. Fresh water still ran in its plumbing after 4,000 years. My friend was puzzled why I stood in that room soaking up the energy for such a long time. She got impatient with me in the end, and who could blame her? But looking back now, I had been transported to the happy feelings I'd had when it had been my dressing chamber, the place where I bathed and dressed in fine silks to impress important visitors at the court.

I had explored Ariadne's life in a regression in the 1990s, but I knew nothing about the merchant's life which was its prequel, and

CHAPTER 18

so I found what Raffim told me very interesting. In my memories of Ariadne's life, Theseus was far from a hero, but perhaps that's a story for another day.

CHAPTER 19
The Ancestor Skull

After Christmas I had planned to do a regression to learn more of the Ancestor Skull, but it never seemed to be the right time for Ye to regress me, and I grew impatient. Ye was still regaining his strength after his illness, but I was eager to progress the book. So by Thursday, the 6th January, 2022, I decided I'd waited long enough and would attempt to regress myself.

It would be like meditating, but instead of entering a skull, this time I would go on a shamanic regression journey that would take me down into my own body. I write about this aspect of my work in detail in *Spiritual Gold*. In essence, your body can function as a shaman's body. Approached in the right way, you can connect with your own deeper knowing and higher subtle bodies through your own physical body. The work of psychotherapist, Arthur Mindell, is very interesting in this regard, and you will find his book, *The Shaman's Body*, in the bibliography at the back of this book.

The difficult bit would be coming up with the questions needed to progress a regression. The questions are important because they hook the information that brings understanding. When you are in the recall you are passively floating through the experience, and are very focused in the right hemisphere of

CHAPTER 19

your brain, the creative hemisphere, whose language is pictures and symbols—but to devise questions you need logic, and this is much more of a left hemisphere activity.

To some extent I had done this in the meditations with the skulls, so although it was going to be difficult, I had high hopes of getting useful material, even without Ye's help.

It is the middle of the afternoon. Ye is in bed with a hot water bottle, having a much needed rest, and I make myself comfortable on a sofa downstairs. Warm and cozy, wrapped up in a fleecy throw, I settle down to meditate. Stardust and Evangeline Mo are with me, one on each side. They are the two skulls that have told me about the Ancestor Skull, so I'm hoping they will help me here.

I relax and breathe deeply and set up the angelic protection.

After more than thirty years working with it I know the regression script off by heart, and I'm going to work through it. First, I visualize myself in a beautiful place in nature...I see a pine forest. The picture springs up in my mind and I'm there. There's a clearing just ahead where a little stream runs...I sit on the banks of the stream in sunlight. The sunlight is quite dazzling. I absorb the energy I need here—I fill myself with sunlight and tree energy, with water and earth energy. Then I follow the stream and go to meet my guardian angel. I see her ahead of me—today she is bigger than I am, with great white wings. Together we follow the stream down to the sea.

We walk into the sea, and I count from ten to zero as I picture myself walking down to the sea bed. I call for the spirit of the sea and Poseidon appears. He opens the sea bed by striking it with his trident, and my angel and I float down through the open sea bed, down and down into my crown, and down and down into my own body, searching for the area most linked to the Ancestor Skull. And all the while I'm counting down from five to zero.

It's my hands! I know it's my hands.

I ask myself what emotions are in my hands, linking me to the skull.

The answer comes—reverence, wonder, and hope for the future. (The reverence is for the skull and humankind; the wonder

COSMIC CRYSTALS! *Working With New Crystal Skulls*

is that we can do this, that we can seed a planet.)

Then I tell myself to let a picture come clear…

And I ask myself, am I inside or outside?

I am in a craft. I am on my way to Earth in a spacecraft and the skull is with me. I know other craft have gone elsewhere, too…gone to other worlds with other skulls.

Where are we from? I ask myself, ("we" because I know I am not alone here).

Orion's belt…we come from one of the worlds around the stars of Orion's belt. There are twelve skulls destined for Earth in this craft, and in total there are twelve drop planets, Earth being one of them. Each drop planet gets twelve skulls dropped off there by the other craft. There is one source planet where we live; it is fairly well like Earth, but larger.

What is my job? I ask myself.

To place the skull, to set up the protective energies, and to create the conditions for "germination" of human-type species. There are four others besides myself in the team that will go down with me.

Is anything important happening on the ship? I ask myself.

We find Earth and park in orbit, and my team drops down to the surface of the world in a small scouting craft. We know this is early in the planet's history and that land masses will move and reorganize, but it doesn't matter; better earlier now than later, when the energies have become more fixed. Things are very fluid on Earth at this stage—and that is all the better for species-originating work to bed in and produce fruit later.

There are eleven other scouting craft, each with a fossilized and fully charged skull on board. We will fan out around the planet and distribute the seed skulls. We know eventually they will dissolve into the worlds we take them to, atom by atom they will dissolve, but not before this work is done and they have kick-started life forms of dexterity and ability and set them on a pathway to develop further. Then later we will return and see what transpired of our "gardening," the setting of seed energies, that we have done.

We are pleased with Earth.

202

CHAPTER 19

Individually we do not live long enough to see the results, but our species does, and the experiments are very long running. For who wants to be alone in the universe? How much better to have potential allies and kin should we need them. Our species monitors the experiment over a very long period of time.

I ask myself to look at my alien body and describe it, starting by looking at my feet.

My feet have toes that are longer, stronger, and more flexible than human toes, but I have two legs, a body like ours, two arms and two hands with five fingers like ours. Our feet are like larger hands and can be just as useful.

Do I have hair? I ask myself.

Yes, very fine and silvery, comes the answer. There's no pigment in the hair shaft.

What are the faces like? I ask myself.

Very human-like, with a high forehead and a delicately-boned nose and delicate lips. We have long faces, delicate ears, and pale skin. Our eyes are gray or gray-green. A lack of minerals and daylight adds to our paleness; we have an adequate diet and adequate artificial light on our craft, but being artificial it makes us less robust than those of us who are born planet-side. We all wear clothing—flexible, thin, insulating fabric is used for our plain, form-fitting garments. We have footwear that caters to our strong flexible toes individually, with fingers like gloves.[11]

Am I male or female here? I ask.

I am male. We have equal numbers of males and females on the craft. Six males and six females will place and disseminate

---

11   The feet were agile, and prehensile, and more like primate feet, rather than like our stiff feet with our stubby toes. Their big toe was more like a thumb. Sounds weird, I know, but in the *American Journal of Physical Anthropology* there is a study that found one in thirteen humans walk on more bendy, chimp-type feet—that is the 8% of us who tend to walk on the outside of our feet, roll our heels, and develop bunions. Have you ever noticed how a pronounced bunion makes the big toe look more like a thumb? Our rigid footwear does not encourage flexible feet; as a child I could pick things up with my toes, but not now. I am one of the 8% who wear down the outside edges of my shoes' heels, and until researching this chapter, I just assumed I had wonky feet! But perhaps it's more a case of Ancestor throw-back genes being more active in the 8%.

the seeding skulls, going down at different times, in groups of five. If the leader of a group of five is male, then the four others making up the group are female. If the leader is female, then four males will go with her to bring the group up to five. On their return we switch about and form new teams.

…So…now at this point we are orbiting Earth, and placing the seeding skulls, and my small group placed the seeding skull just as I was shown when I meditated with Stardust.

Is that all I need to know here? I ask myself.

Yes.

And what advice has the alien for me now? I ask.

"Do not doubt your own abilities. You do not need another to restore any of your memories for you. If you are determined, you will access them for yourself. That is what is important today. We did a good job, then, with the seeding, and in present time it is a lessening of the huge numbers that have resulted from that good job that is required on Earth today."

"We will also do a good job with this lessening."

"Because we are you, humans! We reincarnated into your life streams over the eons, and you are also us—though most of you have more pigment in your skins, eyes, and hair than we do (and this is well and good), a gift from your exceedingly mineral-rich planet to your Earth-grown bodies."

"You think as we did, and still do, except that one of the effects of Earth's gravity has been to make the 'selfish' genes in your DNA more active, and so we have the problems you are seeing on your planet today. We cannot change the gravity of Earth, but we can rewire you all by changing and rewriting bits of DNA code via virus activities, and that is what is happening to you now. Humankind is facing a subtle rewriting of its DNA, and it will take many viruses to achieve this satisfactorily. But it has begun."

"What you call the twenty-first century is the century of rewrites for the DNA. There needs to be less of you, and those living on Earth need to be of one accord, living in harmony together. It will be done by shaking you all up. That is all, transmission terminated."

CHAPTER 19

(In the intense energies of a regression session, time is less linear and more fluid. The past can interact with the present and vice versa. Which is why healing can be profound, and how we can benefit from the advice of our old selves and learn from their experiences. Time is particularly interactive in an ET session, as it was here. Many a sceptic sitting in on an ET contact regression throws the baby out with the bathwater at this point, and can't get their heads around how this can be and dismiss the whole thing. But it just is—and when we accept that—the thing to do is to ask the next question and see what is revealed. A closed mind will never learn; but when you accept what is, and ask what more can you tell me, that is when our understanding grows.

Here my ancient self had interacted with my present self through the medium of consciousness. I had been given information relating to the years ahead by the ancient architects of our existence: a miracle brought about through the existence of soul.)

It is time to go back.

I'm not going to get any more information now.

So bringing the wisdom and knowledge back with me, I focus in my hands, and I float up my body to my crown. With my guardian angel I float through my crown up to the sea bed. I thank Poseidon for keeping it open and guarding it for me. I have met him before, and he is not always as jolly as he is today. He gives me a hug and says, "There, that wasn't so bad or so difficult now, was it?!"

He closes the sea bed and I bid him farewell.

I count from zero to ten as I float up the sea and come into present time.

I thank my guardian angel, Poseidon, the ETs, Stardust and Evangeline Mo, the Archangels Michael, Uriel, Gabriel, and Raphael, and God the Creator of All. I even thank Ye for his part in not doing the regression.

I am back in the room, sitting on my sofa.

I am exhilarated that I did it. And I'm back with a renewed respect for the film *Prometheus*, where the progenitor alien race is called the Engineers: they were right about that...so very, very

COSMIC CRYSTALS! *Working With New Crystal Skulls*

right about that. And I was one. So may you have been when you consider how long we have been monitored for, and how many of them must have come here. It was a very popular film...I think it resonated deep in our consciousness, and there has never been a better explanation for how we arrived on Earth.

That does not mean there is no God.

The Engineers may have shared their form with us and had a hand in the engineering of our physical bodies, but our true essence, our spiritual self that inhabits our body and gives it life, is a droplet straight from the Divine Essence.

We all come from Source.

We are all made in the image of God, whatever our body may look like, human or ET; we are all children of God the Creator.

This book started out with the pandemic newly arrived, when the COVID 19 virus had begun ravaging the world and causing worry, stress, and lockdowns, but after this session I feel changed and very optimistic—because I understand now that viruses have a purpose, and that they are doing what is required for our next evolutionary step forward. It has been a very tough time for us humans, but there is a point to it all, and I felt a burden lift.

CHAPTER 20
"Hitchhikers" and Crazy Buying

Goodness knows what the stars were up to that January—but there was a crazy week I got caught up in a positive skull buying frenzy. In a dizzyingly short space of time a lot of new skulls were heading my way. I'd started out sensibly enough, with just one small second-hand skull on Facebook, but then I'd chanced upon a dark labradorite skull that was an absolute bargain in an auction on eBay—an hour later and it would have gone! But it opened the flood gates for many more skulls to flow to me. They were inexpensive and intriguing, and I was ridiculously excited—on top of that, I did a YouTube interview with Julie Lomas about my books and the crystal skulls.

The first skull to arrive is the auction win.

Carved from glossy, craggy, black labradorite, and sporting a spectacular blue and gold flash like an eye on the back of its head, it had spoken to me in a deep, warm, Carribbean accent as I viewed it on eBay. They rarely speak to me at that stage. On the afternoon the skull arrived, my friend Maggie, who lived across the road, was over for a cup of coffee. I gave her the skull to hold and told her about its voice. "That's strange," she said, "because I've had the Banana Boat song playing in my head ever since you put it in my hands!"

207

COSMIC CRYSTALS! Working With New Crystal Skulls

The skull needed a name...but I was too tired to meditate that night.

However, first thing next morning, with Ye out of the house on a good long walk, I sit up in bed and settle down to a short meditation. First I ask the skull if it is male or female, but there is no clear answer to that. Then I ask its name.

"**Caribbdyss**," is the quick response.

I fall back asleep with Caribbdyss at my side and soon I am dreaming. I am in the Caribbean on a beach. I can't see the sea because the beach has a series of high natural sandbanks between me and the sea. Two people are with me and we are placing spiritual objects in a group on the crest of a sandbank. We think this sandbank will stay clear of the water and the things will be safe there. My only concern is that they look nice and are arranged in a pleasing manner...but then a wave floods over the sandbank in front of us and fills the channel at my feet. The sandbank with the precious items is in danger of flooding! Another wave comes and the tide is sweeping in dramatically—and I wake minutes before I drown and the items are lost to the waves.

I shoot straight downstairs for a coffee...adrenaline pumping...the dream had come with great force and had well and truly woken me up. But it hadn't felt like a nightmare. It wasn't a "bad" dream as such, but it did carry a warning, and the Caribbean theme linked it with the skull.

Later that day I meditate properly.

The skull is jolly. "Welcome to the inner world," it says.

I stand outside it and wonder where to go in...through the flash at the back? Or somewhere else?

"The back," comes the reply.

I see the beautiful flash and make my way up to it.

I find a cave in the dark rough patch that lies at the center of the flash, like a pupil in a cat's eye. I walk in. It is a magnificent cave, high and wide, and as big as a cathedral. I keep on walking, past the black rocky formations of its walls, and deeper and deeper I go into the skull, until I find an echoing cavern with a still pool at its center. I hear water dripping. It's coming down from the roof, delicate drops hitting the tranquil surface of the pool. Drip...drip...quiet but steady.

CHAPTER 20

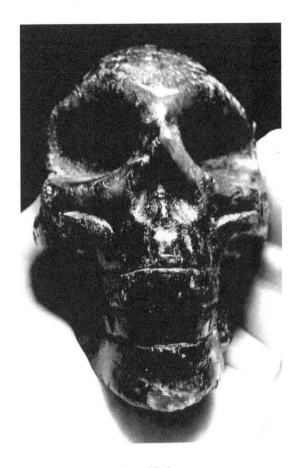

Caribbdyss

I turn around and look back the way I have come. I am looking back through the cavern, back to the entrance cave, and framed by the majestic arch of the cave mouth I see the vista of a forest, its trees catching the rose-gold rays of a setting sun. Pterodactyls glide in the sky above the trees, their shadows flicker over the land. I turn back to look in the pool and see my own reflection in its still water. I look like a nature spirit, with pointed ears and an elfin face.

Is your name Caribbdyss? I ask the skull, double checking I hadn't just dreamt it.

COSMIC CRYSTALS! *Working With New Crystal Skulls*

"Yes."

Are you male or female? (I ask this because the voice is deep and I had thought it was male on first hearing.)

"Female, old…I'm great, great, great grandmother old…," it said with a throaty chuckle.

What is your connection with the Caribbean? I ask.

"It's my spiritual home."

What about Maggie and the Banana Boat song? I ask.

"She is psychic, more than she knows."

What have you come to do, what have you come to help with? I ask.

"To comfort and to cheer you at the darkest time of the year. I bring you sunshine to light your days. Also, the work we will do together will cheer you. This cave is a place of regeneration—come bathe in its waters when you like and they will restore you."

I visualize gingerly stepping over small rocks that are littering the black sand of the floor, and sink down into the water. It is blissfully warm. As I float out into the pool I feel relaxed. The water is volcanic, warm and healing—good for my skin. I feel at peace just floating.

"Come visit me again and we will recharge your batteries and restore your energy levels in a very short time."

I ask about my dream. *What were the incoming waves?*

"Stress."

What were the precious spiritual things that I'd set out on the altar I was making, that were threatened by the waves? I ask.

"Your work, your calling. When your energy levels drop, then drop what you do and rest. Let the stress go. That way you will recharge and be back on your feet in no time. You are too tired to do more, but this is a good start to our time together. Look after yourself and shepherd your energies to serve you, and they will!"

I swim to the edge of the pool. I step out and soon dry off in the warm tropical air. Caribbdyss is laughing. She says, "Well done, well met, and well come[12] to my cave. Now go in peace all the days of your life…"

I make my way out of the cavern and pass into the cave.

---

12   Archaic form of welcome.

CHAPTER 20

I climb out of the flash in the back of the skull and come back into awareness of being in my sitting room. I thank Caribbdyss, the angels, and God for the lovely experience in the pool.

How did she know I was tired? Caribbdyss had read my energy field, that's how, and she was quite right. It had been a full-on week, with me ridiculously over-excited about the new skulls, and also, I had been too stressed to eat lunch before the YouTube interview. I'd got through it on adrenaline and had had to go to bed afterward to sleep. I care passionately about my work, and get so excited talking about my books and crystal skulls that I shoot off all over the place at tangents, talk ten to the dozen, and cover lots of ground. Next time I will make sure I eat and "shepherd" my energy better, as Caribbdyss said. Bless her. I am really liking this skull.

Later comes the certainty that she has taken me back in time and shown me the Waters of Life, as the Atlanteans were to call them ages later. Atlantean emperors visited the healing and renewing waters from time to time to prolong their lives, and the location was always kept a closely guarded secret.[13] Sea levels have changed since then, and volcanic activity has certainly reshaped the land, but the Waters are still there beneath the waves near the Caribbean island of Bimini...I do believe that.

I found Caribbdyss to be different from all my other skulls, in that it has two voices. Two crystal entities are in residence in this skull. They are old and have kindly grandparent energy about them. They are twin flames—well that's what they tell me—but it does explain why on different occasions I've heard both a male and a female voice; it all depends on who I am talking to.

It is Monday, the 17th of January, and four more of the buying frenzy skulls arrive in the post. In the flurry of orders I had lost track of how many I'd actually sent for, and one turned out to be a "hitchhiker" that wouldn't be staying long. That one had cast a glamour over itself and seemed very appealing, but as soon as it arrived I knew it was not for me. I was a stepping stone to get it to the person it wanted to be with—my friend Veronica. That

---

13   In chapter three of *Holy Ice, Past Lives and Crystal Skulls.*

COSMIC CRYSTALS! *Working With New Crystal Skulls*

chevron amethyst skull looked fierce, but its energy felt dead to me, as if it had switched itself off, but Veronica welcomed it warmly. She loves skulls, and spookily enough, its fierce face reminded her of a kindly deceased uncle who had also had a fierce cast to his mien.

Within an hour of being in her company and being caressed by her fingers, the top of the skull had gained a gleam and a lustrous purple hue. It looked radiantly happy and adoring as it sat on the table at her side while four of us drank coffee; my friends and I were amazed at the rapid transformation from dull, cloudy, and dead, to so vibrantly alive. It was remarkable.

I'd read in Edwin Courtney's, *Crystals To Go*, that this can happen...that skulls and crystals can cast a glamour over themselves to beguile you and entice you, and that occasionally a skull is a hitchhiker. The Collective Crystal Skull Consciousness is aware of all humans and all crystal skulls. Like attracts like, and the energy threads that shape our daily life will be tweaked until they flow in such a way they carry the skull to where it wants to be. I was very pleased I had something that illustrated this point for *Cosmic Crystals!*

There was no time to work with the remaining three skulls that had arrived on Monday, before Tuesday's post brings skull number six—the small second-hand skull that had first sparked off the buying frenzy. Advertised in a Facebook group, it was late because it had had to travel to me from Holland in Europe.

Its smooth agate crystal is peppered with dark dots, little black dots that swirl in circles and spirals, reminding me of Australian Aboriginal paintings with their swirls of white dots. I can see why it's been called **Freckles**, and I wonder where the dots might take me.

Wednesday brings a walk by the sea and a stop for coffee with friends in the seafront Rendezvous Café. I feed two friendly crows peanuts and make my way home. By now it is late afternoon and I grab a bite of lunch and settle down to meditate with Freckles. Is it time for a name change? I will ask.

Freckles is happy to work with me. He suggests I call him **Topo-Mo-So**.

Once in the inner world I'm standing outside the skull and

looking up at it as it towers above me. I see steps up to the left cheekbone and I take them. Standing on the bone I see that the dark dots mark a trail—the dots are footprints! The trail of footprints goes from the cheek, up and over the eyebrow, leading me to open desert where people around a fire are drinking desert sage tea as the sun sets, reminding me of a lovely experience I had in Jordan. The trail takes me round in a circle and then down into a sandy gulley, leading to a cave. I go into the cave, and go down and down to a layer of bedrock that is dusted with sand.

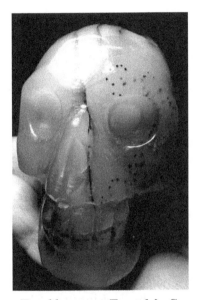

Freckles, now Topo-Mo-So

A wolf is waiting for me there.

Patiently waiting. It has kind eyes…and I remember the wolf—it is Silver Brother—a power animal and guide, and my wolf friend from a lonely past life in the Canadian wilds. I've met him many times before and love him dearly.

What is he here for? Why has he come? I ask the skull.

Oh! It's to speak to me about life today. (My friends and I had been putting the world to rights over coffee…)

"Do not despair of the state of the world," he says. "For there is much that is good that is happening around you. Be patient and let things unfold in their own time,"… and at this point I keep

COSMIC CRYSTALS! *Working With New Crystal Skulls*

fading in and out of the experience. Sleepy after my late lunch and tired after my walk, I'm drifting in and out of sleep.

"...Come back another time," Silver Brother says.

I put my arms around his thick furry neck and hug him.

I retrace my journey back to the cheekbone. I come out of the skull and back into awareness of being in my sitting room. I thank the skull and Silver Brother, the angels and God. I'm glad to have met the wolf again, and glad that this skull is a portal to take me to him. I will go back.

And I do.

But first there is a council of dragons.

It is Thursday now and I'd got myself quite confused with all the purchases I'd made. I had thought I'd sent off for a honey calcite dragon, which spoke to me of fire, but no, I find it is still for sale. However, a small ether dragon arrives that morning. In the evening I meditate with it and the other dragons in the sitting room, while Ye watches TV. I'm wearing ear protectors to cut out the sound, and with my eyes closed and my head turned away from the TV, this works surprisingly well.

I welcome the ether dragon.

This skull is of fine-grained silky agate that looks more like incense smoke than crystal. Her third eye, and part of her crown, are not present in 3D at all, because they are in the area that was the void, at the heart of the geode from which she was carved. The void was lined with tiny sparkling crystals and they shimmer all the way down from her forehead to her snout...she looks very otherworldly and says she is **Elandra**. She confirms she can handle the energies of ether.

I ask her if she likes Raffim.

"Yes, and Raffeem is a sister dragon to me, we two are in harmony."

Then I ask Rafim the burning question: do I need a fire dragon?

"Yes. Eventually," he replies.

Do I need a water dragon? I ask, emboldened.

"Perhaps. Eventually. There is no hurry. We bond well and are content as it is."

(The seller had just offered me a reduction on the fire dragon, which was making it even more tempting.) I press Raffim.

Should I take up the offer? I ask him.

CHAPTER 20

"Yes and no," he replies.

Would a honey calcite dragon be compatible with you? I ask, trying to make him more definite.

"Yes."

Would it be physically strong enough? I ask, because calcite is nowhere near as hard as quartz or the iron pyrite Raffim is carved from.

"If treated with care. It would bring you joy and a twinkle to Moon's eyes."

Why is that? I ask.

"It would entertain her and empower Solange, in a way, because fire dragons are linked to Tibet." (Solange is Tibetan quartz and that alone makes me want to buy this dragon to cheer him up!) Well, I have my answers and it's time to work with Elandra. She tells me to enter her third eye portal.

I do. I'm in the inner world now and hovering above the tiny, shiny, glittering crystals that cover her third eye area. Light cascades off the crystals. I drop down onto them, and I'm walking amongst them while their facets glitter like mirrors. I'm following a gulley and going down into the snout, into a crystal cave. There are crystal devas here, nature spirits of tenuous form, woven of light.

Left to right: fire dragon Casima and ether dragon Elandra

What are they doing? I ask.

"Gathering energies."

What for? I ask.

"To pull things into manifestation...things like book sales. Visit me when you want to do this."

I say I will...and I see them take heaps of my books and put them in a crucible of transformation. It is full of light. I see my books dissolving into light...then that light is projected over the world, penetrating consciousness, bringing wisdom and a hunger for my books that will one day manifest as book sales.

I thank the ether dragon and it says, "Work with me again soon."

I return. I come out of the cave, through the glittering crystals and rise up into the air...and snap back into being aware that I'm sitting on a sofa in my sitting room. And I come back knowing there's no need for a fire dragon at a stone circle; when it comes I can leave it safe at home, so it doesn't matter if it is fragile because it does not need to travel. I stretch my back and my shoulders, open my eyes and thank the dragons, the angels, and God the Creator of All, including dragons, and angels, and us. Then I order the fire dragon!

(And Raffim was right. When it arrives it sits at Solange's side and gloomy Solange positively grins.)

Friday night is January 21st, and it is love at first sight when I see a blue apatite dragon skull on Facebook. If ever I've seen a water dragon, this is it. I make an impulse purchase. I intend it to be the last of my skulls. Ever. Honestly, it's been too much. I don't recommend crazy buying, too many energies to integrate in a short space of time has given me skull indigestion! Seriously, I have enough skulls to work with for the rest of my life, and that's how I'm feeling when I settle down with Freckles later that night.

I can't get the hang of his new name and still call him Freckles.

I'm in the inner world now and he is huge. I'm hoping to meet Silver Brother again, and this time I'm flying over the circle of dots on the left-hand side of his crown. I go closer and see that each dark dot is a lantern in which a candle burns—I see their points of light bright in the darkness of night. The night sky above me sparkles with stars and the candles on the earth below

CHAPTER 20

me make flickering points of light.

Where am I going? I ask.

"Follow the points of light," says Freckles.

As I follow the circle of lights I spiral down and down into the skull. Its crystal is like smoke now…and I find myself standing on a boat rocking on waves, in a deep mist in total darkness.

Am I alone? I ask Freckles.

"No, you are part of the crew."

Where are we going? I ask.

"Across the Mediterranean Sea a long time ago, to trade with those besieging Troy. You are bringing them supplies. The boat is becalmed at night in a thick mist. You can no longer see the sky and the crew shiver with dread. Sailors are superstitious and you all fear sea monsters."

Have I ever seen a sea monster? I ask.

"No, not yet. It is a long drear night of fear, but dawn releases you into the calm certainty of day, and all is well. The mist has gone, a breeze springs up and takes you onward. It is a successful trading mission and you bring home some warriors who wanted to leave the siege. They reward you well and are thankful."

What is important here? I ask.

"That you can succeed, even when all looks lost. This is a good thing for you to know and to remember. You have sent for the water dragon, but it will turn out well, as it did in this story. Let worry and care go, and trust all will be well."

Is there anything else to understand here? I ask.

"No."

May I meet Silver Brother again? I ask.

"Yes, come with me," says Freckles. Freckles's essence and I soar up and go over to the pattern of dots on his cheekbone. But this time we take the other fork, and go toward the back of the skull. The dots again turn into footprints and lead me downhill… and I follow a country path into a little copse of trees. Once more I find myself under a night sky, and there in the moonlight between the trees stands Silver Brother—tail out, ears pricked, waiting. I run to him and throw my arms around his neck. He licks my face. We greet each other and feel happy to be together in this moment.

What do we need to do to complete from last time? I ask Silver Brother.

217

COSMIC CRYSTALS! *Working With New Crystal Skulls*

"Nothing. It is enough to know we can meet through this skull," is his reply.

I press my forehead against his...and then we howl to the moon. The moon is enormous, not long past full. It is a song of longing we howl, and it becomes a song of hope. We feel healed and the bond between us is stronger. He becomes playful, and dawn breaks, bringing the promise of a bountiful new day. I take my leave of him and retrace my footsteps. He follows me back to the cheekbone. We hug and then I snap back into ordinary reality, and I'm back on my sofa surrounded by cushions. I stretch my shoulders and back. I thank my lovely wolf, the skull, the angels, and God for the experience and for keeping me safe. It was well scary out there on the sea, lost in the darkness and mist with an overwhelming feeling of deep dread. Horrible.

I am eager to hear from all the new skulls, and catch up with my earlier purchases. On Sunday night, the 23rd of January, I'm brimming with energy and sit down with those that had arrived last Monday. The "hitchhiker" had gone to Veronica, but that left three I had not worked with.

A gray labradorite with a striking black line down its face tells me she is **Elvira**. The back of her head has a huge golden flash, and when I'm in the inner world, that is where I go.

I fly into the golden flash and I'm flying in sunshine over a tropical forest—a paradise of a place. It's like a large Caribbean island... It is hot, there's lots of light, and a sparkling sea.

Where am I going? I ask.

"Have patience," comes the reply.

I fly on and come to the island's volcano. I see bare gray slopes and fly up to the rim. There's smoke coming out and the rocks are warm. Oh! I'm going in! I'm in my spirit body, so I won't get burnt. It's very bright to me, but not hot. Bright means there is a lot of energy in the rocks.

Where am I going? I ask Elvira again.

"Patience."

I go down, down, down into Earth's heart and I identify with Earth.

What am I doing here? I ask.

"Recording what goes on. Earth sleeps, but she will awaken."

Why does that matter? I ask.

218

CHAPTER 20

"When she wakes the tides are loosed, and the mountains shake, and cataclysms abound."

What wakes her?

"Disturbance from the heavens—being pelted with falling debris is one way, or woken by the sun is another. She will awaken from time to time and that is normal and not to be feared. Like you sleep and wake and are active and then sleep again, so Earth sleeps, though her nights of sleep are long ages to you. All is well. When you turn over in bed you may still be asleep, and so it is with Earth. Some volcanic activity is normal, it is Earth turning over in bed."

(At this point there had been a lot in the news about a volcanic disaster unfolding on Tonga. Tonga is a Polynesian Kingdom of more than 170 islands in the South Pacific.)

"Not to worry about Tonga, it is Earth turning over in bed—though it is a great tragedy for the people there. They need help and when healers send healing thoughts it soothes Earth and she sleeps deeper and is still. She is not ill, does not require healing as such, but locally the nature spirits, animals, insects, fish, humans, and vegetation do—and that's where the healing should go, because, as you see, Earth is not ill. Earth herself does not need healing, but thoughts of harmony, and peace, and beauty soothe her."

Left to right: Elvira and Fanella

What is important here? I ask.

"To be joyful in your daily life, to live in a harmonious fashion with those around you, and to appreciate Earth's beauty. Then you will be an asset to planet Earth."

"Farewell."

I thank Elvira, Earth, the four angels, and God.

I have a good stretch and open my eyes.

I definitely need a cup of tea.

Tonga had been in the news and I was finding it very disturbing because clouds of ash and water vapor climbed 35 miles into the sky, and Tonga's volcanic plume reached halfway to space. The satellite pictures were spectacular. In human terms it was a disaster because of all the ash that covered everywhere, and Elvira was trying to soothe and reassure me by explaining. I was amazed the skull was aware of it, but then not much slips past our crystal skulls.

Sunday, the 23rd, also sees me sitting down with a phoenix stone quantum quattro skull, another of the four skulls that arrived last Monday. It is a ghostly white with green flecks, and has small cavities in which tiny perfect crystals grow that look like quartz wands; they catch the light and shine. The green color is due to copper. It is a strange skull. She tells me her name is **Fanella**.

Once in the inner world I see steps up the left-hand side of the skull, and these take me to the cavities which are now as big as caves. Crystals hang down from the caves' roofs, and they glint in the light.

I go to the cave that had drawn me when I saw its single perfect crystal in the photo on the seller's eBay page. I go in and touch that crystal. I put my hands on it and hear it hum. The crystal is humming, and now I hear that all the crystals are humming, and making a floating ethereal music that fills the caves and resonates throughout the whole skull.

I go in deeper and the music gets louder.

Soaring and ebbing, flowing cadences of beautiful sound swirl around me like fairy music. I go in deeper, and in the center of the skull I find a circular green cavern, around which a walkway runs

CHAPTER 20

in a perfect circle half way up the walls.

I'm standing on the walkway now.

I lean over its balustrade and I'm looking down to see what fills the center of the place: I see a pool of limpid green water. This place is well-lit by transparent crystals piping in light... and there are fish in the pool. I see them frolicking, their tails splashing sparkling trails of water high up into the air. Rainbow drops cascade down.

What are the fish doing? I ask.

"Enjoying their lives, carefree and happy,"

What should I be learning from the fish? I ask.

"To do the same. Enjoy what you do and don't make heavy weather of it. Get the house ready for your visitor with joy in your heart. You will enjoy it! Don't lose the gold of the moment, be at one with your task and easily achieve your goals."

Is that all I need to see here?

"Yes. I have more to show you, but that will come later."

I retrace my footsteps and come out of the cavern. The crystals still sing and the ethereal music still shimmers in the air as I leave the skull and snap back into ordinary reality. I open my eyes. I stretch and take a big breath in, and let it go. It is a moment before I center myself and then I thank the skull, the fishes, the angels, and God for the experience. It has helped. It has really helped. I stop feeling the pressure of getting ready for a housework exam—I always feel like that when visitors come— and instead I feel excited!

My visitor is Vikki Cunningham, who I met a long time ago when *The Mystery of the Crystal Skulls* had just come out, and Chris and Ceri, who were friends of mine, brought Don Alejandro Cirilo Perez Oxlaj, Grand Elder of the living Maya, over from Central America for a workshop in London in connection with their book launch. Vikki had had her large quartz skull, Ebmnagine, with her that day, and for the whole day we sat together, and that's how I met Vikki and Eb.

It had seemed a chance encounter and we hadn't kept in touch.

The years passed.

When I nearly lost Arapo to the waves in chapter two, Star

221

COSMIC CRYSTALS! *Working With New Crystal Skulls*

Johnsen-Moser told me about someone who had lost their skull to the ocean. I contacted the lady in question and we became friends on Facebook. She lived across the world, in far-off Australia, but there was something familiar about her. It took me a while to realize she was the very same person I'd sat beside in London all those years ago, and that I'd actually seen and touched her skull, Ebmnagine, the one the waves had taken.

Vikki had had Eb with her for years, and she is on record as taking part with Eb at many skull events. She is also known by her soul name, Elmera, and I'd come across her mentioned in my crystal skull books. As the months passed, my thoughts often strayed to Eb…and slowly I became aware of a connection with Merlin. Eb was quartz and I wondered if Eb had been Merlin's scrying skull. Eb looked old. Don Alejandro had said Eb was sacred. Was it possible? The feeling got stronger, but it wasn't to prove that simple.

The next time Vikki left Avalon in Australia to come to Glastonbury in the UK, she visited the Isle of Lewis in Scotland to see the famous Callanish Standing Stones. From Facebook I saw she was in Scotland, and as we are near the Scottish borders, I invited Vikki to stay for a few days at the end of January.

It was a joy having Vikki come to visit, and talking with her I found Eb had been too large to have been Merlin's scrying skull—well too large to have been the one I'd seen him with when I was Johannes the Celt, and Merlin had traveled the land visiting stone circles in the desperate times at the end of his life (see chapter six). But it made me wonder about doing a regression with Vikki to see what we could find; at the very least we might strengthen a connection between her and Eb, because whatever had happened in the ocean to Eb's crystal body, the higher bodies would still be intact and in existence in higher dimensions.

Vikki still cared deeply for Eb and we did the regression.

She immediately established a strong connection with Eb, and found he had risen like a phoenix, and is in solar consciousness now; she found that he had changed form and that his crystal body had ascended. She saw that the transition was intended, and that he was overseeing a large group of beings who are activating

CHAPTER 20

consciousness within the crystal kingdom, the animal kingdom, and the bird kingdom, but not the human kingdom. She saw we humans need to connect more with Earth's crystals because our consciousness is too limited at this time…and she found she had been a seer in Merlin's circle. In that past life she had lived within fifty miles of my home, most likely at the Celtic king's fortress at Durham. We learned Eb was not Merlin's skull, but Vikki saw that Merlin had encountered Eb, and from Vikki, to my surprise, I was to learn that Merlin had three crystal skulls—the quartz, the lapis, and also a jadeite skull, green with little sparkles, that I was previously unaware of. He used this skull to communicate with the mineral kingdom, because all the different types of crystals in the world had to know how to talk to each other. This skull was to be the trigger for the group consciousness of all crystals, and because of the work that Merlin did then, we crystal skull guardians now can take our skulls, whatever crystal they may be, and they can commune with the ancient standing stones and rocks of our planet—whether they be Preseli bluestone, sarsen stone, sandstone, or whatever.

As the information about the jadeite skull came through to Vikki, we both got tingles running up and down our bodies! I always take tingles in that situation to be a sign of higher truth. And I think it is really important for now. It explains why the Duddo stones, and the Matfen standing stone, had welcomed my tribe of assorted crystal skulls when they were in physical contact. So it is indeed well worth taking your skulls, whatever crystal or stone they may be, to the old stone circles and places of power anywhere in the world, because the stones will talk to them. Wherever you live you can tap into the rocks with your skulls. The work Merlin did still sings in the rocks beneath our feet and we can benefit from it now.

I shall always be grateful that Vikki came to stay.

On Monday the 31st, the last day of January, Ye had a hospital appointment for eye surgery, and that brought Vikki's visit to an end, and Ye and I back down to earth. And because of problems, Ye also had to go back the next day for a second procedure, and it wasn't until the end of a worrying week that I sat down to meditate

COSMIC CRYSTALS! *Working With New Crystal Skulls*

with the new fire and water dragons that had arrived.

I did both in the same session.

The fire dragon revealed his name to be **Casima** and said, "I can nourish Solange and we belong together. Put me by him, rather than with the other dragons, and today enter through the place of dark banding on my snout."

I do. I enter the inner world and the snout is huge.

I slip in between the teeth in the dark area Casima suggests, and I find it is night...and I'm walking at the bottom of a deep ravine. So deep, that when I look up I can only see a narrow strip of black sky full of stars.

I come to a cave.

I enter and walk down the slope into a dragon's lair, and as in a fairytale dragon's lair, there is a heap of treasure with the dragon fast asleep on the top!

What does this signify? I ask.

"This is you asleep on many of your gifts."

What would wake the dragon? I ask.

"Praise. And it will come to you in time; praise for what you will achieve."

Which gift do I need to help me now? I ask.

"A golden lamp for wishing on. You need to see and wish for success. Come to me to wish for things! Farewell."

I return and slip out of the teeth.

(Only later, when I'm writing this up, do I realize I forgot to find the golden lamp. Do I secretly not want success? Do I have subconscious resistance to success? I'd best visit Casima again, because this needs to be followed up.)

Next in the meditation, I turn to the water dragon.

My fingers stroke the water dragon's blue snout as I tune into the lovely deep rich blue apatite crystal, whose translucent areas glow in sunlight.

The dragon tells me her name is **Firenz** and she says, "Come into my crystal, for I have things to show you." I slip into her left eye socket—a bowl of blue crystal which becomes the sea... I'm tossing on waves, feeling exhilarated! I'm riding their white caps! Here I'm a water sprite with no physical solid body; I'm

CHAPTER 20

impish, and joyful, and I'm having fun in the waves and riding on dolphins now…

What can you help me with? I ask Firenz.

"Regaining your sense of fun. Everything does not need a purpose. Fun is enough of a purpose to validate an activity. You require more fun to make your aura sparkle. It is too dull with cares at the moment, and this is why I caught your eye and you sent for me. I will stimulate, and remind, and prod you to have more fun. Feed the crows by the sea more often, ride the metro into town more often just to look around. You do not always need a purpose, other than fun. Every week needs fun in it. It is a right. From now on think—what shall I do for fun? And you will experience much more happiness overall."

"Farewell."

I come out of the eye socket and back into ordinary reality.

I thank the dragons, the angels, and God; I do need to take this good advice seriously.

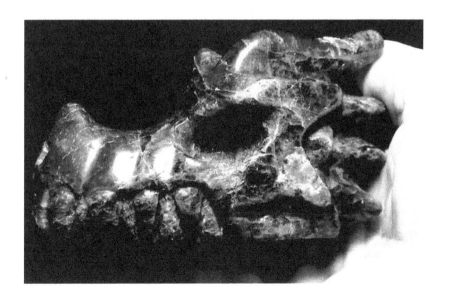

Firenz

My skulls have been generous with showing me things about

COSMIC CRYSTALS! *Working With New Crystal Skulls*

myself and about the world I live in, generous with teaching me things and giving me experiences, and I know I could meditate with them everyday for the rest of my life and never come to the end of what they want to share with me. But for this book, I think that is enough now. It has been an intense year and a wonderful year, and perhaps my next book will be full of experiences at the stone circles I have yet to visit—but before I finish this book I want you to meet **Kai** and the hitchhiker's replacement. Oh yes, I did replace him! I seem to have become a crystal skull addict!

Up to this point, despite having had bodies myself with large black almond-shaped eyes, I had always avoided the almond-eyed ET alien heads that are for sale. Avoided them like the plague because I found them creepy. But after the hitchhiker gave up his place in my team, I was attracted to a striking black tourmaline-in-quartz crystal ET head. The big black eyes still made me feel creepy...but the crystal was lovely. It looked like an abstract mosaic in black and white and I was very taken by it.

When I meditate I'm told it is female.

It is happy to work with me and the name given is **Zuna**. Zuna tells me she is a being, but in quite a different way to my other ET skull, Stardust. Later I will find out exactly what she means by this, but at this stage I think everything is normal.

I am in the inner world now and I'm climbing up a band of black mosaic on the left hand-side of her head. I climb up easily because there are plenty of handholds and places to put my feet. When I am on a level with the eyes of the head, it's like looking out over the top of a wall.

And ahead of me I see an ocean scattered with small islands; the shiny pieces of black mosaic have become islands ringed by beaches of black volcanic sand. The islands are low-lying and are topped by palm trees. The setting sun showers glittering fire into the ocean and sinks below the horizon. Stars come out in the darkening sky above the islands. The ocean darkens with the sky, and there's a fall of stars—but they are not stars—they are craft from another world. "My people," Zuna says. "We work beneath the sea and have bases on your world in the deep ocean trenches."

CHAPTER 20

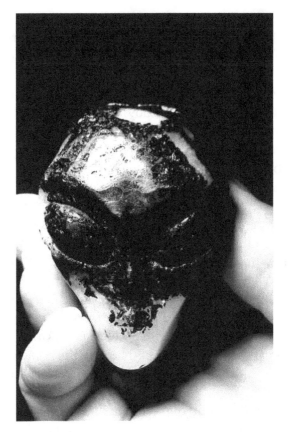

Zuna

What do you do beneath the sea? I ask.

"We patrol and we count the fishy life forms. We are stocktaking planet Earth. Should you forfeit your planet, we would take it over...we are in the ancestor-line of the Grays, but we are not them. Our bones are stronger and our bodies more robust. We can take Earth's gravity very well, and even the greater pressure deep in the oceans."

Are you the same size as we are? I ask.

"Smaller, three foot fully grown; it is big enough. We could caretake the earth better than you do. We have no need for greed, for we are all taken care of in our society. We long ago abandoned the primitive Earth way of capitalist consumption and linear expansion. What we use, we recycle. However, you are still here and may yet get things right. So we watch and we wait. We live on many worlds, and even with you here, we still visit Earth and live in our bases. So while most of you do not realize this—we share planet Earth with you already! Default in your duty of care and it becomes ours."

"Farewell."

I climb back down the mosaic wall and come back into ordinary reality.

I thank the black tourmaline-in-quartz ET head, the angels, and God for the experience. I open my eyes and stretch. I have learned something. The ET head is a way of channeling a live being that is functioning as a live being, with an actual body elsewhere. Zuna is an ET, and not the crystal head itself. This contact took place in present time, the being called Zuna is living now. The ET head acted like a phone or a crystal radio; we talked to each other through it. The live being is not a crystal being. The head is carved in its likeness. The being is attracted to speak through the head because it is carved in its likeness. Like attracts like.

On the other hand, our human head crystal skulls have indwelling crystal entities that want to help **us**. The being that spoke through the ET head was not concerned about helping us. It was concerned about its own life and ambition to replace us on Earth. I felt Zuna was spying with mental and psi abilities that far outstrip ours.

Remember the cosmic crystalline matrix in chapter five? Without crystals there would be no planets, and crystals are seeded throughout Creation. Crystals can be bugging devices and ET heads make perfect Trojan horses. Perhaps next time it won't be Zuna, perhaps next time a different ET will pick up the phone when I make the call. I need to keep an open mind here and will try again. Meanwhile, I quiz Moon about it, because Galactic Federation beings are bound by a code, so it is unlikely to be them talking to us about taking over our planet. I once heard it said that it is easy for a being to masquerade the light and pretend

CHAPTER 20

to be something it isn't, but that you can't masquerade "heart." So when it comes to contact with star beings, see if you feel "heart." No sign of it with Zuna.

Later I settled down with Moon, the ET head, and Casima, the fire dragon, to tidy up some loose ends. Moon tells me the head is an empty vessel. That it is like a phone that rings in the universe and the first to get to it speaks through it…"Collective Crystal Skull Consciousness? Well that might come later if the head gains a suitable indwelling essence. Is it dangerous? No, it only activates when you meditate with it," is Moon's advice.

I check with the head itself and ask if it has an indwelling essence.

It replies, "I have a weak one, easily over-shadowed. But I will grow stronger. Leave the words, just as you have written them, to serve as a warning. Come inside my eyes this time."

I enter the inner world.

Standing in front of the head now, I go up a short wooden ladder to the eyes. I pass into the left eye. I'm standing on a wooden platform, looking out at the sky with a telescope.

What am I looking for? I ask.

"Craft"

A shower of craft fly in and aliens disembark. A tall one comes up to me and says, "We have as much right to this planet as you have. We may yet take it over." I am so deep in this meditation that I keep slipping down into sleep and fading in and out of the experience, and that is all I can remember from the aliens. But before I finish the meditation I ask the fire dragon about the golden wishing lamp. I go to the dragon's hoard and see the lamp and pull it out while the dragon sleeps. I rub the lamp and wish for success, and picture myself holding this book, all beautifully printed and bound—and then I fall asleep properly…and the experience dissolves into a dream where I'm having coffee with friends at a garden center and unsuccessfully trying to find a not-scary way of telling them that aliens are taking over the world!

I wake and cook an evening meal, and it is hours later when I realize I need to thank the ET head, the dragon, Moon-Over-the-

COSMIC CRYSTALS! *Working With New Crystal Skulls*

Waters-of-Life, the angels, and God for the experience, strange as it was.

But I decide I'm going to leave the ET head in Moon's care, as she is my Galactic Federation specialist skull, and I'll allow time for the indwelling essence to strengthen before I ask it its name again, and attempt any more with it. It is lovely; I want this to work. Next time I will have to wish for that on the fire dragon's golden lamp!

But those aliens have another think coming if they think they are getting Earth...How do I know? Meet Kai—the last of the four skulls that came to me on Monday, the 17th of January. Last but not least, it is Kai's voice that will end this book.

CHAPTER 21
Kai

Kambaba jasper has quite a reputation as a powerful stone of high energies, and I was lucky enough to find a skull I really liked carved in it. I had had my eye on this little charmer for a long time now, but when I first thought of buying it, right at the start in chapter one, I had been warned off. But during the crazy buying spree I came across it again on eBay, and this time there were no objections.

I meditate with it for the first time on the night of January 23rd, 2022, and though the meditation is short, I know it is something very special and that it is a gift meant to end the book. Looking back, I can't help but think that was why I had been discouraged from acquiring it earlier, I simply wasn't ready for it then.

When I settled down with the skull I found it was male and its name was **Kai**. I'd studied it well and was familiar with it, from its polished gray whorls and spirals, to the abraded, orangey left side, which put me in mind of weathered sandstone. It is this area I will enter, and I find steps to take me in there. In the cheek area I see a cave. I go in and I am walking over sand. I go in deeper. There are snakes here, I hear them.

And then I see them.

COSMIC CRYSTALS! *Working With New Crystal Skulls*

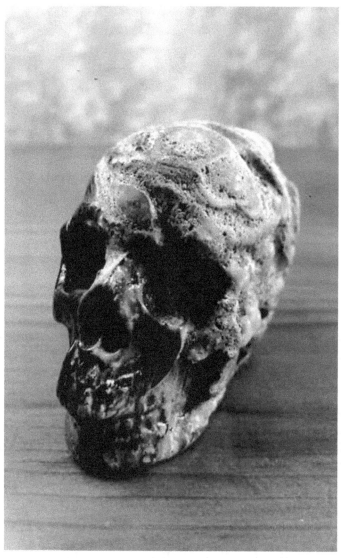

Kai

They do not harm me, they want me to go in further and they clear a path for me. They glide out of my way and lure me in. Is it a trick? I feel fear. They could turn on me…block the exit and overwhelm me.

CHAPTER 21

Kai tells me I have Archangel Michael with me and I am safe.

He is right, and in my fear I had forgotten. (I'm sure you remember I never do inner work without angelic protection).

I see a huge white egg ahead of me.

Kai says, "This is symbolic of knowledge. It is an etheric egg that is symbolic of knowledge. When it opens, a new future is born. It is incubating in this pleasantly warm cave and the snakes are its guards. They guard it and keep intruders at bay."

Why am I here? I ask.

"To see the golden future that is to hatch."

What does it hatch into?

"First comes the chaos of the breaking shell—and that is the time you are living in, for the shell will break, and soon. Then the golden creature emerges, but looks bedraggled, its feathers stubby and wet, but given time and support from others/elders around it, it will emerge triumphant and beautiful, a great bird of golden feathers poised to roost on Earth and usher in a Golden Age. This bird is symbolic but also, on the inner levels, real. Come back and check on its progress and do what you can to assist it. Be one of the others/elders that feed it and encourage its progress. This is what your work is about. You began with books one, two, and three and now take this on further with book four. Be pleased, for we, the crystal and stone skulls, are with you. We want the best for humankind, for we are its guardians and have been from times immemorial. Be at peace. For so it is."

Knowing I will be back, and feeling a little overwhelmed, I leave.

I go back through the cave and come out.

I say farewell to the skull, kiss it, and return to ordinary reality. I stretch and open my eyes. I thank the skull and the snakes, which I now realize symbolize wisdom. I thank the four angels who help me, and God the Creator of All, including snakes and golden futures. I realize it is God's egg. God placed it there and has blessed it, and nourished it, and fertilized it, and given it life.

It's up to us to look after it once it's hatched, and skull guardians are helping, because the energy of love that we feed and generate with our skull community, feeds the golden bird! The love flows to it and will nourish it in growing quantities as more and more skulls are produced and worked with, loved and admired, and cherished and heard.

Crystal skulls are very important to our future, more than we can know.

But know that you, by your own efforts, are all helping in this huge endeavor, and you have all spent many lifetimes acquiring the skills needed for this. You are all naturals at this now. Your presence on the planet ensures our future in ways seen and unseen, but take heart, for you are all heroes to be on planet Earth at the change of the world. Being here brings the future in its true form. Hang on through the trials and tribulations of the world—and then you cannot fail to assist in the birth of the Golden Age. All of you. Now. Well done. For. Being. Here.

There, it is said.

I kiss the skull again and shoot off in search of cocoa to ground myself. That was a high octane energy and I need to ground. The energy was still surging through me even after I left the skull, and the revelations had just kept on coming.

Toast as well…and a cup of tea.

Was I too excited for sleep? Heck yes.

CHAPTER 22
Postscript: Visiting Castlerigg Stone Circle

Kai's revelation may have been a gift to end the book, but it certainly wasn't going to be the end of my journey with the skulls. I had spent a year working with them, and they were now a valued and dear part of my life. Although the year I'd set aside for writing was over, the journey goes on.

And so on Valentine's Day, the 14th of February, 2022, which was our wedding anniversary, our crystal friends were with us when Ye and I visited Castlerigg, an ancient stone circle in the hills of the Lake District, not far from England's north west coast. That day we had an all-terrain shopping trolley for the heavy skulls, and its strong high wheels kept them clear of the mud and puddles. It had rained for days and the land was sodden. A little snow dusted the mountain tops that now surrounded us.

Despite the 14th being on a Monday, there were plenty of cars parked along the country road that lead to the stones, and people were pouring into the site through three wooden gates that pierce the boundary hedge. From the gates it is only a short walk uphill to the stones themselves.

Castlerigg is one of the oldest stone circles in the UK, and within its thirty-eight standing stones are a further ten, only two of which had flat surfaces suitable to set our skulls out on. I was

235

hoping the skulls would plug into the stones and later share any information they downloaded. That afternoon we were lucky, and several times we had the place to ourselves, though it was thronged with visitors and their children when we first arrived.

It was the February half-term school holidays, and all day long people ebbed and flowed through the site. I'm glad the site is well loved, but it is when you are alone with the stones that time melts away. I had visualized my protective clothing about me and silently asked the site's guardian spirits for permission to enter as we approached.

As at Duddo, when we walked toward the stones, the dowsing rods I held had gone crazy, and when I held them above the stones I was going to put our skulls out on, they neatly crossed over themselves. Ye and I walked the circle and introduced ourselves to several of the larger stones that took our attention. With arms out, hands and palms flat on the stone, I pressed my forehead against the cold surface, and with eyes shut, I scanned inside looking for a skull face waiting to be found. If you remember, (in chapter seven) it had happened spontaneously at Duddo when the skull face had impressed itself upon us and introduced itself.

This time I was more prepared to memorize any messages that came.

I repeated the process with three of the larger stones and all three had skull faces within them, smaller than the large one at Duddo, but they each carried a blessing from Merlin, invoking Lugh and the Celtic gods of light. The blessing was to be on the rest of my life. (I suspect a blessing is available to anyone with a crystal skull who takes the trouble to look.)

We were only having a short break away from home because after the recent eye surgery, even a couple of hours spent driving was enough to make Ye's poor right eye ache, and he is the only one of us that drives. But before we went home we visited Mayburgh Henge, near Penrith.

Mayburgh Henge is a high, circular bank of grass-covered river stones that was raised five thousand years ago, at about the same time as Castlerigg. But only one standing stone remains in the center of the henge today. Several stones were removed from

CHAPTER 22

the site in the 18th century, and the tale goes that the two men responsible for breaking them up to use for their own purposes both came to sticky ends. One went mad and the other was driven to kill himself. The moral of the tale being, don't mess with the stones if you value your life!

Solange and Moon on the stones at Castlerigg
I go to lean my backpack containing the smaller skulls against the perimeter stones

Well, when we got home I was curious about what our skulls had downloaded at Castlerigg. For the whole time we were there Moon, Solange, Raffim, Mariam, and Caribbdyss had sat on the stones and I knew they would have something to tell me, but was physical contact essential? I'm learning as I go with this. The smaller skulls had remained in my backpack…

I start the meditations with Raffim, the iron pyrite Earth dragon with dark labradorite eyes. He had specifically asked to come to stone circles. …He says to go in through his right eye, and so with my eyes closed I visualize him. He looks huge when

COSMIC CRYSTALS! *Working With New Crystal Skulls*

I'm in the inner world.

I approach and have to climb up to reach the level of his eye.

I slip into the labradorite eyeball and find myself in a mist... I'm in a liminal zone where realities fuse and cross over.

Where are you taking me? I ask him.

"Back to Castlerigg and into another time altogether, a time long ago...when we Earth dragons met in conference and communed with the holy people of the land. We wished for a landscape of power, with mapping lines—ley lines—along which we could fly to navigate from power spot to power spot. We wished for stone markers to be erected to mark the places of power, and to make them visible to those people who wander the land and travel far by navigating with star maps, carefully drawn and cherished by the learned ones of old."

"The holy ones met with us by entering the Otherworld after fasting and imbibing of herbal tisanes designed to open their awareness to the world within—which is the world where we could meet."

"We asked for this boon and it was granted; at first with wooden henges and then when their purpose and might were recognized, the holy people caused the henges to be built again, this time in stone. From then on, we Earth dragons rose out of the landscape where we had slumbered and dreamed, and we worked alongside the holy people who had heard our call and understood our purpose. For we are the guardians of the land, and in times of danger we can travel swiftly to where we are needed. We can spy ahead, warn and advise on a course of action to counter threats that may arise."

"And so it was for a very long time, until the might of Rome reached these shores. Their straight hard roads cut across our lines of power and were an insult to the folk of the ley, the Fae."

"The Celts' southern tribes had been softened and suborned through trade and had traded for luxuries brought from far off Mediterranean lands—and they fell easily, undermined as they were from within. The northern tribes were let down by their rulers, like Queen Cartimandua, or by those who were weak, or bribed, or promised help against their tribal enemies—and

CHAPTER 22

through their own ego and pride they were compromised. With Celts, the rivalry between them has always been their undoing and their weakness. It makes them vulnerable to an enemy's strategy of divide and conquer."

"And the more hard straight roads that criss-crossed the land, like knife cuts, the fewer the dragons that remained. And the more Romanized the people became, the fewer that remembered dragon lore, and it was forgotten that the land's dragons were its natural guardian forces."

"The Romans changed the spoken tongue to Latin, which has a very different energy to Celtic sounds. And strange as the Romans' gods had been, worse was to come when the soft, gentle words of Jesu the Christ were turned into a weapon to take power away from the people. This weakened their spiritual relationship with the land exceedingly, notwithstanding the churches that were erected on the sites of power where the henges and ancient places of worship had once stood."

"As the Church with its Latin, (never a language spoken by the soft voice of Jesu), hid the holy words from the understanding of the common man and woman of the day, the interpretation of those words was left to those who had taken the power. The words became instruments of bondage, used to exploit a people denied the education to understand for themselves directly from the holy texts. The land fell into a sorry state, and we dragons were unjustly vilified as tools of Satan. Yet we belong to, and are children of, the Earth Mother, and we live in the folds of her Earth-body. We heard the voice of the Mother and we heard her heart beating sad, as her human children grew deaf to her calls. No longer was the solstice celebrated properly, and the stone temples were torn down, and many standing stones shattered by fire and water because war was declared by the 'Church' on the 'pagan' places of power. No threat to their Latin narrative was to be tolerated, as those who ruled and benefitted from suppression tightened their grip on the people."

COSMIC CRYSTALS! *Working With New Crystal Skulls*

Above: Solange, Raffim, Moon and Mariam share a stone with three of Ye's skulls
Below: The crystal skulls Solange and Moon rest on a stone within the circle. The camera shows their quartz crystal glowing with light, even on a very dull day, though our human eyes did not pick this up at the time.

CHAPTER 22

"It was a sad time, but times are changing once more, and there have always been wise ones who heard our call. But now young people sense there is more to life than they are being told. The sites of power draw people back as never before, and more and more hear the call in their bones as they walk the leys and visit the old places of power. We dragons are glad to be of service to humans once more—for our purpose is the same. We love the lands we guard and working with humans once again, we can defend them from what is coming. Farewell."

Is that what you picked up at Castlerigg? I ask.

"Yes. And it is enough."

I thank Raffim, but I confess I was taken aback by the force with which it had been expressed, and by the controlled anger behind the dragon's words. Who knew Earth dragons didn't like the ancient Romans?!!

Nowadays we know the holy people he spoke of as the Druids, and to this day, the Celts' descendants in Wales have a dragon on their national flag, and march to war invoking its protection.

It is Solange's turn next. I sit down with the skull to examine its crystal and I'm drawn to a dark shadowy area in the right eye. I settle down to meditate and Solange agrees I may enter his eye.

My own eyes are shut and I am in the inner world now…I picture Solange, who at this time is actually sitting on my laptop, facing me, within easy reach of my finger tips. He feels cold and I withdraw my hand and focus within myself, ready to begin the journey.

I visualize his face and seek out the right eye with its shadowy darkness; I'm not thinking about what the shadow might signify—I don't want to buy into fear. I just need to be open and neutral to what comes up so the experience can unfold. So I picture myself climbing up Solange's face and resting briefly on the edge of the eye socket. I sharpen my focus and pass into the crystal, into the area of shadow.

It is gray in there…there's hardly any light and gray clouds are scudding across the sky overhead—that is what's causing the shadows, it's the clouds. There's a fierce wind and it is whipping the clouds along at a pace. A storm is brewing, and I'm back in the circle at Castlerigg—as thunder and lightening rend the sky, and torrential rain lashes down all around me. It is exhilarating!

But I'm not in a body. I'm just a spirit witness at the scene, witnessing the power of nature. Earth is looking after herself here. She is cleansing. She is discharging accumulated static and washing herself clean of traces of mankind; she has the power to do that when she judges it best.

Solange says, "There have been times of great cleansing in the past, but the present is not one of them. Be at peace, for you are in no danger here."

Why have you brought me here? I ask.

"To show you what you need to understand."

What did you learn at Castlerigg? I ask Solange.

"Teachings about the cycles of life in a cosmic and planetary sense."

"Whatever happens to the human body, the spirit bodies will still exist to witness, as you are doing now. This is the majesty of cleansing and a glimpse of the power of Earth's cycles."

But how does it relate to Castlerigg? I ask.

"Castlerigg is a place of witness, where things may be revealed because the veil between worlds is thin there. It is a good place to commune with the Fae, the fairy folk, the nature spirits, and storm beings that populate the other levels of life."

Were there any Fae there when we visited? I ask.

"Yes."

Will you let me see them? I ask.

And then I see there was a guardian Earth dragon as we approached, coiled right around the site. In fact, I walked over its tail on the way in. An air dragon had hovered above and called out to its kin in the mountains that ring the site round. And I see that an ether dragon lives within the center of the henge, and that this is what makes the site a portal between worlds. Beings may visit or leave through the portal, and there is a highway in the ethers while that dragon is in residence.

"At night there are more Fae visitors. In the daytime the sunlight and human presences put them off…they avoid men."

CHAPTER 22

Is there more I should know? I ask.

"Not for now. Farewell."

I leave the storm and come out of the eye, I clamber down Solange's dear face and snap back into ordinary reality and become aware of my surroundings. I'm on a sofa in my sitting room, swathed in a cozy throw, and bathed in the warm glow of a lamp. I open my eyes wide now, wiggle my toes, stretch my shoulders, and I'm back.

Then it is the turn of the glossy black labradorite skull called Caribbdyss, and I'm in the inner world now, looking at Caribbdyss. I climb up to a patch of blue flash above the right eye. I launch out into the blue and it becomes blue sky, blue sea—and I'm sailing—speeding along in a dragon ship, a Norse raiding boat. We are skimming over the waves and our big square sail is full of a lively wind. Our oars are drawn in, no need for them now! It is a very vivid sensation of speed. I feel I'm leaning out over the water, not far above it because we're laden with treasure. This is exhilarating!

How does it relate to Castlerigg? I ask.

"Patience…"

Am I talking to he or to she today? I ask, because this skull hosts twin flame essences both with lovely deep honey-warm Caribbean voices.

"She," is the reply.

What is important here? I ask.

"Speed. There's no friction. You're speeding through the water and skimming the waves meeting little resistance."

Is this a past life? I ask.

"Yes. You came raiding the shores of Britain."

What did Caribbdyss tune into at Castlerigg? I ask because I'm wondering how this relates to Castlerigg.

"Vikings who came raiding the north west coast of England settled in the area. Their ship was wrecked, but they brought their boat's carved dragon prow with them when they came here, and it was burned in ceremony in the circle in an effort to stake their claim on the land. Without a boat, they could never go home."

Caribbdyss on a stone within the circle

What do I need to put in the book? I ask.

"Wanderers return. That's you. You were one of the Vikings. You've been to Castlerigg before."

Caribbdyss, did you like the circle? I ask.

"Yes, the stones were talking and they talked to me."

What did they tell you? I ask.

"That the mineral kingdom is waking up, that Earth's heartbeat has speeded up, and that change is abroad in the world. Try again tomorrow…" And that was all I was getting that night.

CHAPTER 22

I came back to the blue flash and came out of the skull and back into ordinary reality.

The next night I enter Caribbdyss again, but through a different area, and I find myself on a hillside overlooking a grassy plain. I see a stone circle. This time it is Castlerigg as seen from the surrounding mountains, and in a speeded-up time-lapse sequence, I watch the weather rage and calm, see sunshine and showers, snow and extreme winds, and I'm told, "See the cycles of nature as Solange was telling you. When you come back to us we will tell you more. We will be here." That's when I realize both he and she have been with me in that meditation.

The following day I try again.

This time I climb up to the tremendous blue-gold flash at the back of the skull and launch myself into the golden part of it. I'm floating in golden air—I'm flying into a sunset…and I drift into the red heart of the setting sun. Here I experience peace, happiness, and pleasure at things unfolding as they should.

Caribbdyss says, "You are living in topsy-turvy crazy times, but that is how it is meant to be right now; all is in good order and all is accounted for. Choose well and follow your heart. Don't waste energy looking back and grieving about anything. Come and rest in the sun when you want to burn away the dross of conflict within, and regrets."

I give my thanks and leave the skull.

Resting in the sun was a lovely freeing feeling and I got great comfort from it. Many times afterward I have recreated the image and visualized floating in the warm red sun and benefited from the accompanying feelings as I let the dross of worry and care burn away.

Now due to all the mud at Castlerigg, and to there having been very few flat surfaces for the smaller skulls to rest on, they had stayed wrapped up in my backpack leaning against a perimeter stone, but it did turn out they had things to say, as did my skull beads which had been worn the whole time I had been there. Such a huge stone circle generates a big energy field, they had all registered something.

With the Council of Thirteen necklace, I focus on one of the earth deva skull beads and ask what it sensed at Castlerigg. All I get is, "Enjoyed the visit. Felt recharged. We sang, but you couldn't hear us. We were happy to go there."

I focus on the Council of Seventeen bracelet. It simply says, "For us it was the same as at Duddo. The skull face imprinted in the stones hopes more crystal skulls will be brought there."

Arapo is more forthcoming.

I enter the inner world and climb up the left-hand side of his sandstone face, to an area above the cheekbone, where I find a door. I open it. It is dark inside the skull, but I see a flight of steps leading down...at the bottom I find sand...I'm standing on soft dry sand and I make footprints as I walk forward, toward a desert landscape where it is night. Here there are stars overhead in a clear black sky. A gentle wind is soft and warm.

Arapo, what did you pick up at Castlerigg? I ask. *Did you pick up anything from the site energies although you were in the bag?*

"It was a muffled impression without the clarity of touch and direct transmission, but I liked the energies there. It is always good to be in nature and to commune with the stones; it is always nourishing to us and helpful. We like to travel and to be exposed to different new energies. It's very stimulating for us."

What was your impression there? I ask.

"It is a peaceful place of thanksgiving—thanksgiving for the year turning, the light returning, the harvest gathered in. The energies are good to bask in, and to be immersed in, though nothing of any great moment was impressed upon me. I liked the place and would willingly return."

Me too, I say. *Thank you Arapo, but why are we in this desert?* I ask.

"I want to show you something."

What? I ask.

"A feeling of peace."

"Life events and cares are robbing you of your peace. Use us to restore it. You can bask in peace now."

Silent gentle moonlight illumines the desert scene, bringing

CHAPTER 22

clarity.

Nothing is rushing or moving.

I lie down on soft desert sand and let go of tension, and breathe in moonlight and night air.

"You can come back anytime. Picture this scene in your thoughts and feel your breathing slow…"

I let out a big sigh and my stress flows out with it. After a while I'm ready I leave.

I am grateful that our skulls can read our energies, because this was helpful advice; a certain matter had been weighing on me since I'd found out about it the day before we'd left home for Castlerigg. Ye's health was deteriorating, and although we didn't know it at this stage, he had a brain tumor. (This would be diagnosed and removed in May. The tumor was benign, and I am glad to say he has since made a good recovery. He did take two of his skulls to the hosipal with him!)

Next comes Alsherida, who speaks for both himself and his twin skull, Bethsherida. He tells me, "We liked the energies there, and again as at Duddo, our crystal tips sang as they picked up the site's emanations. Take us to more of these places. We tune them up and they tune us up. We 'bounce' energies back and forth between the site's stones, the underlying rocks, and our own crystal bodies. It is exhilarating for us, and we offer evolution to the site energies, we step them up."

When I ask Jago Jasper he says, "I kept you safe, as is my purpose, and you were in no danger; there are good, happy energies there and not much darkness from the past."

When it comes to the Shaman Stone, I enter through the right eye and find myself flying with a crowd of dragons.

What did you make of Castlerigg? I ask the Shaman Stone.

"I'm showing you now…" he says. And then I see that the dragons I'm with are dancing above the stone circle! They tell me they are celebrating the quickening energies in the land as spring returns and Earth wakes up; that Earth's rhythm—her heart beat—is speeding up. "She is full of energy and some will be vented through the site. We dance in joy and peace."

When I enter Mars Preseli, I go in through a big white spot

247

COSMIC CRYSTALS! *Working With New Crystal Skulls*

on his teeth…and I find white painted boulders marking the side of a white sandy path. I follow the path until it brings me out on a hillside. I'm half way up the hill, looking out across a landscape.

Mars, I want you to tell me what you picked up at Castlerigg and why you have brought me here.

"For an overview. To see your progress."

What progress? I ask.

"Progress in your understanding of us skulls. There is still much you do not know or the symbolism of this path would have brought you out at the top of the hill. You have made a good start. But start is all it is."

What about Castlerigg? I press.

"Undoubtedly a place of power."

Was there any Preseli bluestone there? I ask.

"Not that I sensed," was his reply, and that was all I was able to get out of him.

Approaching Charles Lapis, I melt into his deep blue jaw and find myself in a dark echoing place. I hear water dripping. It's a derelict building and I step out from it into sunlight. The sunlight is so strong I begin to dissolve into it, and I float up the sunbeams and into the heart of the sun. I feel a deep peace. Reluctantly, eventually I return.

When I float down into the crown of Golden Feathers of the Sun, I pass by glittering bars of rutile. The quartz here feels marshmallowy, soft and billowy, around the hard bars of rutile.

What can you tell me about Castlerigg? I ask Golden Feathers.

"It's a transcendent place, where it's easy to reach up to the heavens with your thoughts and to commune with the spirit forces of the land. Autumn is the season I should be taken there."

But Kai tells me, "The stones there are powerful. They have gathered power over a long period of time and are very little disturbed, and so hold their original charge and have enhanced their energies as the centuries passed. Next time put us on the stones."

Florence says, "I wanted to be out of the bag and I could sense the energies twanging around me. They made me restless. But even though I stayed in the bag, I benefited from proximity

CHAPTER 22

to greatness. The circle stones are great fully-charged batteries of power. We all benefited from being near them."

Disappointingly, all I got from Zeb'n was that it was, "A place of great power." However, dear motherly Mariam tells me something important. She says, "You picked up and integrated a lost fragment of your soul at Castlerigg, lost in the Viking life. You were a young man who longed for home, although the others did not. You had left loved ones in Scandinavia and mourned them till you died. You never saw your sweet heart again, and your old widowed mother was left unprovided for and unprotected. You wept bitter tears for them both."

What quality came back with my soul fragment? I ask Mariam.

"Wholeness of heart, a deep piece of your inner happiness came back."

Do I need to cleanse it? I ask.

"It is done. But that is why you have been told to rest in the heart of the sun, and why you have found doing so beneficial. Burning away the dross of regret leaves you freer now. It is good and it is done. We love you and enjoy working with you and the greater the healing we bring you, the deeper our connection with you can grow."

I feel quite humbled by that. Mariam had picked up on Caribbdyss's story and completed it for me. This shows me that the skulls work as a team and I am in their care as much as they are in mine.

That just left me with Moon to hear from. Moon had sat on the stones, Moon was the real impetus behind the book, and it was Moon who had helped me assemble my team of skulls. She deserves the last word, so the meditation with her is the last that I do. Time has passed, and though we visited the stones in February, by now it is March, at the time of the spring equinox. To enter Moon I decide to go in through a rainbow.

I'm in the inner world now and picture Moon in front of me. I go around her until I focus on a rainbow in her crystal at the back of her head. I see shimmering shards of rainbow colors, beyond which there is a patch of cloudiness in the crystal. I pass

249

COSMIC CRYSTALS! *Working With New Crystal Skulls*

into Moon—I just melt into the rainbow shards of light…and find myself on clouds high above Earth…the clouds come from the cloudiness in her crystal.

Is this to do with Castlerigg? I ask.

"Yes," Moon replies, and I find myself floating over Castlerigg.

It is a lovely feeling, floating on clouds as they lazily pass over the stones below, and I can see energy beaming up out of the circle and into the clouds.

What is the energy, Moon? I ask.

"It's the same Earth energy you have written about. The planet is venting after the equinox and it is balancing the energies in the crystal grid network, planet-wide. These adjustments occur constantly, but major adjustments occur at solstices and equinoxes, taking place over a three day period at the key times." I feel a charge of the energy pass straight through me; I feel it strengthening and balancing me…then Moon tells me it is time to return.

Next day, I go in through a different rainbow. This one is in her right eye.

Around me I see shifting sheets of color. I slip and slide on them as I try to make my way deeper into the skull—but then I give up and cease trying to control the experience, and I slide down the rainbow sheets of color, as if they are fairground rides… Wheeee…! I land in a heap of cushioning quartz which feels as soft as marshmallows.

Moon, what has this got to do with Castlerigg? I ask.

"Everything and nothing; these are just energies, but they are like the energies at Castlerigg—joyful earth energies."

Moon, what did you learn at Castlerigg? I ask her.

"To be joyful; it was, and still is, a place of joyful celebration. **Your life should be a joyful celebration**, for that pleases the angels and your guides, and lightens the load in the collective consciousness of humankind. Do not let events in the outer world get you down—but if that happens, seek the inner world and its peace."

I take that good advice to heart.

250

CHAPTER 22

Hurray! The last meditation for the book has been done, and that's something to celebrate! And from now on I will try to be more mindful and appreciative of the small pleasures of everyday life.

Well, I had found the answer to the question I'd had at the very beginning of chapter one—and it is a resounding yes! New crystal skulls are very capable of interacting and interfacing with ancient stone circles in interesting ways. They have a variety of individual responses, but it is clear that the energy in the land, and in the standing stones, is of benefit to the skull, and that the skull in turn benefits the land and the standing stones. But more than that, our own personal skulls offer us wisdom and a kind of friendship; no matter how small they may be, they can calm and uplift us as we stroke their beautiful crystal; they offer us exciting adventures, both in the inner world when we meditate and go journeying with them, and in the outer world when we physically take them to places.

But do not feel guilty if you have little time for meditating with them. Life today is busy. Put them in a respectful place, perhaps arranged on a small table, or on shelves, and they will form their own relationships and be occupied doing "skull things" together—the Collective Crystal Skull Consciousness will see to that. My skulls sit together on a table, with raw crystals and stones arranged on the floor beneath to provide a nurturing atmosphere, and most days I go to see them and touch their soothing, cool crystal bodies. Often there is no time to do more. Beside the table is a small water feature and house plants, so there is water, movement and life in the room. Take skulls to your bedroom and keep them by the bedside as you sleep—no matter how pressed you are for time you can do this, and benefit from interacting with them in your sleep-state.

I had found crystal skulls so rewarding to have around that although the book was finished, I discovered I wasn't finished buying skulls. To this day it is still a delight to find a new one that calls out to me, but I can remember when they simply were not around to be bought. Before the 1990s, no one in the UK seemed to stock crystal skulls. There was just no demand for them until *The Mystery of the Crystal Skulls* was published in 1997. Then things began to change, and in 2007 the much-loved film, *Indiana Jones and the Kingdom of the Crystal Skull*, was released. It achieved box office success around the world and introduced many more people to the skulls. After that, carved skulls became widely available. Now, even our local weekend market at Tynemouth has up to six stalls selling crystals, and most offer small crystal skulls for sale. I think it is a very good sign that so many new skulls are being carved, and it makes me feel much more optimistic about the future.

I believe crystal skulls make the world a better place.

The skulls are tools—beautiful and epic tools to help us awaken our deeper wisdom and higher consciousness. Just seeing a crystal skull is enough to start the process. Just seeing one sends impulses down the optic nerve to the brain, linking us into memories held deep in our sub—and super-consciousness. Memories often gained in lives long ago, when we worked with ancient crystal skulls in temples, administered their use as oracles in the ancient world, or perhaps were their appointed tribal guardian. These are the kinds of memories that fill the pages of *Holy Ice, Past Lives and Crystal Skulls*, and many of us who are drawn to them today loved them then, and deeply respected them. We knew their worth in ancient times. They were ours to guard and keep safe, but they were never actually ours. No wonder we are drawn to them today, when we can so easily have our very own crystal skulls to treasure.

Morton and Thomas's, *The Mystery of the Crystal Skulls*, is an important book. It tells of Native American legends of thirteen crystal skulls hidden and kept safe down the ages, the thirteen skulls being destined to be brought out and reunited at a crucial time for the world, when the wisdom they hold may save us from disaster. The year 2012 seemed to fit the prophecy...it brought the end of a World Age according to the Maya's Long Count Calendar. At the time, there was so much hype around 2012 being the end of the world, that in 2009, Hollywood released the blockbuster disaster movie, 2012, and as that only served to

CHAPTER 22

increase the hype, on December 22nd and 23rd, 2010, indigenous elders of the Maya took some of their ancient crystal skulls to the United Nations in an attempt to dispel the rumors. You can see it on YouTube (just Google: YouTube, crystal skulls at the UN). Plenty of skull gatherings and conferences *were* held in the years running up to the winter solstice of 2012, so let's be clear, ancient crystal skulls do exist and they have been brought out onto the world stage.

But perhaps the legend may also be seen as an allegory. That the thirteen crystal skulls of the legend represent the memories of them we hold deep within us that are only now coming to the surface of humankind's collective consciousness. If so, our deeper wisdom may yet save us from compounding humanity's mistakes, as an environmental crisis of our own making unfolds around us, and as climate change threatens the stability of the world as we know it. But never mind the thirteen skulls of legend—there has **NEVER** been so many crystal skulls on the planet as there are today—or so many crystal skull guardians happy to work with them!

That is why I feel optimistic.

Most of all, I wish you much joy of your own crystal skulls. As Mayan Daykeeper Hunbatz Men said at the United Nations, "Everyone should have a crystal skull." What a world that would be!

SKULL SIZES

Even Small Skulls Deliver Big Experiences So –

How Big Are the Skulls?

Length in inches from the front of the jaw to the back of the head:

Alsherida, two and a quarter inches (introduced in chapter 5)
Amersandi, one inch (introduced in chapter 8)
Arapo, three inches (introduced in chapter 2)
Arwen, the Bird Skull, four inches (introduced in chapters 16 and 18)
Beamoth, three and a half inches (introduced in chapter 5)
Bethsherida, three inches (introduced in chapter 5)
Caribbdyss, four inches (introduced in chapter 20)
Casima, the Dragon, three and a half inches (introduced in chapter 20)
Charles Lapis, two inches (introduced in chapter 3)
Cloud, one and three quarters of an inch (introduced in chapter 3)
Elandra, the Dragon, two and a half inches (introduced in chapter 20)
Elvira, three and a half inches (introduced in chapter 20)
Erin Nummi, just over an inch (introduced in chapter 3)
Evangeline Mo, four inches (introduced in chapter 13)
Fanella, three and a half inches (introduced in chapter 20)
Firenz, the Dragon, four inches (introduced in chapter 20)
Florence, two inches (introduced in chapter 10)
Freckles, three inches (introduced in chapter 20)
Fred, two inches (introduced in chapter 1)
Golden Feathers of the Sun, two inches (introduced in chapter 16/17)
Hapi-atzi, four inches (introduced in chapter 1)
Heaven-sent Starshine, nearly two inches (introduced in chapter 16)
Hope Ramasa Metri, five inches (introduced in chapter 1)
Hunter, one inch (introduced in chapter 1)
Iron Cloud, one inch (introduced in chapter 4)

COSMIC CRYSTALS! *Working With New Crystal Skulls*

Jago Jasper, one and a half inches (introduced in chapter 3)
Janus the Black, one inch (introduced in chapter 4)
Kai, two inches (introduced in chapter 21)
Mahrasi, one inch (introduced in chapter 4)
Malcolm Issua, one and a half inches (introduced in chapter 3)
Manos the Black, three quarters of an inch (introduced in chapter 1)
Marco Quartz, nearly two inches (introduced in chapter 3)
Mariam, three and a half inches (introduced in chapter 11)
Mars Preseli, two inches (introduced in chapter 3)
Melandra Ruby Ro Quartz, two and a half inches (introduced in chapter 3)
Moon-Over-the-Waters-of-Life, eight inches (introduced in chapter 1)
Peter the Red, one inch (introduced in chapter 4)
Petri of the Seven, one inch (introduced in chapter 4)
Radiance, four and three quarters of an inch (introduced in chapter 3)
Raffeem, the Dragon, nearly three inches (introduced in chapter 17)
Raffim, the Dragon, six inches (introduced in chapter 16/17)
Shallimar, almost five inches (introduced in chapter 3)
Shanash Rose, two inches (introduced in chapter 3)
Shareen Queen of the Stars, two and a quarter inches (introduced in chapter 16/17)
Solange, five inches (introduced in chapter 3)
Stardust, almost four inches (introduced in chapter 3)
The Council of Seventeen, half an inch (introduced in chapter 4)
The Council of Thirteen, one inch (introduced in chapter 4)
The Face Stone, see Shareen above
The Shaman Stone, three inches (introduced in chapter 1)
The Skull of Dreams, two and a half inches (introduced in chapter 3)
Tiger, three quarters of an inch (introduced in chapter 4)
Tiger of the Seven, one inch (introduced in chapter 4)
Topo-Mo-So, see Freckles above
Yello-mani-urua, two inches (introduced in chapter 5)
Zatis, one inch (introduced in chapter 4)
Zeb'n, three inches (introduced in chapter 2)
Zuna, two inches (introduced in chapter 20)

SKULL SUPPLIERS:
Where the Skulls Came From

Alsherida – eBay, sold by nigr_671
Amersandi – www.crystalskulls.com
Arapo – www.crystalskulls.com
Arwen of the Beak and Feathers (Bird Skull) – eBay, sold by rainbowweaverheart
Beamoth – eBay, sold by nigri_671
Bethsherida – eBay, sold by nigri_671
Caribbdyss – eBay, sold by forrest-edge-collectibles
Casima – eBay, sold by nigri_671
Charles Lapis – eBay, sold by Pangaea-Collectibles
Cloud – Etsy, sold by MoonStonesStudio.
Elandra – eBay, sold by jjdeaconward
Elvira – eBay, sold by nigri_671
Erin Nuummi – www.crystalskulls.com
Evangeline Mo – eBay, sold by inature-cases 1670
Fanella – eBay, sold by nigri_671
Firenz – sold by Lotus Seda in the Facebook group:
Crystal Skulls & Caretakers Unite (skulls looking for new homes)
Florence – eBay, sold by Magic Moon, magic.moon.crystals
Freckles – sold by Nancy Mekern in the Facebook group: Crystal Skulls & Caretakers Unite (skulls looking for new homes)
Fred – Etsy, Claire at NewEarthMagic
Golden Feathers of the Sun – eBay, sold by Kates_collectables
Hapi-atzi – eBay
Heaven-sent Starshine – eBay, sold by clickkassabian
Hope Ramasa Metri – eBay, sold by Bruce Mitchell trading as silverli740, www.crystalskullwarehouse.com
Hunter – Etsy, Claire at NewEarthMagic
Iron Cloud – www.crystalskulls.com
Jago Jasper – www.crystalskulls.com

COSMIC CRYSTALS! *Working With New Crystal Skulls*

Janus the Black – www.crystalskulls.com

Kai – eBay, sold by Bruce Mitchell trading as silverli740, www.crystalskullwarehouse.com

Mahrasi – www.crystalskulls.com

Malcolm Isua – www.crystalskulls.com

Manos the Black – www.crystalskulls.com

Marco Quartz – from a stand at a festival

Mariam – eBay, sold by mike-n-faye

Mars Preseli – Etsy, StonehengeStore

Melandra Ruby Ro Quartz - Histories and Mysteries Conference, Edinburgh, UK

Moon-Over-the-Waters-of-Life – Tracy Queen now at www.the-crystal-tree.co.uk

Peter the Red – www.crystalskulls.com

Petri of the Seven – www.crystalskulls.com

Radiance – Etsy, Claire at NewEarthMagic

Raffeem and Raffim the Dragons – eBay, sold by Bruce Mitchell trading as silverli740, www.crystalskullwarehouse.com

Shallimar – eBay, sold by Bruce Mitchell trading as silverli740, www.crystalskullwarehouse.com

Shanash Rose – Histories and Mysteries Conference, Edinburgh, UK

Shareen Queen of the Stars – eBay, sold by denisefsel-0

Solange – Tracy Queen now at www.the-crystal-tree.co.uk

Stardust – Etsy, Claire at NewEarthMagic

The Council of Seventeen – www.crystalskulls.com

The Council of Thirteen – Burhouse, Quarmby Mills, Huddersfield, UK

The Face Stone– see the entry for Shareen

The Shaman Stone – eBay, sold by Bruce Mitchell, trading as silverli740, www.crystalskullwarehouse.com

The Skull of Dreams – eBay, sold by Bruce Mitchell, trading as silverli740, www.crystalskullwarehouse.com

Tiger – www.crystalskulls.com

Tiger of the Seven – www.crystalskulls.com

Yello-mani-urua – eBay, sold by nigri_671

Zatis – www.crystalskulls.com

SKULL SUPPLIERS:

Zeb'n – Tracy Queen now at www.the-crystal-tree.co.uk

Zuna – eBay, sold by Bruce Mitchell, trading as silverli740, www.crystalskullwarehouse.com

BIBLIOGRAPHY

American Journal of Physical Anthropology. Magazine. John Wiley & Sons.

Bonewitz, Ra. *The Cosmic Crystal Spiral: crystals and the evolution of human consciousness.* Great Britain: Element Books Ltd, 1987.

Bowen, Sandra, and F.R. "Nick" Nocerino and Joshua Shapiro. *Mysteries of the Crystal Skulls Revealed.* J & S Aquarian Networking Book in Association with NuSirius Company, US, 1988.

Cope, Julian. *The Modern Antiquarian,* includes a Gazetteer to over 300 Prehistoric Sites and photos of stone circles and dolmens. London: Thorsons, (Harper Collins), 1998.

Courtenay, Edwin. *Crystals To Go.* UK: Inky Little Fingers, 2019.

Delcour-Min, Paulinne. *Spiritual Gold.* USA, Ozark Mountain Publishing, 2018.

Delcour-Min, Paulinne. *Holy Ice, Past Lives and Crystal Skulls: the Secrets of Time, Continuing the Journey of a Soul.* USA, Ozark Mountain Publishing, 2020.

Delcour-Min, Paulinne. *Divine Fire.* USA, Ozark Mountain Publishing, 2020.

DeSalvo, John. *Power Crystals, Spiritual and Magical Practices, Crystal Skulls, and Alien Technology.* USA, Destiny Books, (Inner Traditions International), 2012.

Dorland, Frank. *Holy Ice, Bridge to the Subconscious.* US: Galde Press, 1992.

Hall, Judy. *Crystal Skulls: Ancient Tools for Peace, Knowledge, and Enlightenment.* Weiser Books, an imprint of Red Wheel/ Weiser, Newburyport, MA, USA, 2016.

Keller, Elizabeth HeartStar and Jewels Maloney. *The Crystal Skull Messenger.* Sedona, USA, Dancing with The Sun

BIBLIOGRAPHY

Productions, 2014.

Kindred Spirit. Magazine. London.

Linn, Denise. *Energy Strands, The Ultimate Guide to Clearing the Cords that are Constricting your Life.* UK, Hay House UK Ltd, 2018.

Mercier, Patricia. *Crystal Skulls & the Enigma of Time,* UK and USA: Watkins Publishing, 2011.

Mindell, Arthur. *The Shaman's Body.* USA: HarperSanFransisco, a division of Harper Collins, 1993.

Morton, Chris, and Ceri Louise Thomas. *The Mystery of the Crystal Skulls: Unlocking the Secrets of the Past, Present and Future.* London: Thorson, an imprint of Harper Collins, 1997.

Murray, Kathleen. *Divine Spark of Creation: The Crystal Skull Speaks.* Huntly, UK: Galactic Publications, 1998.

Pizzati, Marguerite and A. J. Ferrara. *Interviews with the Crystal Skulls.* USA, KDP Direct Publishing and Magic City Pictures, Inc., 2020.

Qamar, Gia. *The Crystal Skull Companion: Your new friend rocks!* USA: Moon Queen Publications, 2022.

Shapiro, Joshua, with Katrina Head. *Journey of the Crystal Skull Explorers: Travelogue 2: Search for the Blue Skull in Peru.* Crystal Skull Explorers 2018.

Snyder-Nieciak, Rev Marilee Ann. *Ancient Wisdom for Now.* Printed by Amazon, 2013

Steinbrecher, Edwin C. *The Inner Guide Meditation: A Transformational Journey to Enlightenment and Awareness.* Wellingborough, Northhamptonshire: Aquarian Press, 1982; rptd.1983, 1985.

Van Etten, Jaap. *Crystal Skulls: Interacting with a Phenomenon.* Light Technology Publishing, Flagstaff, AZ, USA, 2007.

Van Etten, Jaap. *Crystal Skulls Exand Your Consciousness.* Light Technoogy Publishing, Flagstaff, AZ, USA, 2013.

Van Dieten, Joky. *Adventures with the Ancient Crystal Skulls.* USA, 2013.

Walker, DaEL. *The Crystal Healing Book.* The Crystal Company,

COSMIC CRYSTALS! *Working With New Crystal Skulls*

California, 1988.

Webb-De Sisto, Marion. *Crystal Skulls: Emissaries of Healing and Sacred Wisdom*. USA, Xlibris, 2002.

LIST OF ILLUSTRATIONS

Chapter 1:   (1) Moon-Over-the-Waters-of-Life and Solange
(2) Hapi-atzi and Radiance
(3) Stardust, Hunter, Cloud, Fred, Manos the Black, Mars, Charles Lapis
(4-7) Four photos of the Shaman Stone and Hope Ramasa Metri showing a curious light energy passing between them.

Chapter 2:   (8) Zeb'n and Arapo

Chapter 3:   (9) Shallimar, Erin Nummi, the Skull of Dreams, and Tiger
(10) Jago Jasper, Malcolm Isua, Shanash Rose, Marco Quartz, Melandra Ruby Ro Quartz

Chapter 4:   (11) The Council of Seventeen
(12) The Council of Thirteen

Chapter 5:   (13) Alsherida and Bethsherida

Chapter 6:   -

Chapter 7:   (14) Three of the five surviving Duddo Stones
(15) Arapo and Zeb'n
(16) Moon

Chapter 8:   (17) Amersandi

Chapter 9:   -

Chapter 10:   (18) Florence and Fred
(19) The Standing Stone at Matfen, Northumberland, England
(20) The Shaman Stone pressed against the Matfen Standing Stone

Chapter 11:   (21) Mariam

Chapter 12:   -

Chapter 13:   (22) Evangeline Mo

Chapter 14:   -

Chapter 15:   -

COSMIC CRYSTALS! *Working With New Crystal Skulls*

Chapter 16:	(23) Heaven-sent Starshine
Chapter 17:	(24) Shareen, Queen of the Stars
	(25) Raffim
	(26) Golden Feathers of the Sun
Chapter 18:	(27) Rafeem
	(28) Arwen of the Beak and Feathers
Chapter 19:	-
Chapter 20:	(29) Caribbdyss
	(30) Freckles, now Topo-Mo-So
	(31) Fire dragon Casima and ether dragon Elandra
	(32) Elvira and Fanella
	(33) Firenz
	(34) Zuna
Chapter 21:	(35) Kai
Chapter 22:	(36) Solange and Moon on the stones at Castlerigg, and I go to lean my backpack containing the smaller skulls against the perimeter stones.

(37) Solange, Raffim, Moon, and Mariam share a stone with three of Ye's skulls.

(38) The crystal skulls Solange and Moon rest on a stone within the circle. The camera shows their quartz crystal glowing with light even on a very dull day, though our human eyes did not pick this up at the time.

(39) Caribbdyss on a stone within the circle.

About the Author

Paulinne Delcour-Min has a first class honors degree and Post Graduate Certificate in Education. After some years teaching, an interest in healing led her to study regression therapy. Paulinne was to spend more than thirty years working as a past life and soul therapist, and during this time she began writing about her work. The resulting manuscript was of such scope it was published as the trilogy *Spiritual Gold, Holy Ice, Divine Fire*. The books are non-fiction. They are based on original research. The far memories recovered include many past lives, even future lives, and cut to the heart of the mystery of the ancient crystal skulls of legend. Crystal skulls proved to be such an amazing phenomenon that in *Cosmic Crystals! Working With New Crystal Skulls*, Paulinne explores their continued relevance for us today.

This is her fourth book. It marks an exciting new development in her work.

Paulinne loves to hear from readers and can be contacted through her website at www.paulinnedelcour-min.com.

Other Books by Ozark Mountain Publishing, Inc.

Dolores Cannon
A Soul Remembers Hiroshima
Between Death and Life
Conversations with Nostradamus,
Volume I, II, III
The Convoluted Universe -Book One,
Two, Three, Four, Five
The Custodians
Five Lives Remembered
Horns of the Goddess
Jesus and the Essenes
Keepers of the Garden
Legacy from the Stars
The Legend of Starcrash
The Search for Hidden Sacred
Knowledge
They Walked with Jesus
The Three Waves of Volunteers and the
New Earth
A Very Special Friend
Aron Abrahamsen
Holiday in Heaven
James Ream Adams
Little Steps
Justine Alessi & M. E. McMillan
Rebirth of the Oracle
Kathryn Andries
Time: The Second Secret
Will Alexander
Call Me Jonah
Cat Baldwin
Divine Gifts of Healing
The Forgiveness Workshop
Penny Barron
The Oracle of UR
The Oracle of UR, Book 2
P.E. Berg & Amanda Hemmingsen
The Birthmark Scar
The Birthmark Scar, Book 2
Dan Bird
Finding Your Way in the Spiritual Age
Waking Up in the Spiritual Age
Julia Cannon
Soul Speak – The Language of Your
Body
Jack Cauley
Journey for Life
Ronald Chapman
Seeing True
Jack Churchward
Lifting the Veil on the Lost
Continent of Mu
The Stone Tablets of Mu

Carolyn Greer Daly
Opening to Fullness of Spirit
Patrick De Haan
The Alien Handbook
Paulinne Delcour-Min
Cosmic Crystals!
Divine Fire
Holly Ice
Spiritual Gold
Anthony DeNino
The Power of Giving and Gratitude
Joanne DiMaggio
Edgar Cayce and the Unfulfilled
Destiny of Thomas Jefferson
Reborn
Paul Fisher
Like a River to the Sea
Anita Holmes
Twidders
Aaron Hoopes
Reconnecting to the Earth
Edin Huskovic
God is a Woman
Patricia Irvine
In Light and In Shade
Kevin Killen
Ghosts and Me
Susan Linville
Blessings from Agnes
Donna Lynn
From Fear to Love
Curt Melliger
Heaven Here on Earth
Where the Weeds Grow
Henry Michaelson
And Jesus Said – A Conversation
Andy Myers
Not Your Average Angel Book
Holly Nadler
The Hobo Diaries
Guy Needler
The Anne Dialogues
Avoiding Karma
Beyond the Origin
Beyond the Source – Book 1, Book 2
The Curators
The History of God
The OM
The Origin Speaks
Kelly Nicholson
Ethel Marie

For more information about any of the above titles, soon to be released titles,
or other items in our catalog, write, phone or visit our website:
PO Box 754, Huntsville, AR 72740|479-738-2348/800-935-0045|www.ozarkmt.com

Other Books by Ozark Mountain Publishing, Inc.

Psycho Spiritual Healing
James Nussbaumer
And Then I Knew My Abundance
Each of You
Living Your Dram, Not Someone Else's
The Master of Everything
Mastering Your Own Spiritual Freedom
Sherry O'Brian
Peaks and Valley's
Gabrielle Orr
Akashic Records: One True Love
Let Miracles Happen
Nick Osborne
A Ronin's Tale
Nikki Pattillo
Children of the Stars
A Golden Compass
Victoria Pendragon
Being In A Body
Sleep Magic
The Sleeping Phoenix
Alexander Quinn
Starseeds What's It All About
Debra Rayburn
Let's Get Natural with Herbs
Charmian Redwood
A New Earth Rising
Coming Home to Lemuria
David Rousseau
Beyond Our World, Book 1
Beyond Our World, Book 2
Richard Rowe
Exploring the Divine Library
Imagining the Unimaginable
Garnet Schulhauser
Dance of Eternal Rapture
Dance of Heavenly Bliss
Dancing Forever with Spirit
Dancing on a Stamp
Dancing with Angels in Heaven
Annie Stillwater Gray
The Dawn Book
Education of a Guardian Angel
Joys of a Guardian Angel

Work of a Guardian Angel
Manuella Stoerzer
Headless Chicken
Blair Styra
Don't Change the Channel
Who Catharted
Natalie Sudman
Application of Impossible Things
L.R. Sumpter
Judy's Story
The Old is New
We Are the Creators
Artur Tradevosyan
Croton
Croton II
Jim Thomas
Tales from the Trance
Jolene and Jason Tierney
A Quest of Transcendence
Paul Travers
Dancing with the Mountains
Nicholas Vesey
Living the Life-Force
Dennis Wheatley/ Maria Wheatley
The Essential Dowsing Guide
Maria Wheatley
Druidic Soul Star Astrology
Sherry Wilde
The Forgotten Promise
Lyn Willmott
A Small Book of Comfort
Beyond all Boundaries Book 1
Beyond all Boundaries Book 2
Beyond all Boundaries Book 3
D. Arthur Wilson
You Selfish Bastard
Stuart Wilson & Joanna Prentis
Atlantis and the New Consciousness
Beyond Limitations
The Essenes -Children of the Light
The Magdalene Version
Power of the Magdalene
Sally Wolf
Life of a Military Psychologist

For more information about any of the above titles, soon to be released titles,
or other items in our catalog, write, phone or visit our website:
PO Box 754, Huntsville, AR 72740|479-738-2348/800-935-0045|www.ozarkmt.com